The God who makes himself known

Titles in this series:

An index of Scripture references for all the volumes may be
found at http://www.thegospelcoalition.org/resources/nsbt.

NEW STUDIES IN BIBLICAL THEOLOGY 28

Series editor: D. A. Carson

The God who makes himself known

THE MISSIONARY HEART OF THE BOOK OF EXODUS

W. Ross Blackburn

APOLLOS

INTERVARSITY PRESS
DOWNERS GROVE, ILLINOIS 60515

Norton Street
Nottingham NG7 3HR, England
Website: www.ivpbooks.com
Email: ivp@ivpbooks.com

Downers Grove, IL 60515-1426, USA
Website: www.ivpress.com
Email: email@ivpress.com

InterVarsity Press®, USA, is the book-publishing division of InterVarsity Christian Fellowship/ USA® <www.intervarsity.org> and a member movement of the International Fellowship of Evangelical Students.

Inter-Varsity Press, England, is closely linked with the Universities and Colleges Christian Fellowship, a student movement connecting Christian Unions throughout Great Britain, and a member movement of the International Fellowship of Evangelical Students. Website: www.uccf.org.uk

Unless stated otherwise, all Scripture quotations are from The Holy Bible, English Standard Version, published by HarperCollins Publishers © 2001 by Crossway Bibles, a division of Good News Publishers. Used by permission. All rights reserved.

First published 2012

Set in Monotype Times New Roman
Typeset in Great Britain by Servis Filmsetting Ltd, Stockport, Cheshire

USA ISBN 978-0-8308-2629-2
UK ISBN 978-1-84474-573-9

British Library Cataloguing in Publication Data

A catalogue record for this book is available from the British Library.

Library of Congress Cataloging-in-Publication Data

Blackburn, W. Ross.
   The God who makes himself known : the missionary heart of the book of Exodus / W. Ross Blackburn.
      p. cm.—(New studies in biblical theology ; 28)
   Includes bibliographical references (p.   ) and indexes.
   ISBN 978-0-8308-2629-2 (paper; usa : alk. paper)—ISBN 978-1-84474-573-9 (paper; uk : alk. paper) 1. Bible. O.T.
Exodus—Criticism, interpretation, etc. 2.
Missions—Biblical teaching. 3. God
(Christianity)—Knowableness—Biblical teaching. I. Title.
   BS1245.52.B53 2012
   222'.1206—dc23

                                                                                    2012007758

P   18   17   16   15   14   13   12   11   10   9   8   7   6   5   4   3   2   1
Y   27   26   25   24   23   22   21   20   19   18   17   16   15   14   13   12

For Lauren

Contents

7

Series preface

New Studies in Biblical Theology is a series of monographs that address key issues in the discipline of biblical theology. Contributions to the series focus on one or more of three areas: 1. the nature and status of biblical theology, including its relations with other disciplines (e.g. historical theology, exegesis, systematic theology, historical criticism, narrative theology); 2. the articulation and exposition of the structure of thought of a particular biblical writer or corpus; and 3. the delineation of a biblical theme across all or part of the biblical corpora.

Above all, these monographs are creative attempts to help thinking Christians understand their Bibles better. The series aims simultaneously to instruct and to edify, to interact with the current literature, and to point the way ahead. In God's universe, mind and heart should not be divorced: in this series we will try not to separate what God has joined together. While the notes interact with the best of scholarly literature, the text is uncluttered with untransliterated Greek and Hebrew, and tries to avoid too much technical jargon. The volumes are written within the framework of confessional evangelicalism, but there is always an attempt at thoughtful engagement with the sweep of the relevant literature.

The God Who Makes Himself Known is a thought-provoking book. Initially, a subtitle such as 'The Missionary Heart of the Book of Exodus' is bound to raise a few eyebrows: has Dr Blackburn tumbled into hopeless anachronism? Yet while remaining sceptical about pieces of the argument here and there, I found the work strangely compelling, drawing me forward to the conclusion that there is much more to the thesis than one might expect. Careful reading of this volume demands frequent pauses for reflection on the inner-canonical connections that Dr Blackburn unpacks with stimulating verve. I am quite certain that most who work their way through this volume will never be able to read

Exodus in the same way they did before doing so – and that is high praise.

D. A. Carson
Trinity Evangelical Divinity School

Author's preface

The following gets to the heart of the most important question we can ask: Who is God? The writing has been a cause of great thanksgiving, for several reasons. First, it is an answer to a prayer ten years ago that the Lord would give me a doctoral project that would help me know him better. Secondly, this work has been a tremendous help in understanding how the Old and New Testaments are to be read together, making clearer, at least to me, how the God-breathed word is meant for our instruction. Finally, it has given me the opportunity to serve and be served by many others, and to put down in an organized fashion much of what I have learned from others over many years.

While my debt to others in this project is legion, I would offer special thanks to several people. Chris Seitz patiently and wisely guided my doctoral work at St Andrews, upon which the following is based. Allen Ross, by his teaching, example and consistent encouragement, has given me a hunger for biblical exposition and a particular love for the Old Testament. The fellowship of Christ the King, Boone, has been an encouragement in every way, supporting me prayerfully and financially, refining my understanding of the Scriptures and giving me the space and resources within our life together to undertake a project such as this. My reluctance to mention names is not due to lack of appreciation, but knowing that I cannot do justice to all who have played a part in this, not least through hidden prayer. However, simply because I know of their earnest prayers for this project in particular, I would mention Carolyn Clement, Darcey James, Matt Foster, Dan Kiser, and Tom and Anna Barry. I would also thank the fellowship for bringing Jonathan Riddle, whose cheerful help in assisting me has freed time to finish this work. My mother and father, Marcia and Bill Blackburn, have always been a tremendous support in just about anything I have done, and particularly this, as has my grandmother, Libby Ross. My children, William, Anna and Joseph are in all things a delight and a cause for great thanksgiving, and I am happy to acknowledge them here. Without Lauren, my wife (and unusually perceptive editor), none of this would be possible.

Thanks to Phil Duce at IVP for his good natured and persistent patience and eagerness to see this work published, for keeping me on track and for attending to all the particulars involved in making it happen, and to Eldo Barkhuizen for his painstaking editorial work, particularly sorting out the bibliography and Scripture references. The precision and perceptiveness with which they work is extraordinary. Thanks also to Don Carson for both initially accepting the work, and for an incisive comment concerning law and gospel that made it much clearer. Writing for the author of *Exegetical Fallacies* I am sure has made this a better work. Erin Thielman's keen eye for detail has been a great help in editing this work.

Finally, I thank God in Christ Jesus, the source of salvation and all sufficiency, who has made Himself known to me at greater depth as a result of this project. My prayer is that, in some small way, this work would be useful to him as he continues to make himself known, from Jerusalem to the ends of the earth.

Soli Deo gloria

Ross Blackburn

Abbreviations

AB	Anchor Bible
ASTI	*Annual of the Swedish Theological Institute*
AUSS	*Andrews University Seminary Studies*
AV	Authorized (King James) Version
Bib	*Biblica*
BibInt	*Biblical Interpretation*
BJS	Brown Judaic Studies
BRev	*Bible Review*
BSac	*Bibliotheca sacra*
BZ	*Biblische Zeitschrift*
BZAW	Beihefte zur Zeitschrift für die alttestamentliche Wissenschaft
CBC	Cambridge Bible Commentary
CBET	Contributions to Biblical Exegesis and Theology
CBQ	*Catholic Biblical Quarterly*
CTJ	*Calvin Theological Journal*
ESV	English Standard Version
FAT	Forschungen zum Alten Testament
HBT	*Horizons in Biblical Theology*
HCOT	Historical Commentary on the Old Testament
HTKAT	Herders Theologischer Kommentar zum Alten Testament
HTR	*Harvard Theological Review*
HUCA	*Hebrew Union College Annual*
Int	*Interpretation*
JANESCU	*Journal of the Ancient Near Eastern Society of Columbia University*
JAOS	*Journal of the American Oriental Society*
JBL	*Journal of Biblical Literature*
JBQ	*Jewish Bible Quarterly*
JETS	*Journal of the Evangelical Theological Society*
JQR	*Jewish Quarterly Review*

JSOT	*Journal for the Study of the Old Testament*
JSOTSup	Journal for the Study of the Old Testament, Supplement Series
NASB	New American Standard Bible
NIB	*The New Interpreter's Bible*, ed. L. E. Keck, 12 vols., Nashville: Abingdon, 1993–2002
NEchtB	Neue Echter Bibel
NIV	New International Version
NJPS	New Jewish Publication Society translation of the Jewish Bible
NKJV	New King James Version
NRSV	New Revised Standard Version
NS	New Series
NSBT	New Studies in Biblical Theology
NTS	*New Testament Studies*
OBT	Overtures to Biblical Theology
OT	Old Testament
OTE	*Old Testament Essays*
NT	New Testament
RB	*Revue biblique*
RSV	Revised Standard Version
SBT	Studies in Biblical Theology
SBTS	Sources for Biblical and Theological Study
SNTSMS	Society of New Testament Studies Monograph Series
TBC	Torch Bible Commentaries
TDOT	*Theological Dictionary of the Old Testament*, ed. G. J. Botterweck, H. Ringgren and H.-J. Fabry, 15 vols., Grand Rapids: Eerdmans, 1974–2006
ThR	*Theologische Rundshau*
TJ	*Trinity Journal*
tr.	translation, translated
TynB	*Tyndale Bulletin*
VT	*Vetus Testamentum*
VTSup	Supplements to Vetus Testamentum
WTJ	*Westminster Theological Journal*
WUNT	Wissenschaftliche Untersuchungen zum Neuen Testament
ZAW	*Zeitschrift für die alttestamentliche Wissenschaft*

Chapter One

Introduction

Concerning biblical mission

The God Who Makes Himself Known will argue that the Lord's missionary commitment to make himself known to the nations is the central theological concern of Exodus. Therefore, a word about the use of the term 'mission' is warranted. One danger of using a well-known term is that ideas commonly connected with the term are often read into the argument, sometimes bringing in unintended associations. For instance, despite its definition as 'any remedial activity pursued with zeal and enthusiasm',[1] it is difficult for the term 'crusade' to be divorced in the minds of many readers from violence and coercion. Likewise, despite its definition as 'a specific task with which a person or a group is charged',[2] 'mission' also carries with it meaning (e.g. direct, usually Christian, evangelistic endeavour) that may be too suggestive to be useful. There are, however, important reasons for using the term. First, the contemporary use of the term 'mission', particularly as defined above, fits the following argument. Many contemporary institutions, whether religious or secular, use the term 'mission' to speak of their purpose; hence the popular use of the term 'mission statement'. However, while the terms 'mission' and 'purpose' overlap, the former has a distinctively proactive sense that the latter often does not. Sunglasses serve the purpose of reducing glare, but one would hardly speak of the mission of a pair of sunglasses. Mission, on the other hand, implies both purpose and the corresponding effort and strategy to achieve that purpose. The word 'mission' therefore fits the following argument, which addresses both the Lord's purpose in Exodus and the means by which he pursues that purpose.

The second reason for using the term 'mission' lies in the context

---

[1] 'Crusade', in Gove 1968.
[2] 'Mission', in Gove 1968.

in which I believe the argument is appropriately considered. Using the term 'mission' positions the following argument in the wider discussion of biblical mission. Too often the concept of mission in the OT has either been generally denied, or the OT has been used as a short prologue to a discussion of biblical mission, which usually means mission according to the NT.[3] Furthermore, many discussions of mission in the OT tend towards a focus on a handful of texts that appear to address more explicitly missionary themes, texts such as Genesis 12:1–3, Exodus 19:4–6 and the book of Jonah.[4] While the importance of these texts cannot be denied, OT mission is much more than a collection of extracted proof texts. In fact, the reason that those texts above are appealed to with such frequency is that we have read the OT through the lens of the NT, particularly the Great Commission (Matt. 28:18–20), and therefore look to texts that explicitly refer to the nations to inform our understanding of mission. The problem is that when this happens, the whole notion of mission in the Bible is severely truncated, even distorted. It is noteworthy that the Great Commission is spoken by Jesus in Matthew, the Gospel that most explicitly and frequently grounds itself in the OT. And yet much of the modern church reads the Great Commission as if Jesus were commanding something entirely new. How is the Great Commission to be carried out? To whom is it given? What is the message? Is proclaiming a message even an appropriate way to understand Jesus' command? What are disciples, and how are they made? These are all issues firmly rooted in the OT. An important implication of the following study is that we cannot even understand mission as expressed in the NT apart from a thorough grounding in the Old.

Two publications help lend definition to the term, at least as used in the following discussion. First, Seitz (2001) has suggested that mission, biblically understood, fundamentally involves God's seeking to put right what has gone awry; that is, the evil inclination of the human heart. Christian evangelistic proclamation, with which mission is commonly associated, may be understood as one means by which God sets right what is wrong, but it is only part of that larger concern:

---

[3] Two major exceptions to this tendency are C. J. H. Wright's *The Mission of God* (2006) and Beale's *The Temple and the Church's Mission* (2004), both of which heavily interact with the OT in their discussions of biblical mission.

[4] E.g. Kaiser 2000.

Mission means getting at the something awry, when we look at the issue theologically and not sociologically. Stated differently, the notion of missionary 'sending' is an earthly subset of a theological reality, and it is this theological reality that makes mission have a divine and not a natural or simply human mandate. Mission is God's address to humanity's forfeit. Understood in this way, it is an Old Testament theme as well as a New Testament theme. Indeed, it could be said to be *the* theme of the Old Testament as such. (2001: 147, emphasis original)

If Seitz's understanding is applied to Exodus, that which has gone awry is a condition in which the world does not know the Lord. 'Getting at the something awry', for Exodus, is simply the Lord's effort to make himself known among the nations for who he is, the God who rules over the universe and redeems those who call upon him. The goal of the following, then, will be to demonstrate that this commitment to right what is awry, or to move Israel and the nations from ignorance to knowing him, is the Lord's motivation behind his actions in Exodus. In this way the theme is missionary. Whether or not mission, thus understood, is '*the* theme of the Old Testament', as Seitz suggests, is beyond the scope of this work, but I do intend to argue that it is the governing theme of Exodus.

The second work, Bauckham's *Bible and Mission* (2003), examines biblical mission in terms of the relationship between the particular and the universal in the Bible. Bauckham understands mission in both the OT and the NT in the light of this movement. The Lord particularly chose Abraham for the universal purpose that all families of the earth might be blessed. The Lord particularly chose Israel for the universal purpose that the nations might acknowledge that he is God. The Lord particularly chose Zion, with its Davidic king, for the universal purpose of extending his rule throughout the earth. In each case the particular always moves to the universal, leading Bauckham to argue that the Lord never chooses a particular person or people for its own sake, but for the sake of the world. This movement, for Bauckham, is biblical mission.

The relationship between particularity and universality is of crucial importance in understanding the book of Exodus, especially in arguing that the central concern of Exodus is missionary. One of the chief burdens of the following argument, then, is to demonstrate that the particular existence of Israel has a universal goal, and that Israel's existence is unintelligible apart from her mission to the nations. In other words the following argument will seek to demonstrate that the existence and nature of Israel cannot be rightly understood apart from the Lord's universal mission.

Finally, a point about the language Exodus uses to express this missionary commitment. Often, mission in Exodus is expressed in terms of knowing the Lord or knowing his name, such as in the oft-repeated phrase 'they shall know that I am the LORD'. Sometimes the Lord's mission is expressed in terms of his being glorified or honoured (e.g. 14:4, 18), and other passages suggest that the Lord acts as he does for the sake of his name (e.g. 32:12). While each of these expressions may have different nuances, they convey the same general meaning. As we shall see, the Lord desires to be known as God, and, further, as a particular kind of God, a God who is both supreme and good. In other words *the Lord seeks to be known for who he is, and* (the corollary, while obvious, needs to be said) *not for who he is not.* Knowing the Lord implies honouring him for who he is. The terms 'honoured', 'glorified' and 'known' will be used at different points in the discussion, depending on which seems to fit best in relation to a given passage. It bears mention, however, that they all point in the same direction.

Purpose and approach

The New Studies in Biblical Theology series of which this volume is a part seeks to address one or more of three areas: issues related to the discipline of Biblical Theology, the exposition of the structure of thought of a particular book or corpus, and the delineation of a particular theme across part or all of the Scriptures. The following work seeks to address all three.

First, recognizing that hermeneutical decisions often turn on the contexts in which particular passages are interpreted, *The God Who Makes Himself Known* makes a case for the importance of canonical context in interpretation.[5] As Olson (1985: 3) writes, 'A

---

[5] While there are differences in approach between interpreters who identify their method as canonical, Schultz (2002: 96) cites five common commitments among canonical interpreters, all of which describe the approach of this work: (1) canonical approaches focus on the final form of books, rather than reconstructed histories, (2) theological reflections are based on the canonical presentation of history (regardless of the assessment of historical validity), (3) the Bible is viewed as theologically normative, (4) theological unity is emphasized, and (5) an

major obstacle to the appreciation and interpretation of any literary work is a perceived lack of coherence or organization'. One of the problems of much critical interpretation is that it has increasingly assumed a lack of coherence,[6] which has led some interpreters increasingly to explain difficulties in the text by resorting to different sources, traditions or editorial processes. Now, of course, some will argue that critical scholarship has not *assumed* a lack of coherence, but rather has demonstrated it.[7] Aside from the obvious point that there is significant difficulty in assessing coherence, particularly in a text far removed both temporally and culturally, one's assessment of what a text *is* informs how it will be read. Practically, the more that one fragments the text, the greater the tendency to fragment it further becomes. This is not to say that there are not places of real difficulty in the text, some of which have been brought to light by critical scholars. But it is to say that the impulse has made interpretation increasingly difficult.[8] If A does not appear to fit with B, it may be that we are discerning different sources or editorial layers, or it may be that we simply have not yet discerned how they do indeed fit together. For example, is Van Seters's (1994: 323) judgment that Exodus 33:18–23 is 'so entirely out of character with [33:12–17] that it must be considered an addition' an accurate reading of the text, or might there be a connection between the two sections that Van Seters misses? It is noteworthy that Van Seters's assessment closes down theological discussion, for he simply asserts 33:18–23 as an addition without enquiring as to its theological function. The point of this work is not to repudiate critical scholarship, per se, but rather to demonstrate that the impulse to retreat to sources or editorial histories is sometimes due to the fact that

---

effort is made to preserve the distinctive voice of the OT so as not to be silenced by the NT.

[6] Following Sailhamer (1995: 87–88), the term 'critical' is used to speak broadly of various types of historical, source, literary and form criticism, which base their theological judgments upon historical or literary reconstructions, rather than on the final canonical form of the biblical text.

[7] E.g. Barton 1996: 24: 'Literary criticism begins with the attempt to understand and make sense of the text; and its conclusions about the composite character of many texts arise from noticing that the text actually cannot *be* understood as it stands, because it is full of inconsistencies, inexplicable dislocations of theme, form, style, and so on, which make it impossible to know what to read it as' (emphasis original).

[8] In the words of Childs (1974: xiv–xv), 'The concentration of critical scholars on form-critical and source analysis has tended to fragment the text and leave the reader with only bits and pieces.'

we have not taken the canonical context of the Scriptures seriously enough.

In addressing this hermeneutical concern, each chapter follows a similar pattern. Beginning with a (usually well-known) hermeneutical problem, each chapter moves to argue that the particular section at hand points to the Lord's missionary commitment to be known as God, then ends with a suggestion of how appreciating that missionary commitment helps make sense of that hermeneutical problem. In addition, occasionally I suggest specific examples where critical decisions have been made, to my mind unnecessarily, on theological grounds or due to a lack of appreciating the canonical movement of the text. In order not to discourage readers not primarily interested in these matters, I have left these examples mainly in the footnotes.

Secondly, this volume argues that the Lord's missionary commitment to be known as God governs the book of Exodus. Breaking the book up into five commonly accepted divisions, I have sought to demonstrate that this missionary commitment is the reason why the Lord does what he does in each section, whether it is the manner of Israel's deliverance from Egypt, the giving of the law, or the Lord's response to Israel after she made the golden calf.

The effort to argue for a governing trajectory in Exodus brings up another, related, issue in Biblical Theology that has brought forth much discussion: whether or not it is appropriate to speak of a 'centre' of Biblical Theology.[9] The objection to searching for a centre is the very real concern of imposing a particular theme or structure that would in effect flatten or silence the sometimes diverse voices of the Scriptures. Yet the corresponding danger of such a fear is to rule out the possibility a priori, and therefore possibly miss ways in which the Scriptures might be read as a coherent whole. In the end, whether or not there is a centre of Biblical Theology is an issue that cannot be settled theoretically, but must be joined exegetically, with proposals being offered and subsequently evaluated. Whether or not one wants to use the term 'centre', the argument in this volume is that the Lord's commitment to be known as God throughout the earth governs all the Lord does in the book of Exodus.

Consistent with my own commitments, this work is written from a confessional evangelical perspective. I bring to the work an understanding of Scripture as the word of God, and thus an expectation

---

[9] For an overview of the discussion concerning a centre of Biblical Theology, see Hasel 1991: 139–171 and Baker 2010.

that it is the product of a unified voice. As suggested above, this commitment can mute our understanding of the Bible's witness, which is of particular concern when arguing for a 'centre'. However, it must be recognized that more critical approaches to the Bible can have a similar effect. Barton's (1996: 84) critique of Childs's canonical method is pertinent:

> But doesn't this all amount simply to a return to pre-critical exegesis? If we are going to read Scripture as a unified work, doesn't that mean that we are going back to all the old abuses – allegory, harmonization, typology, and even downright falsification of the text – from which the historical critical method has freed us?

While Barton rightly raises several potential dangers, his allusion to the historical-critical method as a type of hermeneutical saviour from pre-critical exegesis suggests not only a deep scepticism of attempts to read the OT as a unified whole, but also an approach to the text that is less concerned with understanding how the Bible might fit together, thus running the danger of muting the witness of the biblical text from another direction. If, however, the Bible is given by God, then its unity and coherence should be able to be discerned exegetically (even if imperfectly). In the end, it is my hope that this work will serve as an encouragement to take difficult texts and read them in the light of the whole, listening to them as they are given to us in their canonical form. The unified voice of the Bible, if real, need not just be insisted upon a priori, but ought to be increasingly appreciated as we continue to engage with it.

This leads to one further comment concerning the perspective of the work. Writing from a confessional evangelical perspective (and particularly admitting it!) has the effect of ruling out one's contribution in some circles of biblical scholarship. We do well to recognize, however, that prior commitments are unavoidable in all interpretation. For example, in arguing for the academic community as the appropriate community for Biblical Theology, Collins (1990: 8) writes:

> We are shaped by the rational humanism that underlies our technological culture and political institutions, no less than by the Bible (usually far more so). It is possible to have critical dialogue between our modern world view and the Bible,

but we cannot simply abandon the twentieth century for the ancient world.

In referring to 'the twentieth century', Collins speaks not of a period in time as much as a viewpoint informed by rational humanism. However, it cannot be said that all people in the twentieth century (or all people living in the West) hold that particular perspective, as Collins seems to assume. The 'we' to whom Collins refers is a particular community, the academic community, which, by his definition, holds the presuppositions (or dogma) of rational humanism. Whether or not this is true of the academic community *in toto*, Collins is clear that he approaches the text from a humanistic perspective as 'confessional' as the one he dismisses, even though his perspective rules out God. In all cases interpreters inevitably are governed by specific assumptions and concerned with specific questions.

Finally, the work is concerned with a biblical theme that spans the whole Bible. As mentioned above, mission is a theme of tremendous biblical importance, but not adequately appreciated in the OT, which runs the risk of distorting our understanding of biblical mission as a whole. In seeking to draw this theme out more broadly, I have sought to make connections throughout the Bible, Old and New Testaments. There are, of course, certain dangers here, particularly the temptation to read canonically later writings back into Exodus. However, to read Exodus apart from the later canonical witness, while perhaps safer in a certain way, would significantly impoverish its message. Aside from the myriad NT allusions to the Old, Jesus explicitly taught that the OT bore witness to him (John 5:39), and interpreted it accordingly (Luke 24:27). In dealing with this tension, I have sought to refer to later canonical writings by way of illustrating or confirming a point made in Exodus, extending a line of thought discerned in Exodus itself or drawing out the implications of what Exodus reveals about the Lord or his mission. I have tried, to the best of my ability, to steer clear of reading later canonical writings back into the earlier. An implicit argument of this work is that appropriate interpretation must take into account the canonical form of the Bible as a whole, and honour its movement. Whether or not I have been successful is for the reader to discern.

In the end, this work is about knowing God, for Exodus itself is about knowing God, knowing God for who he has made himself known to be, rather than for who we might think he is, imagine him to be or wish him to be. In the ancient words of Augustine, 'Who can call on Thee, not knowing Thee? for he that knoweth Thee not, may call on Thee as other than Thou art.'[10] The mission of God is God's commitment to be known for who he is, among his people, and through them, among all peoples.

---

[10] Augustine, *Confessions* 1.1.

Chapter Two

The name of the redeemer (Exod. 1:1 – 15:21)

If it had not been the LORD who was on our side –
   let Israel now say –
if it had not been the LORD who was on our side
   when people rose up against us,
then they would have swallowed us up alive,
   when their anger was kindled against us;
then the flood would have swept us away,
   the torrent would have gone over us;
then over us would have gone
   the raging waters.

Blessed be the LORD,
   who has not given us
   as prey to their teeth!
We have escaped like a bird
   from the snare of the fowlers;
the snare is broken,
   and we have escaped!

Our help is in the name of the LORD,
   who made heaven and earth.

(Psalm 124)

Whatever the precise referent, Psalm 124 well describes the exodus, Israel's deliverance from Egyptian slavery: the rising of an angry people in pursuit, great waters threatening to wash Israel away, the escape from bondage as a bird from a snare. Likewise, the psalm reflects Israel's response: blessing the name of the Lord, and proclaiming the Lord as her help. In this song of ascents the memory of the past leads to praise in the present, and faith for the future. For the Lord has revealed himself as being willing and able to do Israel good, and so Israel proclaims, 'Our help is in the name of the LORD'.

Names in the Bible are not mere labels, but often stand for the character and/or destiny of the bearer.[1] Abram becomes Abraham (father of many) upon the impending arrival of Isaac, through whom Abraham will become the father of many nations. Jacob is named Israel (God fights) after wrestling with God, a name then aptly applied to the nation of Jacob's descendants. Moses' name reflects his origin, and perhaps destiny, as one drawn out of water. Jesus is so named because he will bring salvation to his people.[2] In other words a name often suggests content and contours, which define who a person is. So when the psalmist speaks of the name of the Lord in Psalm 124:8, he speaks specifically of one who has a character that can be known. Through what the Lord has done, he has revealed who he is. And, thus, Israel knows his name. To know the name of the Lord implies knowing the Lord, not simply the label by which he is called. 'Our help is in the name of the LORD'.

The problem: Exodus 6:3 and the name of the Lord

One of the most important critical problems in modern biblical scholarship has to do with this very issue, the name of the Lord. In what would become one of the central texts of the Documentary Hypothesis, Exodus 6:3 states, 'By my name the LORD I did not make myself known to [the patriarchs],' a statement that appears to contradict the frequent use of the name in Genesis. Rowley (1950: 25) put the matter most starkly:

> Obviously it cannot be true that God was not known to Abraham by the name Yahweh [Exod. 6:3] and that He was known to him by that name [Gen. 15:2, 7]. To this extent there is a flat contradiction that cannot be resolved by any shift.

The traditional critical solution argued that different sources reflected different understandings of when the name was revealed to

---

[1] Adler 2009: 265: 'Names in the Tanakh are never meaningless. Rather, there is a pronounced trend in biblical Hebrew to functional or objective eponymy – that is, the names of things or people are given to describe something about them. A name is an attempt to define the character of the named thing in essence.'

[2] The Gospel of John in particular demonstrates the equivalence of believing in Jesus and believing in his name (e.g. John 1:12; 3:18).

Israel. Although widely acknowledged that the presence (or absence) of the divine name did not perfectly match the typically accepted source divisions, the theory nonetheless held. Noth's words (1981: 23) concerning the call narratives of Exodus 3 and 6 reflected the perspective of many:

> Regardless of scholarly ingenuity, no one has offered a more plausible explanation of the usage of the divine names than the view that these were two originally independent narrative works, the 'Yahwist' and the 'Elohist,' which were later combined.[3]

Others, however, were unconvinced, some arguing that the contrast implied in 6:3 had not to do with *when* the name was revealed, but rather *what* the name revealed. It was argued that it was not the name per se that was new, but that a new and more complete understanding of the name was being revealed. In other words the emphasis fell not upon the label by which the Lord was called, but rather upon the nature and character of the Lord now being revealed as something new in the experience of Israel. Motyer's rendering of 6:2–3 (1959: 12) reflects this sense:

> And God spoke to Moses, and said to him: I am Yahweh. And I showed myself to Abraham, to Isaac, and to Jacob in the character of El Shaddai, but in the character expressed by my name Yahweh I did not make myself known to them.[4]

Of those who see a change in significance in the divine name between Genesis and Exodus 6:3, most commonly understand the name as referring to the fulfilment of the patriarchal promises. Childs (1974: 115) expresses it well:

> for the biblical writer the revelation of different names is important because it made known the character of God. He had made a covenant with the patriarchs as El Shaddai, but they had not experienced the fulfillment of that promise. Now

---

[3] A few have sought to resolve the problem linguistically. See G. R. Driver 1973; Andersen 1974: 102; Whitney 1986.

[4] See also Abba 1961: 323–324; Buber 1958: 49; Freedman 1960; Gianotti 1985; Martens 1994: 19.

> God reveals himself through his name as the God who fulfills
> his promise and redeems Israel from Egypt.

According to this view, the period prior to the Egyptian deliverance
was a time of anticipation, for the promises made to the patriarchs
had yet to be fulfilled. The character of the Lord as expressed in 6:3
is one who is faithful to his covenant commitments. The fulfilment of
the promises will bring with it an understanding of the Lord as one
who fulfils his word.

In looking at 1:1 – 15:21 canonically this chapter follows Childs
and others in arguing that what is new in 6:3 is an interpretation of
the divine name, and not the name itself.[5] However, I will argue that
the fulfilment of the patriarchal promises, while important, is not
what ultimately distinguishes the significance of the name Yahweh
from Genesis to Exodus, but rather that, in the light of the narrative
context of 1:1 – 15:21, what is new in 6:3 is the revelation of the Lord
as Redeemer, the God who, being supreme over all creation, is willing
and able to deliver his people. To make that argument, I begin by
setting the problem in its canonical context, seeking to demonstrate
that the driving theological concern of 1:1 – 15:21 is the Lord's commitment to be known to Israel, Egypt and throughout the earth.

That the name be known (Exod. 1:7)

Exodus begins by connecting itself to the past, recounting the names
of Jacob's sons who settled in Egypt, and then commenting on the
passing of that generation. We are told nothing of the life of the
Israelites in Egypt, save for one detail: 'The people of Israel were
fruitful and increased greatly; they multiplied and grew exceedingly
strong, so that the land was filled with them' (Exod. 1:7). Serving a
far greater purpose than simply alerting the reader to the growth of
Jacob's family into a nation, the description of Israel's fruitfulness
takes us back to two cardinal passages in Genesis that speak to the
purposes of God. The first is God's mandate to humanity in Genesis
1:28:

> And God blessed them. And God said to them, 'Be fruitful
> and multiply and fill the earth and subdue it, and have domin-

---

[5] Seeing 6:3 as referring to the meaning of the name need not be driven by canonical concerns. For linguistic arguments to that end, see Motyer 1959.

ion over the fish of the sea and over the birds of the heavens
and over every living thing that moves on the earth.'

When interpreted firmly within the context of Genesis 1, God's
mandate to be fruitful and exercise dominion has the distinctly missionary purpose of making himself known throughout creation.
Because humanity is the image of God (1:26),[6] the command calls
for God's image to spread throughout, and ultimately fill, the earth.
Furthermore, as humanity spreads throughout the earth, he is called
to exercise dominion, governing God's creation as befits his status
as God's image. The effect of the commandment, then, is that life
on the earth would witness to the character of God, as God's image
spreads and governs according to his likeness and character. The
implied purpose of God in Genesis 1 is expressed throughout the
Bible:

> Blessed be his glorious name for ever;
>   may the whole earth be filled with his glory!
> Amen and Amen!
>
> (Ps. 72:19; cf. e.g. Isa. 6:2; Hab. 2:14)

The second passage to which Exodus 1:7 calls attention is Genesis
12:1–3:

> Now the LORD said to Abram, 'Go from your country and
> your kindred and your father's house to the land that I will
> show you. And I will make of you a great nation, and I will
> bless you and make your name great, so that you will be a
> blessing. I will bless those who bless you, and him who dis-
> honours you I will curse, and in you all the families of the
> earth shall be blessed.'

Inaugurating his call to Israel, the Lord promises to make Abraham
a great nation, through which all the families of the earth will be
blessed. From the beginning, the call of Abraham has a worldwide
scope. This promise of nationhood, and hence the worldwide blessing that would come from that nation, depends on Abraham's fruitfulness: 'I will make you exceedingly fruitful, and I will make you
into nations, and kings shall come from you' (Gen. 17:6; cf. 26:2–5,

---

[6] For a defence of the translation 'as God's image', see Clines 1968.

24; 28:14). The connection between Genesis 12:1–3 and Exodus 1:7 is further supported by the reference to Jacob's descendants in Egypt in Exodus 1:1–6, demonstrating that God's promise to Abraham is being fulfilled.

The convergence of Genesis 1:27 and Genesis 12:1–3 in Exodus 1:7 is important on at least three levels. First, it suggests that Israel is living under the blessing of God. It is noteworthy that in both Genesis passages blessing is connected with multiplication, the bearing of children being an expression of God's blessing.[7] In the words of Psalm 105:24, concerning Israel in Egypt, 'The LORD made his people very fruitful and made them stronger than their foes.' Furthermore, given that both Genesis texts reflect God's commitment to be known, Israel's fruitfulness indicates that God's missionary purposes were going forward in Egypt. While this inference will need to be confirmed as we read further, the convergence of these two cardinal texts suggests, from the beginning, that mission is very much in view in the book of Exodus.

Secondly, the recognition of God's larger missionary purposes sets up the coming conflict with Pharaoh in the broadest terms possible. It is precisely Israel's multiplication that Pharaoh seeks to restrain. Again in language reminiscent of Genesis 1:27, and in response to Exodus 1:7, Pharaoh gives the reason for his ensuing oppression of Israel: 'Behold, the people of Israel are many and stronger than us' (1:9, my tr.; cf. 1:7). The nature of the conflict becomes clear: Pharaoh directly (albeit unwittingly) seeks to undermine God's purposes not only for Israel, but also for the world. Understanding Exodus 1:7 in connection with God's purposes in creation and for Israel exposes what is ultimately at stake in the coming conflict with Pharaoh, which dominates Exodus 1:8 – 15:21: Pharaoh's opposition threatens God's purposes to be known throughout the world.[8]

Finally, the allusions to Genesis 1 and Genesis 12 in Exodus 1:7 point to an important insight concerning God's purposes in Exodus.

---

[7] E.g. Deut. 7:13–14; Pss 127, 128. Conversely, barrenness is roundly lamented in the Bible (e.g. Sarah, Rachel, Hannah, Elizabeth).

[8] When Pharaoh's attempt to stem Israel's growth through brutal slavery fails to work, Pharaoh directly attacks Israel's growth by calling for Israel's infant boys to be killed. The account of the midwives whom Pharaoh commanded to kill the male children (1:16) encapsulates the conflict. Caught between the will of God and the will of Pharaoh, they are forced to choose sides, disobeying Pharaoh explicitly because they fear God (1:17). In response (and in a hint of God's eventual triumph over Pharaoh), God rewards the midwives with families, further extending his will that Israel be fruitful and multiply.

In Genesis 1:27 the implication of God's call to humanity is that the earth reflect his nature as it is filled with his image. In other words God's call is for the sake of his glory, that he might be known for who he is throughout creation. In Genesis 12:1–3 the Lord's purpose in calling Abram is explained from a different angle: God's intention through Abraham is blessing, for Abraham's descendants and, through them, the world. In other words Genesis 12:1–3 suggests that God's missionary purpose is for the good of the world. These two angles work together to suggest within Exodus the conviction held by the church through the ages: God does what he does for his glory and for the good of his people.

The name unknown (Exod. 1:8 – 2:25)

Yet, despite Israel's living under the blessing of God, Exodus begins with a problem. Whereas Exodus 1:7 speaks of God's purpose to make himself known throughout the earth, Exodus 1:8 introduces a world ignorant of the Lord. Characteristic of Exodus 1 – 2 is a curious and noteworthy absence of the name of the Lord, an absence particularly striking in the light of the abundant presence of the Lord's name from Exodus 3 onwards. In fact, save for the comment that Hebrew midwives feared God, there is no indication that Israel even acknowledged the God of their fathers in Exodus 1 – 2. Israel cries out under their affliction, and their cries are heard by God, but the text does not indicate that Israel cried out *to* God. This inference that the Lord was largely unknown, admittedly argued from silence, is supported both by Moses' asking for the Lord's name (3:14)[9] and by Pharaoh's question 'Who is the LORD that I should obey his voice and let Israel go?' (5:2). Whereas early in Genesis 'people began to call upon the name of the LORD' (Gen. 4:26), Exodus begins with an apparently universal ignorance of the Lord's name. Thus, at the beginning of the narrative, two inferences can be made: God is clearly at work among Israel, and yet Israel, like the rest of the world, appears to be ignorant of her God. The rest of the narrative concerns both – God continues to work in and through Israel for the sake of the world, as he reveals himself to Israel as her God. In this

---

[9] Moses' question does not require that Israel would not have known the name. Seitz (1998: 236–237) suggests that Moses asks for the name in anticipation that Israel will test Moses to ensure he comes in the name of the God of their fathers. For reasons stated above, and further below, the absence of the name in Exod. 1 – 2 suggests this interpretation is unlikely.

way the problem with which Exodus is chiefly concerned is brought forth from the beginning of the narrative.[10]

The corollary to Israel's ignorance of God is the situation in which she finds herself in Exodus 1. The description of Israel's plight is given immediately after Pharaoh's decree to 'deal shrewdly' with Israel, in order to stem their growth:

> So they ruthlessly made the people of Israel work as slaves and made their lives bitter with hard service, in mortar and brick, and in all kinds of work in the field. In all their work they ruthlessly made them work as slaves. (Exod. 1:13–14)

Two matters are particularly important to note. First, Israel does not know the Lord, and finds herself serving Pharaoh. Presumably due to the desire for more interesting prose, this emphasis on Israel's *serving* (Hebrew root *'bd*) Pharaoh is typically obscured in most English translations. The verses immediately above can be translated more literally as follows:

> And the Egyptians forced the sons of Israel to *serve* with violence. And they caused their lives to be bitter with hard *service*, with mortar and with brick and with all kinds of *service* in the field. In all their *service* with which they *served*, in violence. (Tr. and emphases mine)

The repetition of the verb 'to serve' highlights Israel's slavery, that Israel is not her own master, but rather the forced servant of another.

Secondly, the nature of their service is deeply and violently oppressive. This oppression begins with Pharaoh's afflicting them with heavy burdens as they are exploited for economic profit while they build Pharaoh's cities. Beatings were apparently common. That the incident of an Egyptian's beating a Hebrew (2:11–15) is not an isolated event is made plain when we are later told that the Egyptian taskmasters beat the Hebrew foremen (5:14). Finally, and most chillingly, when Israel continues to multiply in the midst of such oppression, Pharaoh issues the order to kill Israel's infant boys. While the text does not specifically report the death of any children, that Moses' mother hid him for three months after birth before releasing him to an uncertain future (and possible death) suggests that the threat was very real indeed.

---

[10] Supporting this inference, see Ps. 106:7 and Ezek. 20.

Because many modern readers, particularly in the West, are unfamiliar with what is involved in brickmaking, we are warranted in exploring further what other readers would intuitively understand:

> [B]rickmaking operations are big business in several developing nations. Usually resembling a rustic fortress, most are surrounded by walls seven or eight feet high – to keep brick poachers out, and to keep slave laborers in. They have a dark, otherworldly presence to them because of the dust and smoke that hang constantly in the air, coating everything within the walls with gray-red dust and soot. . . . The kilns require extra labor, because someone has to stoke the charcoal first constantly to keep them at their optimum temperature. This is one of the worst jobs in an operation defined by awful jobs – excruciatingly hot, dirty, and sticky, the workers covered with charcoal dust that mixes with the dust of clay and dirt until sweat-soaked skin begins to harden and crack.
>
> Before the bricks are ready for the kiln, they must be shaped and predried in the sun. All day long, slaves perform the backbreaking labor of packing wet clay and straw into molds that form the bricks. They slap the clay into the molds forming row after row, then other workers, usually children, carry the bricks on their heads to set them out in the sun to dry. When they are dry enough to fire, the slaves carry them to the kiln to be baked. Hour after hour, day after day, weeks that flow into months, months that fade into years . . . some of these slaves have been at this dirty, tedious, painful work for decades with no relief in sight. Until now.[11]

This account of modern-day slave labour might well have been written of Israel's life in Egypt: an oppressed people living as slaves under the threat of death, subject to physical brutality, making bricks for the economic profit of their oppressors. Lingering here is important, for if we don't understand the plight of Israel from the beginning, we will fail to appreciate both the magnitude of the deliverance that communicates the nature of God and thereby reveals his name, and the difference between Israel's serving Pharaoh and serving the Lord.

---

[11] Haugen 2005: 22. Childs (1974: 106) comments on the consistency between ancient brickmaking practice and the description in Exod. 5:10–21.

Thus at the beginning of Exodus we see Israel's plight. Ignorant of her God, she serves another in great affliction. Here we see two conditions that, in the Scriptures, always go together, for it is in knowing and serving the Lord that the people of God find blessing, and are freed from masters that bring harm, not good. As Israel forsakes the Lord she ends up serving others, whether the Philistines, the Midianites, the Assyrians or the Babylonians, masters that oppress, not bless. But the lesson runs deeper. An important implication of Jesus' words 'no one can serve two masters' is that everyone will serve one, a truth that Paul addresses foundationally in his claim that unless one is a servant of Christ, he is a servant of sin (Rom. 6:15–19). The plight of Israel in Egypt illustrates this larger truth that runs throughout the Scriptures.

The name made known (Exod. 3 – 14)

If Exodus 1 – 2 presents the problem, that the name of the Lord is not known, Exodus 3 begins the solution, where the Lord makes his name known. A key passage concerning the divine name in all of the OT, here the Lord's name first appears in Exodus, and is explained.

Our task is to discern the meaning of the divine name firmly within the literary context in which it first appears in Exodus. While literary context is always important in biblical interpretation, it is particularly important here for two reasons that will become apparent as we press into Exodus. First, the ambiguous nature of the name as given to Moses makes it more tempting to interpret it outside its literary context, a tack that has often been taken in OT scholarship. The most basic item to note in this regard is that the Lord gives his name to Moses in response to a specific question. Our starting point in understanding the meaning of the name is to understand it, not as an independent datum concerning the nature of God, but as the answer to a question. The context of that question is crucial.

Secondly, the meaning of the name is perhaps the primary burden of the book of Exodus as a whole. Brueggemann (1997: 124) has gone so far as to suggest that 'it is plausible that the entire Exodus narrative is an exposition of the name of Exod 3:14, requiring all its powerful verbs for an adequate expression'.[12] If it is the case that the

---

[12] Cf. Jacob (1992: 76–77) who writes, imagining the voice of God, 'Should someone wish to question My name, he is right, for he will discover that He who is Almighty and helpful will indeed help.'

whole book of Exodus is concerned with explaining God's name, as I will argue it is, then it is particularly important that we begin carefully. In a flight from Boston a few degrees at the beginning can mean the difference between landing in Seattle or Los Angeles.

Exodus 3 finds Moses, a refugee from Egypt tending sheep in Midian, in his first encounter with the Lord, who commissions him to lead Israel out of Egyptian slavery. Fearful concerning the task before him, Moses presents a hypothetical question: What if the people of Israel ask Moses, 'What is his [God's] name?' (Exod. 3:13). In asking for God's name Moses is not asking the philosophical or existential question, but is rather concerned for his life and the lives of the Israelites should they attempt to escape from Egypt.

> God said [*wayyōmer*] to Moses, 'I AM WHO I AM' ['*ehyeh 'ăšer 'ehyeh*]. And he said [*wayyōmer*], 'Say this to the people of Israel, "I am has sent me to you."' God also said [*wayyōmer*] to Moses, 'Say this to the people of Israel, "The LORD, the God of your fathers, the God of Abraham, the God of Isaac, and the God of Jacob, has sent me to you." This is my name for ever, and thus I am to be remembered throughout all generations.' (Exod. 3:14–15)

Some modern scholarship has seen this response, particularly with its threefold 'and he said' [*wayyōmer*] as 'garbled', 'overcrowded' or 'swollen'.[13] Another possibility is that these statements actually work together to suggest the meaning of the name Yahweh, articulated in 3:15. If so, how are these statements related? The following will suggest that the Lord's answer to Moses is given in three stages, each building upon the one before, together giving an interpretation of the name that addresses Israel's hypothetical concern of 3:13. We will take each of these statements in order.

'I am who I am'

As has been noted by many, 'I AM WHO I AM' (*'ehyeh 'ăšer 'ehyeh*) in 3:14 looks back to 'I am with you' (*'ehyeh 'immāk*) in 3:12.[14] The Lord has appeared to Moses and has called him to go to Pharaoh and bring Israel out from Egypt. Moses responds with the question,

---

[13] See, respectively, Fishbane 1979: 67; Noth 1962: 43; Arnold 1905: 130.

[14] The common practice of translating 3:12 as 'I will be with you,' allowed by the flexibility of the Hebrew imperfect, often causes this connection to 3:14 to be missed.

'Who am I that I should go to Pharaoh and bring the children of Israel out of Egypt?' (3:11). The question is not existential (Moses knows who he is), but rather an expression of doubt concerning whether or not he can succeed. Responding to Moses' real concern, the Lord answers, 'I am with you,' an answer that says nothing about Moses, but much about the Lord. Implied in the Lord's answer is both his presence with Moses in his task, and his power to enable Moses to succeed.[15]

Moses then asks for a response should Israel ask him the name of the 'God of your fathers'. The Lord responds with 'I am who I am,' a reply that has engendered great discussion.[16] Several translations are linguistically possible, accounting for the multitude of suggestions.[17] Citing the flexibility of the imperfect tense, Brichto argues for the legitimacy of multiple translations, each of which suggests important nuances of the name.[18] The linguistic flexibility in Hebrew of 'I am who I am' suggests that a more fruitful approach would be to examine a particular interpretation in the light of the immediate canonical context, and then to rule out certain readings, rather than to insist on a precise English translation. Two elements are important in understanding 'I am who I am.' First, the relationship between 3:12 ('I am with you') and 3:14 ('I am who I am') suggests that the meaning of 3:14a is related to the promise of success, for the

[15] The two other appearances of *'ehyeh* in Exodus (4:12, 15) carry the same sense.

[16] For an extensive bibliography, see Sæbø 1998: 78–79.

[17] Most proposals follow the traditional pattern 'I am/will be who/what I am/will be'. Proposals offered as an alternative to the traditional possibilities fall into two broad categories. One alternative, offered by Albright (1924), finds YHWH to be a hiphil of the verb *hāyah* (to be), and supports an emendation that he renders, 'I cause to be what comes into existence.' Freedman (1960) largely follows Albright, by translating the phrase as 'I am the creator,' although he argues that the parallel between 3:14 and 33:19 makes the emendation unnecessary. The weakness of the above proposals, however, is that each ultimately relies upon conjecture, either upon textual emendation or a hypothetical hiphil form of 'to be' that occurs nowhere else in the Masoretic Text (the causative stem for *hayah* being the piel). The other alternative, proposed by Schild (1954) and Lindblom (1964), suggests that the relative clause 'that I am' is governed by the first *'ehyeh*, rendering the translation 'I am he who is.' Albrektson (1968) argues for a return to the traditional possibilities, convincingly demonstrating that the parallels upon which Schild's and Lindblom's proposals are based are not adequate parallels to 3:14a. Following Albrektson, the present argument will work with the understanding that the Hebrew phrase is best rendered according to the traditional pattern.

[18] Brichto (1983: 29) argues for every combination of 'I was'/'I am'/'I will be', saying, 'The multivalence and ambiguity of the imperfect tense in biblical Hebrew is often exploited by Scripture's authors to make a statement in a broadly inclusive sense even while it is addressed to a particular context.'

Lord will be present as Moses and Israel carry out his will. Secondly, the ambiguity of 'I am who I am' must be honoured. While not a rebuff or refusal to answer, the Lord's response in 3:14a is nonetheless vague, and certainly not a complete answer. As Zimmerli (1978: 21) has written, 3:14 'refuses to "explain" the name in a way that would confine it within the cage of a definition'. One effect of this is to give the divine name a future orientation, opening the possibility, even expectation, of further revelation. Any 'definition', or understanding, of the name would become clearer as God makes himself known in rescuing Israel from Egypt.

'I am' has sent me to you

The second stage in the revelation echoes 3:14a: 'And he said [*wayōmer*], thus you shall say to Israel, "I am" has sent me to you' (my tr.). Whereas 3:14a was given for Moses, 3:14b is given for Israel, in direct response to Israel's hypothetical question. The nature of Israel's question has been much discussed, mostly along the lines of whether Israel would be asking for a name previously known, in order to test Moses' claim to speak for their God,[19] whether Israel would be enquiring concerning the character of God,[20] or whether Israel was enquiring concerning a previously unknown name.[21] Here again the literary context helps us. The similarity between the Lord's answer to Israel ('I am') and the Lord's answer to Moses ('I am who I am') may suggest a similar question. In a manner comparable to Moses' own need for assurance in going before Pharaoh, Moses envisions Israel's having similar misgivings, and therefore needing similar assurance that this mission would be successful.[22] In response to this desire for assurance the Lord tells Moses to answer Israel in a manner that would reflect the promise of his presence: 'I am has sent me to you,' thereby assuring Israel of the success of the upcoming exodus.[23]

---

[19] So Seitz 1998: 236–237; Mowinckel 1961: 126; Houtman 1993: 366–367; Clements 1972: 23.

[20] So Abba 1961; Buber 1958: 48; Gianotti 1985: 39.

[21] So Moberly 1992: 24–26; deVaux 1970: 49; Noth 1962: 43.

[22] On linguistic grounds, Buber (1958: 48) has argued that the Hebrew expression does not ask for God's name, but is rather a question concerning the character of God. See Abba 1961: 323, and especially Motyer (1959: 17–24), who has tested Buber's suggestion throughout the OT.

[23] In favour of such a reading is the sense it makes of the sequence between 3:14a and 3:14b. It has been widely recognized that 'I am who I am' is not a direct answer to Moses' question, leading some (e.g. Arnold 1905: 129–130; cf. Bernhardt 1978:

'The LORD, the God of your fathers . . .'

Assurance of the presence of Moses' God, however, would not be enough for Israel, for 3:14 has not formally answered the question that Moses envisions Israel asking. This leads to the Lord's third reply to Moses, where the name Yahweh is specifically given. The giving of the name completes Moses' answer to Israel, assuring Israel that the God of Moses is the God of Israel. Particularly notable is the almost identical wording of 3:14b and 3:15a:

> 3:14b: Say this to the people of Israel, I AM has sent me to you.

> 3:15a: Say this to the people of Israel, the LORD, the God of your fathers, the God of Abraham, the God of Isaac, the God of Jacob, has sent me to you.

Except for the rendering of the divine name, where 'I AM' in 3:14b directly parallels 'the LORD, the God of your fathers, the God of Abraham, the God of Isaac, the God of Jacob' in 3:15a, the above sentences are identical. Considering that 'I AM' is not, strictly speaking, the divine name itself, the parallel suggests that 'I AM' is an interpretation, or explanation, of the name of the God of their fathers. Put differently, the linguistic similarity between 3:14b and 3:15a suggests that the meaning of 'I AM' is equivalent to the meaning of 'the LORD, the God of [the patriarchs]'. Given what we have discovered concerning the significance of 'I AM' in 3:12 and 3:14, the name 'the LORD' in 3:15a therefore carries with it the promise of God's presence in leaving Egypt and the corresponding assurance of success. Confirming this inference are the Lord's words in 3:16, where the Lord goes on to assure the people that, as the God of their fathers, he will deliver them from Egyptian oppression and bring them into an abundant land.

376–381; Noth 1962: 43–44; Phillips and Phillips 1998: 81–83) to assume that it is an interpolation. However, if the function of 3:14b is to provide assurance to Israel that what Moses anticipates will be needed, then 3:14b becomes dependent upon 3:14a, thereby eliminating the need for an interpolator. Furthermore, it also addresses Arnold's contention that 'I am' was substituted for 'the LORD' in 3:14b due to respect for the divine name, for an introduction of the divine name without the prior explanation of 3:14 would have yielded a much different sense. Rather than being a problem, the threefold 'and he said' (*wayyōmer*) marks a logical progression leading to an understanding of the name in 3:15.

Understood in this way, the Lord's answer to Moses becomes less problematic. The threefold repetition of God 'said' (*wayyōmer*) is not needlessly repetitive, but marks an answer in three stages, each building upon the previous one, together answering Moses' (and by implication Israel's) concern. Israel will be delivered, because the God of their fathers has heard their groaning, and is willing and able to deliver them. Furthermore, the Lord has given his name in such a way that has not exhausted its meaning. The rest of the book of Exodus, and in particular the manner in which the Lord will deliver Israel, will shed further light on the meaning of the name. And Israel will come to know her God.

'I am the LORD'

Not only does 3:14–15 not exhaust the meaning of the name, but it suggests a future orientation, for the 'I AM' begs the questions 'You are what?' or 'Who are you?', questions that await an answer. A specific illustration of the name begging such a question can be found in Jesus' words to the Jews, where 'if you do not believe that I am,[24] you will die in your sins' provokes the reply 'Who are you?' (John 8:24–25). In Exodus this implied question 'Who are you?' is addressed with the very specific phrase 'I am the LORD.' As we will see, the principal burden of Exodus 5 – 15 is to give meaning to that name.

In a manner similar to the revelation of the name in Exodus 3, the revelation of the name in Exodus 5 – 15 is also introduced by a question. In response to the command of the Lord to release Israel, addressing Pharaoh as a subject in language that Pharaoh uses to address Israel, Pharaoh asks a question to which the rest of 5 – 15 will be the answer: 'Who is the LORD, that I should obey his voice and let Israel go? I do not know the LORD, and moreover, I will not let Israel go' (Exod. 5:2). Unlike Moses' question of 3:13, however, Pharaoh's question is not one of enquiry, but of defiance. Goldingay's translation of 5:2 (2003: 340) captures the sense well: 'Who is Yhwh that I should listen to his voice and let Israel go? I do not acknowledge Yhwh. No, I will not let Israel go.'[25] In a further comment on 5:2 Goldingay (2003: 341) writes that Pharaoh

---

[24] My tr. *Egō eimi* used here is the LXX translation of *'ehyeh* in Exod. 3:14. The common translation 'I am he' adds a 'he' not present in the Greek NT, thus obscuring the connection to Exod. 3:14.

[25] Cf. Childs 1974: 153–154; Brueggemann 1995: 36.

'is declining to recognize Yhwh's authority. He is laying down his own gauntlet for the fight that Yhwh also wishes to have.' The conflict between Pharaoh and the Lord, only implicit in 1:8, becomes explicit. Pharaoh's defiant response, then, serves as the theological context for the section.[26] The remainder of the exodus account is the answer to Pharaoh's question.

It would be difficult to overestimate the importance of 'I am Yahweh' in the exodus narrative, for knowing the Lord is the theme and ultimate goal of the plagues.[27] As Zimmerli (1982: 9) has argued in his broader study titled 'I am Yahweh',

> [t]he phrase 'I am Yahweh' carries all the weight and becomes the denominator upon which all else rests. . . . [E]verything Yahweh has to announce to his people appears as an amplification of the fundamental statement, 'I am Yahweh.'

Applied to the exodus narrative, Zimmerli's statement is most strongly supported by the Lord's words to Pharaoh:

> For this time I will send all my plagues on you yourself, and on your servants and your people, so that you may know that there is none like me in all the earth. For by now I could have put out my hand and struck you and your people with pestilence, and you would have been cut off from the earth. But for this purpose I have raised you up, to show you my power, so that my name may be proclaimed in all the earth. (Exod. 9:14–16)

The above statement is critical for understanding the purpose of the plagues. While Israel's liberation is crucial in Exodus, the Lord's words make it clear that liberation is not the reason for the succession of plagues. This is not to downplay the Lord's compassion for Israel or his remembering his covenant, but simply to say that neither of those things accounts for the *manner* in which the Lord overcame Egypt and released Israel. If Israel's liberation was the

---

[26] Sailhamer 1992: 249. According to Carpenter (1997: 102), 'Exod. 5:1–2 is a programmatic piece that illustrates the concerns to be dealt with throughout chs. 5–17.'

[27] Fretheim (1991b: 387) observes that, rather than plagues, the language of Exodus most often refers to signs (4:17; 7:3; 8:17; 10:1–2) or wonders (4:21; 7:3, 9; 11:9–10), an emphasis more in keeping with the ultimate goal of communication in the plague narratives.

controlling issue, the narrative might have quickly moved from 5:2 to 14:30a: 'Thus the LORD saved Israel that day from the hand of the Egyptians.' Rather, it is the Lord's desire to be known throughout the land that accounts for the plagues, and therefore the narrative of chapters 5 – 14. As Fretheim (1991a: 95) claims, 'there is a fundamental *mission orientation* to the entire plague cycle' (emphasis original).

God is great: the Lord is God

If the primary purpose of the signs and wonders was not deliverance, per se, but rather communication, that raises the questions 'What was "I am the LORD" intended to communicate? What kind of God did the Egyptian deliverance reveal the Lord to be?' A survey of these statements (and several closely related statements)[28] in 1:1 – 15:21 points to the Lord's unrivalled superiority over creation, which can be divided into three areas: supremacy over humanity, over nature and over other gods. We will explore these in order.

'*I am the LORD*' *declares the Lord's supremacy over humanity.* The Lord's supremacy over man is first seen in his claim to be the creator of humanity. When Moses objects that he cannot speak well, the Lord asks, 'Who made the mouth of a man? . . . I am the LORD, no?' (Exod. 4:11, my tr.). This first appearance of 'I am the LORD' is easily missed in English translations, for, readily apparent in Hebrew, the statement is difficult to render as an interrogative into English and preserve intact (as the awkward translation above suggests). In a rhetorical response to Moses' misgivings about his speech, the Lord assures Moses that he made Moses as he is, and therefore can enable him to carry out this calling. The assurance is grounded in the Lord's being the creator.

The Lord's supremacy over man is further apparent in his interaction with Pharaoh, perhaps best represented by 14:4: 'And I will harden Pharaoh's heart, and he will pursue them, and I will get glory over Pharaoh and all his host, and the Egyptians shall know that I am the LORD.' This verse speaks to the Lord's supremacy over humanity in two different ways. First, 14:4 alludes to the Lord's supremacy over Pharaoh, evident in his ability to harden Pharaoh's heart. Although there has been much discussion concerning the relationship between the Lord's hardening Pharaoh's heart and

---

[28] E.g. Exod. 8:10[6]; 9:14–16; 9:29; 11:7.

Pharaoh's hardening his own heart,[29] the narrative makes it clear that the Lord controls Pharaoh's heart.[30] Secondly, 14:4 addresses the Lord's supremacy over the Egyptian army. As we will see in our discussion of Exodus 15, Exodus portrays the crossing of the sea as a military conflict between Egypt and the Lord in which the Lord triumphs, with no hint that he suffers at all in the battle, or that the outcome is ever in doubt. Not only is the Lord supreme over an individual ruler, but he is supreme over that ruler's army. 'I am Yahweh' would convey that even the armies of nations cannot withstand the Lord's power to exercise his will.

'I am the LORD' declares the Lord's supremacy over nature. That 'I am the LORD' communicates the Lord's mastery over nature can be seen most explicitly where knowledge that 'I am the LORD' is given as an intended result of a particular plague (7:17; 8:22[18]; cf. 8:10[6]; 9:14, 29). The plague narrative is fraught with indications that the Lord, not Pharaoh, is supreme over nature. For instance, dramatic actions demonstrate unambiguously that the plagues were the Lord's doing: the river became blood after Aaron smote the Nile with a rod,[31] Moses threw dust into the air to inaugurate the plague of boils in Pharaoh's presence (9:10), he stretched out his hands over the land to bring the locusts (10:13) and the darkness (10:22), and he stretched his staff towards the heavens to bring the hail (9:23). Precise predictions concerning an upcoming plague, including its beginning and/or ending also demonstrate the Lord's precise control over nature (8:9[5]; 8:23[19]; 8:29[25]; 9:5; 9:18; 9:29). The Lord further demonstrates his command over nature by controlling precisely the extent of a particular plague by making a distinction between Israel and Egypt (8:22–23[18–19]; 9:26; 11:7; 10:23; 12:23). While still refusing to submit to the Lord's command to release Israel, even Pharaoh acknowledges the Lord's power in

[29] It is, of course, well recognized that Exodus attributes Pharaoh's hardening both to Pharaoh (8:15[11]; 8:32[28]; 9:34; 13:15) and to the Lord (4:21; 7:3; 9:12; 10:1, 20, 27; 11:10; 14:4, 7, 17), and often simply comments that Pharaoh's heart was hardened (7:13, 14, 22; 8:19[15]; 9:7, 35). For recent attempts to relate these differing conceptions, see particularly Beale 1984; Childs 1974: 170–175; Cassuto 1967: 54–58; Fretheim 1991a: 96–103; Gunn 1982; Räisänen 1976; Wilson 1979.

[30] See particularly 4:21 and 7:3, both of which suggest beforehand that it is the Lord who hardens Pharaoh's heart. Cf. Noth (1962: 68), who contends that, based on 7:3, 'We shall have to assume the narrator to mean that right from the beginning it was only Yahweh who was really at work.'

[31] Note that the Lord tells Pharaoh that he himself will strike the river with the staff 'in my hand', even though the river was struck by Aaron (7:19–20).

his repeated petitions that Moses stop the plagues (8:8[4], 28[24]; 9:27–28; 10:16–17; 12:31–32).

As has been noted by several interpreters, this demonstration of control over nature points to the Lord as the creator.[32] Zevit has drawn connections between the plagues and creation in Genesis 1 – 2, arguing that the plague account is carefully structured to make this very point. The end of the plague narrative, he argues, shows a land without people, animals and vegetation, '[a] land in which creation was undone' (Zevit 1976: 210). Fretheim likewise sees creation as the fundamental background of the plagues, arguing that the conflict between the Lord and Pharaoh comes from the fact that Pharaoh's sin is 'anticreation'; that is, Pharaoh's attempt to curb Israel's growth goes against God's creational purposes.[33] Because Pharaoh's sin is anti-creational, the Lord's response to judge Egypt by subverting creation to a pre-creation state is possible because, as the Creator, he can. Or, in the words of Dozeman (1996: 119), 'The [I am Yahweh] motif . . . transforms the exodus into a polemical story whose goal is to confront Pharaoh and the Egyptians with Yahweh's power as a creator God, who controls all land, including Egypt.'

'I am the LORD' declares the Lord's supremacy over other gods. Finally, 'I am the LORD' was intended to communicate that the Lord has unrivalled power over all other gods. The phrase is explicitly connected to the Lord's supremacy over other gods only in 12:12, where the Lord declares that, in bringing death upon the firstborn, 'on all the gods of Egypt I will execute judgments: I am the LORD'.[34] Whether 'execute judgments' is best understood as punishing Egypt's gods for Israel's oppression, as referring to a display of divine power, or both, the inescapable implication of the phrase is that the Lord

---

[32] Fretheim 1991b; Dozeman 1996: 101–152; Enns 2000: 192–239; Zevit 1976. Propp (1998: 345–346) is unconvinced of the connection to creation, particularly as conceived by Fretheim and Zevit.

[33] Fretheim 1991b: 385; cf. 1991b: 106–107.

[34] Cf. Num. 33:4. While 12:12 is the only verse that explicitly mentions other gods in connection with 'I am the LORD,' several related passages imply the Lord's superiority over other gods. For instance, in 8:10[6] Moses pledged to remove the frogs, that 'you may know that there is no one like the LORD our God'. In 9:14 the signs were sent that 'you may know there is none like me in all the land'. The lack of a specific referent in each verse gives the contrast with other beings the widest possible scope, which would include other gods among those who cannot be compared to the Lord. The explicit reference to other gods in 12:12 and 15:11 (cf. 20:2–5; 22:20; 23:32; 34:11–16) shows that Exodus is aware of other gods, and thus provides solid warrant to see 8:10[6] and 9:14 as including other gods as among those who cannot compare to the Lord.

is incomparable, supreme over the gods of Egypt.[35] As Zevit (1976: 198) wisely observes, 'The fact that plagues did affect the Egyptians adversely led to an intertwining of the two motives, but, as has been mentioned above, for Pr [the writer] their significance did not lie in their destructive aspect but in their heuristic one.'[36]

The implications of the Lord's supremacy over all creation are severalfold. First, the Lord claims authority over Egypt. That the plagues implicitly point to the Lord as the Creator becomes particularly important, for it establishes his rightful ownership and rule over the earth. The goal of the hailstorm is the purpose of all the plagues: 'that you may know that the earth is the LORD's' (9:29). Whether the Hebrew word *hā'āreṣ* (earth, land) refers to the whole earth or just the land of Egypt, the force is the same: despite the pretensions of Pharaoh or the Egyptian gods, Egypt belongs to the Lord. Psalm 24 articulates later what is implicit in the exodus accounts:

> The earth [*hā'āreṣ*] is the LORD's and the fullness thereof,
>   the world and those who dwell therein,
> for he has founded it upon the seas
>   and established it upon the rivers.
>
> (Ps. 24:1–2; cf. 95:3–5)

Why does the whole earth belong to the Lord? Because he is the Creator.

Secondly, the supremacy of the Lord exposes Pharaoh and the gods of Egypt as helpless to save. The division between Israel and Egypt declares simultaneously that Pharaoh and the Egyptian gods cannot protect their people or land, while the continued welfare of Israel in the midst of disaster declares that the Lord can do both. Again, the connection between the Lord as Creator and his ability to save is not incidental, but rather imperative, and expressed elsewhere in the Scriptures. 'Have you not known? Have you not heard? / The LORD is the everlasting God, / the Creator of the ends of the earth' (Isa. 40:28) is a word of comfort to a captive people, and articulates the foundation of Israel's confidence in the Lord's promise to deliver them. Or, negatively, Jeremiah declares, 'The gods who did not make the heavens and the earth shall perish from the earth and from under the heavens' (Jer. 10:11). The Lord's might to save and

---

[35] See e.g. Propp 1998: 399–400; Goldingay 2003: 321.
[36] Cf. Greenberg 1971b.

the impotence of false gods go hand in hand. We will return to this point below.

God is good: the Lord is the God of Israel

Not only does the Lord's name suggest that he is God, supreme over all, but it suggests that, in a particular way, the Lord is the God of Israel. This is first apparent, of course, in the initial revelation of the name in Exodus, where the Lord reveals himself to be 'the LORD, the God of your fathers, the God of Abraham, the God of Isaac, and the God of Jacob' (Exod. 3:15–16). Just as the Lord communicated the meaning of his name through mighty acts meant to declare his greatness, so also the name suggests covenantal loyalty to Israel. The Lord's declaration that he is the God of the patriarchs harkens back to the promises made in Genesis:

> I will establish my covenant between me and you and your offspring after you throughout their generations for an everlasting covenant, to be God to you and to your offspring after you. And I will give to you and to your offspring after you the land of your sojournings, all the land of Canaan, for an everlasting possession, and I will be their God. (Gen. 17:7–8)

Here the promise contains both a provision of a home and a special relationship with the Lord as their God, throughout the generations.

What is particularly interesting about the above passage is that it is introduced by the Lord's appearing to Abraham as *El Shaddai*: 'I am God Almighty' (Gen. 17:1). Returning to Exodus 6:3, the Lord makes it clear that he appeared to the patriarchs as *El Shaddai*, but did not make himself known as Yahweh. This raises the question 'What will be revealed about God to Israel in the exodus that was not made known to Abraham, Isaac and Jacob?'

The answer to this question is suggested in Exodus 6. After acknowledging that he did not reveal himself to the patriarchs as Yahweh in 6:3, the Lord immediately does so to Moses. What the Lord will reveal to Israel about himself is stated explicitly, as he tells Moses what to say to Israel: 'Say therefore to the people of Israel . . .' (Exod. 6:6a). The speech can be structured as follows:

A: I am the LORD.
    B: And I will bring you out from under the burdens of the
      Egyptians, and I will deliver you from slavery to them,

> and I will redeem you with an outstretched arm and with
> great acts of judgment.
> C: I will take you to be my people, and I will be your God,
> and you shall know that I am the LORD your God, who
> has brought you out from under the burdens of the
> Egyptians.
> B': I will bring you into the land that I swore to give to
> Abraham, to Isaac, and to Jacob. I will give it to you for
> a possession.
> A': I am the LORD. (Exod. 6:6b–8)

Several items are worthy of note here. The speech is bracketed by
'I am the LORD,' suggesting that what falls between A and A' lends
further definition to the declaration. The structural centre, C, is the
goal of the Egyptian deliverance – that the Lord would bring them
out from slavery and take them for himself, knowing him as their
God. Particularly interesting here is how the Lord defines himself as
the God who delivered them from Egypt. While B and B' speak to
what the Lord will do on behalf of Israel, in redeeming them from
Egypt and bringing them into the land, it is the Egyptian deliverance that takes centre stage, as the Lord defines himself as the one
who brought them out of slavery. As we will see later, the Egyptian
deliverance becomes the cardinal event that defines the relationship
between Israel and her God. What is particularly important here
is the recognition that something new is indeed being made known
to Israel as the Lord defines his name. The promise of the land had
already been given, as had the special covenant between the Lord
and Israel, as seen above in Genesis 17:7–8. What is new now, which
could not have been known by the patriarchs, is that the Lord would
redeem Israel from Egyptian slavery.[37] In other words, in the exodus
from Egypt Israel would come to know the Lord as, in the words of
6:6, One who brings out, Deliverer, Redeemer. Before all else, this is
what it means for Yahweh to be the God of Israel.

Greatness, goodness and the judgment of God
'The LORD reigns; let the peoples tremble!' (Ps. 99:1). To this point,
we have sought to understand the Lord's greatness in terms of his

---

[37] In Gen. 15:13–14 the LORD reveals to Abraham that he will bring Abraham's
descendants out of Egyptian slavery, looking ahead to the time when Israel will know
the LORD as redeemer.

supremacy, and his goodness in terms of his commitment to the welfare of his people. One issue the exodus forces us to address is the relationship between the character of God and his judgment. How is the Lord's greatness related to his judgment? Can God be good, and at the same time bring such devastating judgment?

The exodus raises several specific issues that are dealt with throughout the Scriptures. First, the Lord humbles those who exalt themselves. The problem with arrogance is, at bottom, a fundamental misunderstanding of who the Lord is. The plagues communicated that Egypt belonged to the Lord (8:22[18]; 9:29), thereby testifying to the Lord's rightful authority over Egypt. Pharaoh is not, ultimately, the ruler of Egypt. Rather, he is a vice-regent who rules at the Lord's pleasure, who in the end serves the Lord, as the manner in which the Lord addresses Pharaoh as his subject suggests. To obey the Lord would require Pharaoh to acknowledge his position of submission and dependence in relationship to the Lord, that he rules at the Lord's pleasure, and by his permission.

Pharaoh's humiliation is in large part due to his refusal to learn what Nebuchadnezzar later had to learn, 'that the Most High rules the kingdom of men and gives it to whom he will' (Dan. 4:25, 32). Haughty and at ease, Nebuchadnezzar provides a good illustration of what, ultimately, the Lord required of Pharaoh as the ruler of a people. The Lord's will for Nebuchadnezzar? 'Break off your sins by practising righteousness, and your iniquities by showing mercy to the oppressed, that there may perhaps be a lengthening of your prosperity' (Dan. 4:27). However, enamoured of his kingdom and crediting himself with its glory, Nebuchadnezzar must be humbled, and the kingdom is taken from him until he acknowledges that the Lord is king, even over Babylon. Nebuchadnezzar's praise of the Most High demonstrates that he has learned his proper place:

> For his dominion is an everlasting dominion,
>   and his kingdom endures from generation to generation;
> all the inhabitants of the earth are accounted as nothing,
>   and he does according to his will among the host of
>   heaven
>   and among the inhabitants of the earth;
> and none can stay his hand
>   or say to him, 'What have you done?'
>
> (Dan. 4:34–35)

When Nebuchadnezzar acknowledges that the Lord reigns, his kingdom is restored: 'Now I, Nebuchadnezzar, praise and extol and honour the king of heaven, for all his works are right and his ways are just; and those who walk in pride he is able to humble' (Dan. 4:37). As a result of his humiliation, Nebuchadnezzar came to know God.[38] Pharaoh, on the other hand, did not. The words of Psalm 2 get to the heart of the Lord's expectation of both Pharaoh and Nebuchadnezzar:

> Now therefore, O kings, be wise;
>> be warned, O rulers of the earth.
> Serve the LORD with fear,
>> and rejoice with trembling.
>
> (Ps. 2:10–11)

This leads to the second point. Part of what it means to rule at the Lord's pleasure is to rule righteously, seeking justice and shunning oppression. What is said of Josiah, and what we saw of Nebuchadnezzar above, is true of all kings who know the Lord:

> He judged the cause of the poor and needy;
>> then it was well.
> Is not this to know me?
>> declares the LORD.
>
> (Jer. 22:16)

While it would be too much to say that rulers of the nations would know the Lord as did the kings of Israel, it is nonetheless incumbent upon kings to rule with justice (see e.g. Amos 1 – 2). Part of what it meant for the Lord to reveal himself to Israel, Egypt and the world would be to make clear that he will not tolerate injustice, particularly the oppression of the vulnerable. And what is true for all peoples is certainly true of Israel in her vulnerability. As the LORD declared in his initial missionary call to Abraham, 'I will bless those who bless you, and him who dishonours you I will curse' (Gen. 12:3).

The plagues make clear God's intolerance of oppression. As discussed above, the situation from which Israel was delivered was severe physical oppression and the murder of their infant boys.

[38] While Nebuchadnezzar never speaks the Lord's name, he does refer to the God of Heaven or the Most High God, whom he knows as the God of Shadrach, Meshach and Abednego.

Both the first and last disasters call to mind Pharaoh's murderous decree: the Nile turning to blood, having claimed the lives of infants thrown in, and the death of the firstborn sons of Egypt. Perhaps less explicitly, the livelihood of Egypt, much of which was built upon the backs of Israel, was systematically destroyed, with Israel leaving with Egyptian wealth, such that Exodus comments, 'Thus they plundered the Egyptians' (12:36). Important to note is that these judgments were public judgments, making it clear to Israel, Egypt and the world that the Lord would not tolerate the oppression of Israel. This also is what it means to know the Lord, for in failure to bring judgment for Egypt's oppression of Israel, the Lord runs the risk of being misunderstood as either unwilling or unable to deal with such oppression. Thus, to borrow Paul's words concerning the cross, the judgment against Egypt 'was to show God's righteousness, because in his divine forbearance he passed over former sins' (Rom. 3:25).[39] The need to make a public statement of judgment may help explain the controversial notion of the Lord's hardening Pharaoh's heart, so that judgment may be complete and the Lord not misunderstood. The Lord will publicly humble Pharaoh, he will judge Egypt for her oppression and he will redeem Israel. And, in so doing, the world will come to know the Lord, and what kind of God he is.

This leads to the third implication of God's greatness and goodness: other gods can't save. Whatever the nature of the gods of Egypt, neither they nor Pharaoh could deliver Egypt from the disasters that befell her. Pharaoh implicitly acknowledges this by turning to Moses, rather than to his own magicians, for relief from the plagues. That some in Egypt learned this lesson is apparent in several ways. The first acknowledgment of the Lord's superior power comes early in the succession of signs, as the Egyptian magicians become aware that the Lord can do things that they cannot (8:19). As the disasters continue for Egypt (while Israel is protected), some begin to heed the word of the Lord, as illustrated in Egypt's response to the announcement of the coming hail:

Whoever feared the word of the LORD among the servants of Pharaoh hurried his slaves and his livestock into the houses, but whoever did not pay attention to the word of the LORD left his slaves and his livestock in the field. (9:20–21)

---

[39] The Lord's making himself known through judgment is particularly evident in Ezekiel, where coming to know 'I am the LORD' is the central thrust of the book.

As the plagues continue, Pharaoh's servants understand what needs to be done, and press Pharaoh to release Israel: 'Let the men go, that they may serve the LORD their God. Do you not yet understand that Egypt is ruined?' (10:7). Whether or not this suggests a full submission to the will of God, it is clear that the servants of Pharaoh were well aware that only Moses' God could halt the plagues. In the acknowledgment that the Lord brings calamity is the implicit hope that the Lord brings deliverance.

The most important way in which Egypt understood this lesson is an inference we can make concerning the last disaster, the death of the firstborn. While it must be acknowledged that the text does not say this explicitly, there are good grounds to suggest that some Egyptians were delivered from the final plague. First, the means of deliverance was not nationality, per se, but rather the presence of blood over the doors of each house that responded to the Lord's command. Secondly, as we have seen, before the coming of the hail there were Egyptians who were already responding to the word of the Lord. Finally, Exodus 12:38 tells us that a 'mixed multitude' left Egypt. That this mixed multitude did not refer to Israel is apparent, for the text explicitly speaks of the Israelite men, women and children, and the mixed multitude with them. It is clear, then, that whoever this group of people was, they were not Israelite. Given that Exodus gives no hint of other peoples living in Egypt (be that as it may), it is probably a reference that includes Egyptians. If this is the case, then the plagues not only served as a means of judgment, but also as a means of mercy, that the Egyptians might come to know the Lord as God, and in so doing find refuge from the judgment that was to come upon the whole land. The wider biblical parallels – a universal judgment coming, from which one might find refuge through identification with the people of God, and sheltered by blood – are plain.

Israel's continued acknowledgment: ceremonies of deliverance

The importance of knowing the Lord as Redeemer is further emphasized in the institution of the ceremonies of Israel's deliverance: the Passover (12:1–13), the Feast of Unleavened Bread (12:14–20; 13:3–10) and the Consecration of the Firstborn (13:1–2, 11–16). Although the position of these ceremonies in the narrative has struck many as awkward, their appearance here supports the inference that the LORD is now known to Israel as Redeemer.

The three ceremonies have much in common. First, they all commemorate the death of the firstborn in Egypt, the plague that finally broke Egypt and brought about Israel's deliverance. The Passover commemorates the Lord's protecting Israel from the destroyer (12:23), the Feast of Unleavened Bread commemorates the hasty flight from Egypt that same night (12:17), and the practice of redeeming the firstborn memorializes the Lord's killing the firstborn in Egypt (13:14–15).[40] Secondly, each ceremony serves as a memorial for future generations. For each, the Lord gives explicit instruction concerning how the feasts are to be explained to Israel's descendants, indicating the importance of remembering and faithfully interpreting the events. The interpretations of each ceremony are remarkably similar. In addition to each crediting the Lord with Israel's deliverance from Egypt, two explicitly recall the slaying of the Egyptian firstborn (Passover, 12:25–27; Consecration of Firstborn, 13:14–15), while two credit the Lord for delivering Israel with a strong hand (Unleavened Bread, 13:8–10; Consecration of Firstborn, 13:14–15).

The interpretations of the ceremonies are not designed, however, simply to impart information to generations removed from the exodus. Rather, the ceremonies draw future generations and the events of the exodus together, so that Israel's descendants might, through ritual, *participate* in the Egyptian deliverance. In each case the Israelites are bidden to re-enact an event that happened on the night of the exodus: Passover through the consumption of the lamb in haste (dressed accordingly), Unleavened Bread through the eating of unleavened bread akin to that which had not risen when Israel left Egypt in haste, and Consecration of the Firstborn through the sacrifice or redemption of the firstborn, because the Lord killed the firstborn of Egypt. The purpose of this ritual re-enactment, however, is not simply to remember a past event through drama, but rather to bring the past and the present together for subsequent generations. Childs (1962: 66–70) has argued that the noun *zikkārôn* (memorial), which describes both the Passover (12:14) and the Feast of Unleavened Bread (13:9), has an active sense that points to something beyond itself as worthy of remembrance. As he writes (1962:

---

[40] The significance of these events is supported by the severity of punishment for eating leaven during Unleavened Bread (12:15, 19; cf. Num. 9:9–14) and in the Lord's declaring the month of the exodus to be the first month, which Durham (1987: 153) sees as signifying both the start of the calendar year and the theological importance of the events associated with it.

68) concerning 12:14, 'The particular concern of the P [Priestly] writer is not the reliving of a past historical event so much as the maintaining of a reality which indeed entered history, but is now an eternal ordinance.'[41] To observe the ceremonies was to participate in the events themselves. Applied to the ceremonies of the exodus, Hendel's reference to Faulkner is apt: 'The past is never dead. It's not even past.'[42]

The need for Israelites to know the Lord as their redeemer becomes evident in a myriad of ways through the Bible, perhaps well illustrated in a survey of a few psalms. The psalmist of Psalm 77 finds comfort in his despair precisely by remembering the wondrous works of the Lord in delivering Israel from Egypt, and taking the same lesson his ancestors did on the other side of the sea: 'What god is great like our God?' (Ps. 77:13). Psalm 78 speaks to the importance of remembering for the sake of obedience. Beginning with a pledge to 'tell to the coming generation the glorious deeds of the LORD, and his might, and the wonders that he has done' (v. 4), the psalmist gives the reason: 'they should set their hope in God and not forget the works of God, but keep his commandments' (v. 7). Psalm 106 looks at this issue from the side of unfaithfulness through a historical lesson from the Egyptian deliverance. Having described the drowning of the Egyptian army, the psalmist declares that 'they believed his words; / they sang his praise. / But they soon forgot his works' (106:12–13; cf. Exod. 14:31 – 15:1), leading to their murmurings in the wilderness, the opposition to Moses, and the worship of the golden calf. 'They forgot God, their Saviour, / who had done great things in Egypt' (106:21). In each case the psalmist makes plain that the faithfulness of the succeeding generations lies in remembering the great things the Lord has done for them. In Israel's continued participation in the exodus event, through these ceremonies, the future generations would know the Lord as their redeemer.

---

[41] Mann (1996: 242) goes a step further: 'The Passover narrative is arguably the most important section of the entire book because it is primarily here that the experience of exodus is communicated not simply as a moment in historical time (in the past) but as a perennially recurring moment in the present life of these for whom the story is sacred. ... The Passover narrative elicits a communion between past and present, and joins past and present together in anticipation of the future.'
[42] Faulkner 1951: 51, cited in Hendel 2001: 601.

The name known (Exod. 15)

Whereas Exodus 1 introduces the conflict between the Lord and Pharaoh, Exodus 15 concludes it. While questions concerning tradition history and dating have dominated much modern study of Exodus 15, the song has an important theological function of demonstrating what Israel came to know of the Lord during the Egyptian deliverance.[43] To this point we have seen how communicating 'I am the LORD' was the underlying reason for the Lord's actions in the Egyptian deliverance. Now, for the first time, Israel herself proclaims, '[T]he LORD is his name!' (15:3). Israel now knows the name of the Lord. But what did that mean to Israel? What did Israel learn of the Lord in the Egyptian deliverance? Canonically speaking, Exodus 15:1–21 is Israel's response to the Lord's intention that Israel know that 'I am the LORD.' Because the song speaks to what Israel learned of the Lord, it can therefore serve to test the inferences we have made to this point concerning what the name of the Lord was meant to communicate to Israel.

We begin with the short exclamation, in Hebrew parallelism, 'The LORD is a man of war; / the LORD is his name' (15:3) and ask what it meant for Israel to understand the Lord as a man of war. As we have seen beginning in Exodus 1:8, the conflict is not firstly between Israel and Egypt, but the Lord and Egypt, now reiterated in Exodus 15 as Egypt is referred to as the Lord's enemy. Israel came to know the Lord as a man of war, who overcame his enemies for the salvation of Israel.

The implications of such an understanding are severalfold. First, Israel knew the Lord as her redeemer. As Moses sings, 'The LORD is my strength and my song, / and he has become my salvation' (15:2), the implication being that Israel understood her deliverance to be the sole work of the Lord. While there is abundant praise for the Lord in defeating the Egyptians, there is no hint in the poem that Israel contributed to the Lord's victory. The east wind of 14:21 becomes the wind of Yahweh's nostrils in 15:8, Moses plays no active role (it is the right hand of God extended over the waters, 15:12) and there

---

[43] Although see Smith 1997: 205–218; Watts 1992: 41–62. Noting the emphasis on critical questions, Childs (1974: 248) writes, 'An equally important and usually neglected exegetical task is to analyze the composition in its final stage. Regardless of its prehistory, the fundamental issue is to determine the effect of joining the poem to the preceding narrative.'

is no mention of an angel, a cloud or any other intermediary.[44] This understanding of ultimate agency renders curious Fretheim's (1989: 36, emphasis original) reflections on the plagues:

> The divine working in nature is usually in coordination with human activity. Hence, the use of the rod by Moses/Aaron in the plagues or at the sea crossing or in the wilderness is an integral element in what happens in the natural order. . . . There is a complex understanding of agency in connection with each of the plagues. Moses and Aaron would not be effective without God's power working in and through them, and God is dependent upon Moses and Aaron, working in the world of *nature* in and through that which is not divine.

Aside from the logical fallacy that finds the Lord's *use* of human activity to indicate *dependence* upon human agency, the fact that Exodus 15 nowhere mentions human agency suggests that Israel understood her role in the exodus to be immaterial. The idea that the Lord was in any manner dependent upon human assistance in the exodus is foreign to the thought of both Exodus 15 as well as the plague narrative itself.[45] In fact, the lavish nature of the praise given the Lord is precisely due to the fact that Israel understood the Lord to be solely responsible for Pharaoh's defeat. As seen above, the conflict is portrayed from the beginning of Exodus as between the Lord (not Israel) and Pharaoh. That this conflict is resolved by the Lord alone is recognized by all parties: Moses exhorts Israel, 'The LORD will fight for you, and you have only to be silent' (14:14), the Egyptians recognize that 'the LORD fights for them' (14:25), and the narrator comments that 'the LORD threw the Egyptians into the midst of the sea' (14:27). According to the song of Exodus 15, the Lord is the warrior (15:3), the Egyptians are his enemies (15:7) and it is the Lord's arm that wrought the victory (15:1–2, 4, 6–8, 10, 12).[46]

The corollary to Israel's recognition of the Lord as her redeemer

---

[44] Sarna 1991: 75.

[45] Furthermore, it is not the case, as Fretheim suggests, that there is human participation in 'each' of the plagues (cf. 8:24[20]; 9:6, where the Lord is the only agent).

[46] Jacob (1992: 418) contrasts Exod. 15, with its theocentric perspective, with the victory song of Judg. 5, which exalts human participation (cf. Hauser 1987). On a broader level, Noth (1981: 47) observes that, in Israel's faith-statement that God led Israel out of Egypt, 'God is regularly the grammatical or, at least, the logical subject, and it is equally remarkable that "Israel" as a totality always appears as the object.'

is seeing herself as a people redeemed: 'the people whom you have redeemed' (15:13), and 'The people . . . whom you have purchased' (15:16). Redemption now defines what it means for Israel to be the Lord's people, and for the Lord to be their God. The relationship between Israel and the Lord articulated in Exodus 6:7 has taken effect:

> I will bring you out . . . I will deliver you . . . I will redeem you . . . I will take you to be my people, and I will your God, and you shall know that I am the LORD your God, who has brought you out from under the burdens of the Egyptians. (Exod. 6:6–7)

Now, the people have been redeemed, so that they might be God's people, dwelling with him in his sanctuary (15:13, 17). In fact, it is here that Israel first explicitly acknowledges the Lord as her God (15:2), the acknowledgment of the redeemed to the redeemer.

Secondly, Israel came to know the Lord as supreme above all gods and earthly rulers, one of the primary purposes of 'I am the LORD' to this point in Exodus. The Lord's defeat of Pharaoh is the inevitable outcome of who he is.

> Who is like you, O LORD, among the gods?
> Who is like you, majestic in holiness,[47]
> awesome in glorious deeds, doing wonders?
>
> (15:11)

The statement of incomparability is particularly important in the light of the fact that other gods are mentioned explicitly only in 12:12 (and implicitly in 8:10[6] and 9:14). Israel's declaration of Yahweh's supremacy over other gods in 15:11 demonstrates that the Lord's supremacy over other gods is at stake in chapters 3–14, despite the fact that other gods are rarely mentioned.[48] Likewise, Israel came to recognize that no earthly ruler compares to the Lord, as is clear in their exultant claim that the nations (Philistia, Edom,

---

[47] The phrase *ne'dar baqōdeš* can be translated 'majestic among the holy ones' (cf. Ps. 89:5; Job 5:1; 15:15), which Sarna (1991: 80, 248) suggests may be another reference to other gods.

[48] This inference is further confirmed later in 18:11 in Jethro's confession upon hearing of the Lord's mighty deeds against Egypt: 'Now I know that the LORD is greater than all gods.' Jethro's confession will be treated in greater detail in chapter 3.

Canaan) will fear the greatness of the Lord. The events of the exodus communicated that the Lord was like no other (cf. e.g. Deut. 4:34–35; Ps. 135).

The implications of understanding the Lord's supremacy reach beyond the events of the exodus, giving Israel confidence in her God. If the Lord were simply superior to Egypt, there would be no grounds for confidence in the face of another threat. This is precisely the mistake of the Rabshakeh, who sought to discourage Hezekiah by speaking of Israel's God as another national deity, who in the end would be unable to rescue Judah from the Assyrian king. Hezekiah, however, knew the Lord as Israel came to know him after the exodus:

> O LORD, the God of Israel, enthroned above the cherubim, you are the God, you alone, of all the kingdoms of the earth; you have made heaven and earth . . . O LORD our God, save us, please, from [the Assyrian king], that all the kingdoms of the earth may know that you, O LORD, are God alone. (2 Kgs 19:15–19; cf. Isa. 37:16–20)

It is precisely the supremacy of God over all that brings assurance and courage to Israel, regardless of the enemy. In fact, the deliverance from Egypt became paradigmatic for the Lord's ultimate redemption of Israel, prophecy couched in the very language of Exodus 15:

> Behold, God is my salvation;
>   I will trust, and will not be afraid;
> for the LORD GOD is my strength and my song,
>   and he has become my salvation.
>
> (Isa. 12:2)

The prophets can comfort Israel centuries hence precisely because 'the LORD will reign for ever and ever' (Exod. 15:18). He is for ever known as the redeemer of his people.

Conclusion: concerning Exodus 6:3

We now return to Exodus 6:3. As has been indicated above, if the source-critical hypothesis is not taken, the apparent newness of the name Yahweh in Exodus must somehow be accounted for.

Therefore the question becomes, what does the Lord make known about himself that was not known to the patriarchs? What about the character of the Lord is genuinely new in the experience of Israel?

As we have seen, one of the primary burdens of 'I am the LORD' was to reveal that the Lord is supreme, in such a way not yet apparent in Genesis. While Genesis speaks of the Lord's receiving worship, and being the God of Abraham, Isaac and Jacob, nowhere in Genesis does the Lord explicitly demand exclusive worship, nor is the Lord compared to other gods. The book of Exodus exhibits a marked change in this perspective, introducing a polemic against other gods and authorities absent in Genesis. The plague accounts in Exodus are explicitly designed to reveal the Lord as supreme not only over Pharaoh, and but over all creation, and in so doing to expose all else, including other gods, as inferior and insufficient.

The display of the Lord's supremacy, however, serves a particular end, the redemption of Israel from slavery. The meaning of the name is not exhausted by recognizing his supremacy, for 'I am the LORD' intends to communicate that the Lord is the God of Israel. Throughout Exodus, the Lord is known as the God of a particular people, and is not known apart from them. Each plague is designed, not only to demonstrate the Lord's supremacy, but to force Pharaoh to free Israel from slavery. Indeed, it is precisely Pharaoh's pledge to release Israel that stops a particular plague, and the reversal of his decision that brings another. The message that the Lord intends to free Israel, bringing judgment upon Egypt in the process, is not lost on the Egyptians, who increasingly become aware that the Lord is Israel's God. In fact, as discussed above, it seems likely that some Egyptians, as part of the mixed multitude that left Egypt, came to know the Lord as their redeemer as well, as they joined the people of Israel and obeyed the command to apply blood to their doorposts.

These revelations of the Lord as supreme and redeemer are, of course, inseparable, for the supremacy of the Lord is the foundation for his redeeming of Israel. The corollary of the display of the Lord's greatness in Genesis is the exposure of Pharaoh and the gods of Egypt as futile and unable to save. The supremacy of the Lord ensures Israel that their God can deliver. 'O God, save me by your name, / and vindicate me by your might' (Ps. 54:1). 'The name of the LORD is a strong tower' (Prov. 18:10).

This connection between the supremacy of the Lord and his being the Redeemer of his people is both logical and biblical. Psalm 115 is an excellent example of how the name of the Lord simultaneously speaks to the supremacy of God and his desire to redeem:

Not to us, O LORD, not to us, but to your name give glory,
for the sake of your steadfast love and your faithfulness!

Why should the nations say,
'Where is their God?'
Our God is in the heavens;
he does all that he pleases.

Their idols are silver and gold,
the work of human hands.
They have mouths, but do not speak;
eyes, but do not see.
They have ears, but do not hear;
noses, but do not smell.
They have hands, but do not feel;
feet, but do not walk;
and they do not make a sound in their throat.
Those who make them become like them;
so do all who trust in them.

O Israel, trust in the LORD!
He is their help and their shield.
O house of Aaron, trust in the LORD!
He is their help and their shield.
You who fear the LORD, trust in the LORD!
He is their help and their shield.

The LORD has remembered us; he will bless us;
he will bless the house of Israel;
he will bless the house of Aaron;
he will bless those who fear the LORD,
both the small and the great.

(Ps. 115:1–13)

Three things are noteworthy in the light of our reading of Exodus. First, the psalm is explicitly about glorifying the name of the Lord, and for a reason – for his steadfast love and faithfulness. Secondly, the Lord is supreme, doing everything he pleases, unlike the gods of the nations who can do nothing, and therefore cannot be trusted. Thirdly, because of the Lord's power and his love for his people, Israel can trust the Lord, as one willing and able to secure their good. Finally, there may be a hint of the kind of broader application that the exodus suggests. The blessing upon Israel, the house of Aaron and those who fear the Lord may not be simple parallelism, but may rather suggest that, as the Lord is the shield of Israel, he is likewise the shield of all who fear him, regardless of nationality. If so, the suggestion fits the Egyptian deliverance. Pharaoh does not fear the Lord's bringing judgment upon Egypt ('But as for you and your servants, I know that you do not yet fear the LORD God,' Exod. 9:30). Yet there appear to be some Egyptians who learn to fear the Lord. The comment on the plague of hail reveals two kinds of Egyptians: those who feared the Lord and brought their animals under cover, and others who did not pay attention to the Lord's word (9:20–21; cf. 10:7–8). The mixed multitude that left Egypt presumably included Egyptians, those who feared the Lord, and therefore obeyed his word. If so, the blood of the lamb protected their firstborn. The Lord was their shield, the redeemer of those who trust him.

The name of the Lord indicating redemption does not stop in the OT, but spans the entirety of Scripture. Two examples will suffice. First, in what has become known as the high priestly prayer in John 17, Jesus defines his ministry in terms of God's name. Not only does Jesus confess to the Father, 'I have manifested your name to the people whom you gave me out of the world' (17:6; cf. v. 26), but he prays, 'Holy Father, keep them in your name, which you have given me' (17:11). And what is that name? Distinctive in John is the manner in which Jesus takes 'I am' upon his lips, applying the exact words of Exodus 3:14 (LXX) to himself, and continuing to fill with content the question that the name begs. One of the striking features of the way Jesus uses 'I am' is that in almost every instance he refers to life. In the seven well-known 'I am' statements Jesus speaks of himself as 'bread of life' (6:48), 'the light of the world' who brings life to those who follow him (8:12), 'the door' entering through which leads to abundant life (10:9–10), 'the good shepherd' who lays down his life so that his sheep may be protected and live (10:11–15), 'the way, the truth, and the life' (14:6), and 'the vine' to whom the disciples must be connected if they are to live and bear fruit (15:1–6). In each case Jesus refers to the need to be delivered from death, whether articulated in terms of hunger, darkness, enemies or even

God himself as the vinedresser who cuts away the barren branch. Similarly, in Jesus' words to the Jews the name suggests salvation: 'unless you believe that I am he you will die in your sins' (8:24). Jesus' words to his storm-weary disciples struggling in the boat, translated 'It is I; do not be afraid' by the ESV, is a word of comfort using 'I am' from the one who walks towards them and will deliver them (6:20; cf. Matt. 14:27; Mark 6:50). As we saw of the name in Exodus, likewise in John. The name of the Lord, the name given to Jesus, points to salvation.

Secondly, in a cardinal passage that speaks of the Lord as both incomparable and redeemer, Isaiah writes:

> Turn to me and be saved,
>   all the ends of the earth!
>   For I am God, and there is no other.
> By myself I have sworn;
>   from my mouth has gone out in righteousness
>   a word that shall not return:
> 'To me every knee shall bow,
>   every tongue shall swear allegiance.'
>
> Only in the LORD, it shall be said of me,
>   are righteousness and strength . . .
>
> (Isa. 45:22–24a)

This is a word offering salvation, salvation for all the earth through the Lord, and only the Lord. Yet, as we know from the great hymn of Philippians 2, it is the name of Jesus to which every knee will bow and swear allegiance. The angel's words to Joseph 'You shall call his name Jesus, for he will save his people from their sins' (Matt. 1:21) are given practical expression in the willingness of the Son to empty himself, even to death on a cross, precisely for the salvation of his people, and the glory of the Father. The name Jesus, like 'the LORD' in the OT, signifies sovereignty, for every knee will bow. And it signifies redemption.

The name that was unknown to the patriarchs, then, was not the label, but rather the character of the Lord as the supreme redeemer, a characteristic of the Lord that Israel had not known, and could not have known apart from being delivered from bondage. In this way yes, Israel came to know the name of the Lord as one who fulfils his promises. But far more than learning that the Lord was faithful to his word, Israel came to know the Lord who is faithful. In fact, the reason that the Lord is faithful to his word is because he is sovereign, and he loves his people. God is great and God is good, indeed. 'His name is the LORD' (Ps. 68:4).

Chapter Three

Training in the wilderness (Exod. 15:22 – 18:27)

My son, do not regard lightly the discipline of the Lord,
  nor be weary when reproved by him.
For the Lord disciplines the one he loves,
  and chastises every son whom he receives.

(Hebrews 12:5–6)

While rarely embraced with enthusiasm, it is the testimony of Scripture that the Lord disciplines his own, often using difficulty to shape and perfect his people, and to display his glory. As Spurgeon wrote, in typical eloquence,

[h]e brings His people ofttimes into straits and difficulties, that, being made conscious of their own weakness, they may be fitted to behold the majesty of God when He comes forth to work their deliverance. He whose life is one even and smooth path, will see but little of the glory of the Lord, for he has few occasions of self-emptying . . .[1]

Or, in the words of my argument thus far, God uses difficulty to make himself known.

For our purposes, there are several observations to make concerning the Hebrews passage above. First, the discipline mentioned does not appear to be punishment, for the passage does not appear to be addressing sin.[2] Secondly, discipline is not a means to sonship, but rather comes upon those who are already sons. In fact, Hebrews argues that the lack of discipline indicates a lack of sonship (12:8). Thirdly, discipline serves God's glory and the good of his people: 'he disciplines us for our good, that we may share his holiness' (12:10).

---

[1] Spurgeon 1991: 402.
[2] Koester 2001: 526–528. For a helpful look at the relationship between Hebrews and Israel's wilderness wanderings, see Thiessen 2009.

Finally, discipline is a means of training, so that sons so trained will receive 'the peaceful fruit of righteousness' (12:11). As we will see, each observation well describes the Lord's dealings with Israel in the wilderness.

The problem: the significance of the wilderness

Compared to other sections in Exodus, the wilderness material has not received a great deal of attention in biblical scholarship,[3] a lack due in part to the perception by some that the wilderness material is of secondary importance. An illustration of this can be found in the work of Martin Noth. For Noth, the main blocks of tradition that formed the foundation of the Pentateuch were the guidance from Egypt and the guidance into the land. The wilderness material, which he understood as a compilation of somewhat unrelated narrative traditions, functioned as a bridge between these two main traditions (Noth 1983: 115). Consequently, Noth (58) found the wilderness material to be subordinate to the other great themes of the Pentateuch, arguing that it is 'obvious that this is not a very important or really independent theme'. The paucity of independent work on the wilderness material, compared to other sections of Exodus, reflects a general (if implicit) agreement with the assessment of Noth.

While Noth's observation that the wilderness section is not an independent theme is surely correct, its dependence need not imply that the wilderness material is therefore less important. In fact, it is the relationship to both the preceding exodus narrative and the Sinai material following that makes sense of the wilderness material, and indeed that makes it so important. If the wilderness material is not understood in the light of the exodus and Sinai, but rather seen as an independent theme sitting awkwardly between them, it can be asked if either the exodus or Sinai have been appropriately understood. The theological importance of the wilderness material lies in large part in the manner in which it helps the reader understand this relationship between the exodus and Sinai, which, in turn, helps the reader understand both. If it can be said that this chapter addresses a particular problem, it would be the general lack of appreciation for how the wilderness functions in the theological movement of Exodus.

---

[3] See the comparatively scant attention given to the wilderness in Vervenne's review of Exodus scholarship (1996: 23–27).

In the last chapter I argued that the purpose of God in the Egyptian deliverance was missionary, that the Lord delivered Israel as he did so that Israel, Egypt and the nations would know him. In this chapter we will see how the wilderness material carries this missionary purpose forward, and how this purpose connects, theologically, the exodus and Sinai. In short, I will argue that the wilderness section describes how God makes himself known *to* Israel, so that he might make himself known *through* Israel.

Exegesis of the wilderness section

Exodus 15:22–27

Exodus 15:22–27 is the first of three murmuring passages in the wilderness material and, perhaps due to its brevity, the most straightforward. The movement of the narrative is simple. Having travelled three days into the wilderness and unable to find drinkable water, Israel murmurs against Moses. In response to Moses' cry the Lord shows him a tree, Moses casts it into the water, and the bitter water becomes drinkable.

Theologically, the weight of the section falls on 15:25b–26, which gives the rationale behind the Lord's action:

> There the LORD made for them a statute and a rule, and there he tested them, saying, 'If you will diligently listen to the voice of the LORD your God, and do that which is right in his eyes, and give ear to his commandments and keep all his statutes, I will put none of the diseases on you that I put on the Egyptians, for I am the LORD, your healer.'

The interpretation of this passage turns on the clause 'the LORD made for them a statute and a rule, and there he tested them', which Wellhausen (1885: 343) argued 'stands there quite isolated and without bearing on its context'. First, the phrase 'a statute and a rule' presents a difficulty, for it is unclear to what the phrase refers, since no formal law had been given at this point. Does it refer to previously given laws now lost (Sarna 1991: 85)? To the Sabbath command (Ruprecht 1974: 298–302)? To other laws (Jacob 1992: 436–437)? Houtman (1996: 313) has offered a compelling suggestion that honours the canonical text, without speculating about editorial purposes or what may have been left out. For Houtman, 'statute' and 'rule' are not collectives, but should rather be understood as a hendiadys, 'a binding statute'. The function of the hendiadys, Houtman suggests, is to indicate from the beginning the Lord's requirement of obedience as 'the *charter, the constitution, for YHWH's relationship with Israel*' (emphasis original). Similarly, Brueggemann (1994: 807–808) captures well the implications, commenting that 15:25b–26

> makes unmistakably clear that the liberation from Egypt does not lead to autonomy for Israel, but rather to an alternative sovereignty that imposes an alternative regimen on the liberated slaves. This single verse presents Yahweh as the God who commands, and it anticipates the larger tradition of command in the Sinai meeting to come.

Whether or not it is possible to assert a precise referent for 'a statute and a rule', the unambiguous implication of this ambiguous phrase is that Israel's welfare will depend upon obedience to the voice of the Lord.

The connection between Israel's obedience and her welfare leads to the second phrase in 15:25b that requires attention: 'and there he tested them'. The phrase is particularly important in that it addresses the Lord's purpose for Israel at Marah. However, the precise meaning of 'test' in the present context is not entirely straightforward. For instance, Noth (1962: 129) finds the idea that the Lord tested Israel a 'rather vague observation', which was 'attached only loosely to what goes before'. How does testing fit the context?

The traditional translation 'test' for the Hebrew root *nsh*, if simply seen as the Lord's seeking to know Israel's inclinations, is inadequate to the context of 15:25b.[4] While there may be an element of seeking to know Israel's inclinations, the emphasis falls upon teaching or instruction. First, the crisis at Marah concludes with the Lord instructing Israel that in her obedience she would find her welfare. If the Lord were simply testing Israel to know whether she would obey, there would be no need for the subsequent exhortation concerning obedience. Secondly, the appearance of 'I am the LORD' in 15:26 suggests instruction, given that it has been used consistently to this point in Exodus in the context of teaching Israel, Egypt and the nations who the Lord is. Finally, a wordplay in 15:26 may suggest

---

[4] Greenberg (1960) makes a similar argument for the use of the root *nsh* in Exod. 20:20.

instruction. Often noticed, the phrase 'and the LORD showed', referring to the log of 15:25, comes from the Hebrew root *yrh*, rendered (in the hiphil) as 'teach' or 'instruct'.

A helpful suggestion, appropriate to the present context, is Eissfeldt's suggestion of 'train' (1955: 235–236), a translation that fits the passage nicely in that the Lord's goal at Marah is to fashion a people who will obey.[5] The Lord trains Israel to obey in 15:22–27 firstly through establishing trust by reminding her of who he is and what he has done. 'I am the LORD' would remind Israel of the lesson she learned in the exodus, that he is willing and able to do her good. The restoration of the waters would point to the Lord's ongoing commitment to Israel, communicating that the Lord's help to Israel is not confined to deliverance from Egypt, but will include providing for her in the wilderness as well. Appended to 'I am the LORD' in 15:26 is 'your healer', further engendering trust in the Lord.[6] The trust the Lord seeks to foster in Israel forms the foundation for the Lord's requirement of obedience in 15:26. The reference to Israel's stay at the springs of Elim serves as an affirmation to Israel of the way in which the Lord can provide, and ultimately offers a glimpse of the possibilities of the life a faithful and obedient Israel can expect in the Promised Land (Enns 2000: 324).

The conditional nature of 15:26 indicates that the Lord's provision for Israel is not automatic, but is rather contingent upon Israel's obedience. This leads to a second means by which the Lord seeks Israel's obedience: through instilling fear. The corollary to the Lord's not visiting the disasters of Egypt upon Israel if she obeys is that he will bring disaster if she does not.[7] In this way the use of *nsh* in 15:25b is similar to its use later in 20:20, where the purpose of the terrible theophany at Sinai is to instil fear: 'Do not fear, because

---

[5] A good illustration of this use of the verb can be found in 1 Sam. 17:39, where David declines Saul's armour to fight Goliath because David has not trained (*nsh*) with it. Instead, David defeated Goliath with a sling and stone, a means with which David was apparently familiar.

[6] Normally translated as 'heal', the Hebrew verb *rāpā'* here probably does not refer to the eradication of disease, given that the 'healing' of 15:26 is the provision of drinkable water, and that the 'diseases' inflicted on the Egyptians were not generally sicknesses, but rather disasters. In addition to healing disease, *rāpā'* can be used for such varied processes as repairing an altar or a pot (1 Kgs 18:30; Jer. 19:11), restoring waters to their normal position (2 Kgs 2:22) or turning salt water into fresh water (Ezek. 47:8–9). The sense here might be well understood 'I am the LORD, who maintains your welfare,' giving Israel a much broader assurance than typically understood by healing.

[7] Cf. Deut. 11:1–9.

God has come to test [root *nsh*] you, in order that his fear may be before you, that you may not sin' (my tr.). Thus instilling fear becomes the corollary to instilling trust, both serving the same end of leading Israel into a life of obedience.

Understanding 'testing' in terms of training and/or instruction does not require replacing the idea of testing, but must certainly qualify it.[8] The Lord tests primarily to instruct. If Israel 'passes' the test, then the Lord's faithfulness to maintain her well-being, demonstrated in the exodus from Egypt, is further confirmed in a new setting. Israel can expect the Lord, who delivered her from Egypt, to sustain her after she has left Egypt. If Israel 'fails' the test, as in 15:22–27 (demonstrated by Israel's murmuring), the failure provides the opportunity for explicit instruction concerning both the Lord's expectations for Israel and the consequences Israel can expect for her compliance or lack thereof. In either case the testing provides Israel the opportunity to know the Lord her God.

Exodus 16:1–36

After a stay at the springs of Elim, Israel is confronted with another challenge: a lack of food. Like the previous section at Marah, the theological rationale for the manna section is relatively straightforward, articulated explicitly in 16:4–5:[9]

> Then the LORD said to Moses, 'Behold, I am about to rain bread from heaven for you, and the people shall go out and gather a day's portion every day, that I may test them, whether they will walk in my law or not. On the sixth day, when they prepare what they bring in, it will be twice as much as they gather daily.'[10]

Again the Lord tests Israel, using the same root *nsh* used in 15:25b. As in the previous section, the sense of 'test', if simply understood as the Lord's seeking information, is inadequate to the context. Brueggemann's suggestion (1994: 813) that 'God resolves to "test"

---

[8] See Deut. 8:2–5, where testing (*nsh*) 'to know what was in your heart' and instruction are the stated goals of the wilderness.

[9] Despite their importance in the theology of the text, critical scholars have generally considered 16:4–5 to be problematic in Exod. 16, finding them an intrusion of J into the larger context of P. See Childs 1974: 271–202; Frankel 2002: 63–117.

[10] There has been much discussion as to whether these verses are a command, an announcement of a miracle, or both. See Beuken 1985.

Israel in order to determine whether Israel is prepared to receive bread and life under wholly new terms and completely changed conditions' therefore only partially addresses what is at stake in the Lord's testing. If, as in the last section, the Lord seeks to teach/train Israel through the provision of food, the question then becomes, what does the Lord seek to impart to Israel through giving the manna daily, with a double portion given on the sixth day? Or, anticipating our larger question, 'How does the Lord's giving of the manna help prepare Israel for the law?'

The manna material prepares Israel for the law in, at least, two important ways. First, as we saw concerning the bitter water, the Lord's provision is meant to foster trust in Israel by reminding Israel of who he is and what he has done for her, here indicated by the reminder that the Lord brought Israel out of Egypt, and the reappearance of 'I am the LORD.' This same Lord, who in delivering Israel demonstrated his superiority over all creation, is the one who provides for Israel in the wilderness. Such a reminder would have the effect of strengthening Israel's confidence in the power and willingness of the Lord to provide. Furthermore, 'I am the LORD' would effectively remind Israel of the Lord's promise to escort her into the land. As we have seen in 6:6–8, the promise of deliverance from Egypt and provision of the land are bracketed by 'I am the LORD' (6:6, 8), with 'you shall know that I am the LORD your God' in the centre (6:7), both structurally and theologically. Moses' reiteration of the Lord's words 'I am the LORD your God', last spoken directly to Israel in 6:7, should remind Israel that the Lord's promise of 6:6–8 included both deliverance from Egypt and guidance and protection into the land. Knowledge that the Lord promised Israel the land should serve to confirm that he will provide for her in her journey to the land, thereby fostering Israel's trust in the Lord.

The *manner* in which he provides for Israel further underlines the Lord's intention to foster trust in Israel. The issue in Exodus 16 is, of course, the lack of food. The Lord addresses this lack by providing Israel with food one day at a time, save the special circumstance of the seventh day, effectively re-presenting every evening the very circumstance about which the Israelites were complaining – the lack of food. The lack of a sustainable food source would be a constant reminder that the Lord was Israel's provider. While there is an element of truth in von Rad's (1962: 282) comment concerning the manna, that 'daily sustenance by God demanded a surrender without security', it must be stressed that the experience with the manna was meant to teach Israel that security *could* be found in the Lord, through obedience to his word.

To appreciate the connection between trust and obedience, a brief look ahead is warranted, for what is hinted at in the wilderness material is brought out clearly in Israel's sin with the golden calf (32 – 34). The issue that led to Israel's idolatry is precisely fear that comes through lack of trust. Anxious concerning Moses' extended absence, Israel charges Aaron, 'Up, make us gods who shall go before us. As for this Moses, the man who brought us up out of the land of Egypt, we do not know what has become of him' (32:1). The charge to Aaron is driven by the people's anxiety about having no one to go before them, probably a reference to the upcoming journey into the land. In other words Israel's idolatry is driven by fear concerning her welfare. Exodus 32:1 suggests that a stable trust in the Lord would have precluded Israel's disobedience concerning the calf. It is precisely this issue – trust leading to obedience – that becomes the theological thrust of Exodus 16. Israel's obedience (or lack thereof) is shown to be dependent upon her trust in the Lord's promises of protection and provision. The provision of the manna as a *daily* provision is precisely meant to train, repeatedly instilling in Israel the kind of trust in the Lord that is so foundational in preparation for the giving of the law.[11]

The second way the Lord uses the manna to teach/train Israel prior to giving the law is through the pattern of the Sabbath. Here the emphasis falls not just on provision, but also on imitation. The absence of bread on the Sabbath indicates that the Lord, by not supplying bread, rests. This calls for another look ahead, for what is hinted at in Exodus 16 becomes clearer in the formal institution of the Sabbath in 20:8–11, and its further explanation in 31:12–17. The pattern of six days of work followed by a day of rest, practised by the Lord in Exodus 16, is grounded in creation, and becomes the foundation upon which the Sabbath is formally instituted at Sinai: 'For in six days the LORD made heaven and earth, the sea, and all that is in them, and rested on the seventh day. Therefore the LORD blessed the Sabbath day and made it holy' (20:11). The implication here is that the Sabbath is observed in imitation of the Lord. Concerning

---

[11] That daily provision depends upon trust is essentially Jesus' point in Matt. 6, when he teaches the disciples to pray for daily bread (6:11) and exhorts them not to be anxious for food, drink or clothing, but to rely upon their heavenly Father who will provide for them as they seek his kingdom and his righteousness (6:25–33).

the reference to God's seventh-day rest in Genesis 2:1–3, von Rad (1961: 60) comments, 'The Sabbath as a cultic institution is quite outside the purview. The text speaks, rather, of a rest that existed before man and still exists without man's perceiving it.' Or, in the words of Buber (1958: 80) concerning Exodus 16, 'Sabbath does not exist exclusively in the world of human beings; it also functions outside their world.'

The lesson the Sabbath provided for Israel is, at least, twofold. First, the Sabbath would communicate that Israel's whole life was to be lived in imitation of the Lord. This implication is further apparent in 31:12–17. Here the Lord singles out the Sabbath from all the commandments as a sign between himself and Israel, to be observed throughout the generations. Whatever other reasons there may be that the Sabbath specifically was chosen as a sign, it is interesting that, of all the commandments in the Decalogue, only the Sabbath is mentioned as something the Lord himself observed. In other words the sign of the covenant between the Lord and Israel (31:16–17) is rooted in her imitation of the Lord. The keeping of the Sabbath has a familiar purpose, 'That you may know that I am the LORD, who makes you holy' (31:13, my tr.). That the Sabbath, which calls for Israel's imitation, is the sign of the covenant suggests that, in effect, the whole law was obeyed in imitation of the Lord. Or, to say it another way, in her obedience to the law, Israel conformed to the character of the Lord. As the Lord is, so he calls his people to be.

Secondly, the Sabbath taught Israel that obedience would not come at her expense. The extra portion provided on the sixth day gave Israel the ability to carry out the Sabbath command. That the Sabbath served as the continuous sign of the covenant would communicate something very important about the law as a whole: Israel would not suffer deprivation as she carried out the Lord's commands. In fact, as we will see below, observing the Sabbath is a gift ('See! The LORD has given you the Sabbath,' 16:29), a pledge of the blessing that comes with keeping the law.[12] The weekly rhythm of the Sabbath would be a weekly reminder of the nature of the law, and of the Lord's faithfulness to provide for Israel as she obeyed it. Realizing that she does not obey the Lord at her own expense is another way that Israel knows 'I am the LORD.'

---

[12] The Scriptures are replete with statements that indicate that Israel would be blessed in her obedience. Cf. e.g. Deut. 28:1–14.

Exodus 17:1–7

The discussion of the final murmuring section may be brief, for the section reiterates many of the same themes of the first two sections, particularly those of 15:22–26: the lack of water, the murmuring, the miraculous provision of water through Moses, the naming of the place. As seen previously, the Lord seeks to foster trust in Israel by supplying her lack in a time of need. Noteworthy in the light of the first two episodes is the absence of 'I am the LORD' as the goal of what the Lord seeks to teach Israel. However, present in this particular section is the staff of Moses, which may serve a similar function. The same staff that represented the power of the Lord in the plague accounts (4:17; 7:9–12, 17–20; 8:5[1], 16–17[12–13]; 9:23; 10:13; 14:16) represents that same power as the Lord provides for Israel in the wilderness, this time as Moses strikes the rock with the staff, the sign that initiates the Lord's action on Israel's behalf.

One significant difference between 17:1–7 and the two prior episodes warrants mention. Whereas in 15:22–26 and 16:4 the Lord is the subject of *nsh*, here Israel is the one to test the Lord. The sense of the verb is different, however, since the idea of teaching/training would not apply to the Lord in the same way it does to Israel. Rather, Israel's testing has more to do with doubt concerning the Lord's willingness and/or ability to care for Israel (Helfmeyer 1998). The difference in the subject of *nsh* in a passage that is otherwise so similar to 15:22–27 and 16:1–36 suggests mutual testing in all three narratives, albeit of course in different manners. The idea that Israel was trying the Lord's patience is not explicit in 15:22–27, but is strongly suggested in the Lord's response to Israel regarding their disobedience over the manna: 'How long will you refuse to keep my commandments and my laws?' (16:28). That the Lord was training Israel in 17:1–7, while not explicitly stated, is nonetheless clear in the manner in which the Lord provides for Israel's need, in a manner almost identical to 15:22–27.

Psalm 95 reflects upon this incident in a very instructive, if sobering, manner. After opening with an extended call to worship the Lord, the creator who is great above all gods (what Israel learned of him in the exodus), the psalmist exhorts the people:

> Today, if you hear his voice,
>> do not harden your hearts, as at Meribah,
>> as on the day at Massah in the wilderness,

when your fathers put me to the test
and put me to the proof, though they had seen my work.
For forty years I loathed that generation
and said, 'They are a people who go astray in their heart,
and they have not known my ways.'
Therefore I swore in my wrath,
'They shall not enter my rest.'

(7–11)

There are two matters worthy of note here, both of which concern preparation for the law. First, the lesson drawn by Psalm 95 concerns obedience, for the call of the psalmist is to respond faithfully to the voice of the Lord, unlike the wilderness generation. It is interesting that Psalm 95 charges the wilderness generation with hardening their hearts, the same language used of Pharaoh in Exodus.[13] Hebrews, drawing on Psalm 95, echoes this warning against 'an evil, unbelieving heart, leading you to fall away from the living God', that 'none of you may be hardened by the deceitfulness of sin' (Heb. 3:12–13). The call is to obedience to the word of the Lord, so that, unlike the Israelites in the wilderness, the people will be able to enter rest: 'Let us therefore strive to enter that rest, so that no one may fall by the same sort of disobedience. For the word of God is living and active . . .' (Heb. 4:11–12).

Secondly, it is noteworthy that it was not Israel's testing the Lord at Meribah and Massah that directly led to her forty-year wandering, but rather her refusal to enter the land in Numbers 13 – 14, despite the assurances of Caleb and Joshua that 'the LORD is with us' (Num. 14:9). The point is not that the psalmist and Numbers disagree (indeed, Ps. 95 does not suggest that Massah and Meribah directly led to the wanderings), but that it is precisely Israel's lack of trust exposed there that lay behind her fearful refusal to enter the land God had promised her. In other words, while Exodus 17:1–7 speaks of grumbling, not disobedience, there is a *trajectory* evident at Meribah and Massah that leads away from trusting God, and therefore towards disobedience. In the end Israel's lack of trust is a rejection of the Lord: 'How long will this people despise me? And

---

[13] Exodus uses three verbal roots to describe what most English Bibles uniformly translate as 'harden': *ḥzq* (4:21; 7:13, 22; 8:19[15]; 9:12, 35; 10:20, 27; 11:10; 14:4, 8, 17), *kbd* (7:14; 8:15[11]; 32[28]; 9:34; 10:1) and *qšh* (7:3; 13:15). The root in Ps. 95:8, *qšh*, is the least used of these roots.

how long will they not believe in me, in spite of all the signs that I have done among them?' (Num. 14:11). Whereas 15:22–29 and 16:1–36 speak to the Lord's training Israel to obey, Exodus 17:1–7 suggest that the lessons are not being learned, even if the outworking of Israel's lack of trust in disobedience has yet to be fully realized.

Exodus 17:8–16

The encounter with Amalek in 17:8–16 brings Israel to yet another trial. Although the form of the danger is different (being military, rather than hunger or thirst), the threat is ultimately the same: Israel's existence is threatened, and the patriarchal promises endangered.

The passage alternates between two scenes: Joshua and the Israelite army in battle with the Amalekites, and Moses with Aaron and Hur upon the mountain. The primary focus of the narrative, however, is not Israel's army, but Moses, which suggests that it is not military strength, but Moses' presence upon the mountain that is decisive in the battle. Of particular importance are Moses' hands, the position of which seems to determine the course of the battle.[14]

The exact function of Moses' hands is not explicit in the text. Several options have been proposed.[15] Some have argued, based upon the lack of mention of God in 17:8–13, that Moses' raised hands suggest a magical effect (e.g. Noth 1962: 142), some have suggested Moses' raised hands indicate prayer (e.g. Cole 1973: 136–137),[16] while others have posited that he carried some kind of ensign that encouraged the Israelites in battle when they gazed upon it,[17] an interpretation encouraged by the reference to a banner in 17:15. While perhaps not ruling out any of the above options, the text makes a special point of indicating that Moses had the 'rod of God' in his hand, suggesting that the rod is significant in interpreting Moses' actions. As mentioned above in reference to 17:1–7, the

[14] Robinson 1985: 15 suggests a chiastic structure to 17:8–16, which finds the position of Moses' hands at the centre of the narrative, and therefore theologically central.

[15] For an overview of the options, see Houtman 1996: 383–384. Enns (2000: 344–364) has a particularly lengthy and thoughtful reflection on 17:8–16.

[16] Buber (1948: 90) suggests that the change from the singular 'his hand' in 17:11 to the plural 'hands of Moses' in 17:12 is an editorial change due to the supposition that Moses' action referred to prayer. Houtman (1996: 383) has suggested that Moses alternated hands when each grew too heavy, a suggestion that does not require the supposition of an editorial change. Cf. Jacob 1992: 482; Propp 1998: 618.

[17] E.g. Buber 1958: 91; Fretheim 1991a: 193; Clements 1972: 103–104.

staff would serve to signify the Lord's power. Prior to Moses' use of the rod on the mountain, the rod functioned in conjunction with the Lord's intervention on Israel's behalf, particularly in public demonstrations of the Lord's power: in demonstrating his superiority over Pharaoh's magicians, and in bringing water out of the rock. Here the Lord's power is again emphasized, this time signifying the Lord's ability to bring military victory, in a manner similar to the Lord's victory over Egypt at the sea. As in Exodus 14, where Moses waves the staff over the waters (both to divide them and to bring them back together, 14:16, 21, 26–28) to bring military victory, so functions the rod in the battle against Amalek. The presence of the rod in Moses' hands, therefore, points to the Lord as the ultimate power behind Israel's victory over Amalek. In a manner reminiscent of the song of Exodus 15, the war is described in 17:16 as being between the Lord (not Israel) and Amalek, a further indication that Moses' hands indicate the power of the Lord.

The comparison between the victory over Egypt and the victory over Amalek suggests another way in which the Lord prepares Israel for the law in the wilderness. Whereas Israel was passive in the destruction of the Egyptian army, Israel is required to fight against Amalek. This signals a change in Israel's role from being entirely passive to becoming increasingly active. Israel's more active role, however, must be understood carefully, for it implies neither that the Lord is somehow insufficient to bring about victory for Israel, nor that Israel is sufficient in herself. Concerning the first, while Fretheim (1991a: 193–194) rightly calls attention to Israel's active role in the battle, to suggest as he does that God somehow *needs* Israel to fulfil her part goes beyond the sense of the text, which is focused upon Moses on the hill, and is inconsistent with what Exodus has communicated to this point concerning the power of God. Nor, concerning the second, does the smaller stature of the Amalekites as compared to the Egyptians mean that the army is small enough for Israel herself to fight, as Propp (1998: 617) implies. Rather, the Lord's work here is not done with Israel in a passive role. That Israel fights marks an important shift in the manner in which the Lord works out his missionary purpose in Exodus. While a fuller discussion must await the ensuing discussion of 19 – 24, a simple observation may be made here. Whereas in 1:1 – 15:21 the Lord sought to reveal himself to the nations as he delivered Israel through signs and wonders, with Israel's remaining passive, in 19 – 24 the Lord will seek to reveal himself through the active participation of

Israel, who will make the Lord known to the nations through obedience to the law.

Exodus 18:1–27

Chapter 18 differs from 15:22 – 17:16 in several respects. First, and most obviously, the section centres on the character of Jethro, who is absent from 15:22 – 17:16. Secondly, the two episodes of chapter 18 are not centred on immediate crises. While some have suggested that Moses' difficulty in applying the law in 18:13–27 is a crisis (e.g. Isbell 2002: 53–55), it is nonetheless of a different order than those of 15:22 – 17:16 in that Israel's existence is not threatened. Thirdly, unlike the previous material, 18:1–27 does not record any direct action of the Lord. Finally, from a critical perspective, chapter 18 has been generally viewed as a literary unity, in Durham's (1987: 241) words, 'a literary and thematic unity virtually unparalleled in the narrative chapters of the Book of Exodus'.

The chapter divides naturally into two sections: these are the meeting between Moses and Jethro (18:1–12), and Jethro's subsequent advice to Moses concerning the administration of justice in Israel (18:13–27). The theological climax of 18:1–12 comes in the confession of Jethro, who, after hearing of the Lord's intervention on Israel's behalf, declares, 'Now I know that the LORD is greater than all gods, because in this affair they dealt arrogantly with the people' (18:11). Jethro's confession has been interpreted in several ways. Some have argued that Jethro became a worshipper of the Lord (Cole 1973: 139), others that hearing Moses' testimony deepened Jethro's already existing faith,[18] and others that Jethro simply acknowledged the Lord's incomparability (Houtman 2000: 97). Common in the above interpretations is the recognition that Jethro acknowledged the Lord as supreme, and there seems little reason to deny that Jethro worshipped, particularly given his participation in activities associated with worship, such as the sacrifices and the common meal shared with the elders of Israel (18:12).[19] As Carpenter notes, Jethro's

---

[18] Childs 1974: 329; Durham 1987: 244; cf. Rowley 1948: 150.

[19] Jethro's participation in Israelite worship, which may suggest that Jethro was the initiator of the sacrifice (although see Cody [1968], who suggests that Jethro accepted the sacrifices as part of a covenant ceremony between himself and Israel), is one of the pillars of the Kenite hypothesis, a history of religions project which argues that Jethro brought to Israel the knowledge of YHWH, who was already worshipped in Midian. The conflict between the Kenite hypothesis and the canonical text is a good example of how the methodologies and presuppositions of a history of religions approach and a canonical approach can conflict with one another and lead to

confession provides the proper response to Pharaoh's question of 5:2, 'Who is the LORD . . . ?' Unlike Pharaoh, Jethro's recognition of the Lord's incomparability leads appropriately to worship.

Jethro's confession, however, is much more important to the narrative than just the testimony of one individual, for it serves as a specific fulfilment of the Lord's primary goal in 1:1 – 15:21, that other nations would come to know his supremacy. The use of 'know' in Jethro's confession not only brings to partial realization the purpose statement of 9:14–16, but also connects Jethro's confession to the familiar phrase 'then they will know that I am the LORD' so prominent to this point in the narrative. That Jethro is a non-Israelite is particularly important given the scope of the Lord's commitment to be known, for Jethro's confession suggests that the intended goal of the plagues is being realized on an international scale, thereby fulfilling the Lord's goals in the exodus. As Carpenter (1997: 98) expresses it, 'The purpose of the deliverance of Yahweh finds expression in microcosm in Jethro.' Jethro stands as an instance that the Lord's missionary purposes in the exodus are being realized.[20]

The second section, 18:13–27, takes a different trajectory. Jethro observes Moses' judging the people, sees a problem, and instructs Moses accordingly. The issue here is entirely practical – despite his ability to make known the Lord's statutes, Moses is unable to manage the load that such a task requires. Jethro's solution, for Moses to share the burden with God-fearing men in positions of authority, allows the resolution of disputes and the teaching of the Lord's statutes to be carried out among the people. In other words it is a practical measure that enables Israel to be governed under the law of the Lord. As such, it anticipates the coming legal material of 19 – 24. In addition, Moses' language of 18:16 concerning 'the statutes of God and his laws' looks back to language already encountered in the wilderness section ('statutes' in 15:25–26 and 'law' in 16:4). As with the earlier wilderness material, 18:13–27 anticipates the giving of the law.

Concerning the relationship of 18:1–12 and 18:13–27, Carpenter (1997: 92) has made a compelling argument that Exodus 18 serves the dual function of being an epilogue of Exodus 1 – 17 and a prologue to 19 – 40:

widely divergent conclusions. In support of the Kenite hypothesis, see Rowley 1948: 149–163; and against, Buber 1958: 94–100.

[20] Cf. e.g. Exod. 15:14–16; Josh. 2:9–13; 9:9–10; 1 Sam. 6:5–6.

The chapter serves artistically as both an epilogue to the preceding materials of Exodus and as a prologue to the remaining sections of the book. Its positioning helps the reader grasp the overall content and meaning of the book. It helps to emphasize and make clear two ways of knowing Yahweh, that are, indeed, complementary: (1) the knowledge of Yahweh available in and through the event of the exodus itself and its recitation (18:7–8); and (2) the knowledge of Yahweh found in the way (דרך) of Yahweh – his Torah.

Thus, for Carpenter, Exodus 18 serves as the theological centre of the book of Exodus, which is concerned with the communication of the knowledge of the Lord. This is particularly important because, as mentioned earlier, the role of Israel changes significantly between 1 – 15 and 19 – 40 from being passive to active. Although he does not pursue the missionary trajectory of Exodus, Carpenter's observations demonstrate how the theme of knowing the Lord can remain central in Exodus while, at the same time, undergoing a significant change in the way that knowledge is communicated.

Conclusion: the theological function of the wilderness section

As stated above, the function of the wilderness material cannot be appreciated fully outside the larger context of the giving of the law, beginning in chapter 19. In this way Noth's comment that the wilderness is not an independent theme is surely correct. However, to argue, as Noth does, that the wilderness is therefore less important suggests that, for Noth, the theme of the wilderness is fundamentally different from the themes of deliverance and the giving of the law.

Noth's assessment of the wilderness highlights the importance of reading the Bible canonically. As I have argued, the wilderness is not fundamentally different in trajectory or theology from the exodus, but rather demonstrates how the Lord's concerns in the Egyptian deliverance are carried forth in the life of Israel, now a free but yet to be settled people. The God who delivered Israel is the God who trains Israel to remember, practically, that he is Israel's God. The one who delivered Israel is the one who sustains Israel, and the one who will give Israel the law. His character and purposes remain the same. He is the same yesterday, today and for ever.

This is essentially the perspective of Deuteronomy's reflections on the wilderness, where the Egyptian deliverance and the wilderness wanderings are seen in continuity with one another (e.g. Deut. 8:14–16). Particularly helpful for our purposes is the way that Deuteronomy articulates the purpose of the wilderness wanderings in terms of training:

> You shall remember the whole way that the LORD your God has led you these forty years in the wilderness, that he might humble you, testing you to know what was in your heart, whether you would keep his commandments or not. And he humbled you and let you hunger and fed you with manna, which you did not know, nor did your fathers know, that he might make you know that man does not live by bread alone, but man lives by every word that comes from the mouth of the LORD. (Deut. 8:2–3)

The goal of this training is Israel's obedience, in order that she might not forget the Lord as she begins life in the land. How Israel's obedience is related to Israel's missionary calling will be explored in the next chapter. For now, it is sufficient to recognize that the wilderness essentially prepares Israel for what Peterson (2000; with apologies to Nietzsche) called 'a long obedience in the same direction' (the title of his book).

Reading the wilderness section in the light of the larger canon reveals a striking continuity in both the missionary purposes of God and the manner in which he prepares his people to carry out those purposes. To return to the Hebrews passage with which we began, the purposes of God in trial are 'that we may share his holiness', yielding 'the peaceful fruit of righteousness to those who have been trained by it' (12:10–11). Interestingly, the words of assurance to God's children that their suffering is unto training to holiness, peace and righteousness immediately precedes an allusion to Sinai, that holy mountain that cannot be touched (12:18–20). How peace and holiness are related to Sinai remains to be seen in the next chapter, but the connection is worth stating here, for it is through a people formed as a 'holy nation' (Exod. 19:6; 1 Pet. 2:9) that the Lord realizes his missionary purposes throughout the world.

Although not all later biblical reflection concerning training explicitly refers back to the wilderness section, as does Hebrews, the concerns at stake are carried forward throughout the Bible. For Paul, we rejoice in our sufferings, knowing that suffering produces endurance, and endurance produces character, and character produces hope, and hope does not put us to shame, because God's love has been poured into our hearts through the Holy Spirit who has been given to us. (Rom. 5:3–5)

That Paul himself learned from suffering is evident in his own testimony:

I have learned in whatever situation I am to be content. I know how to be brought low, and I know how to abound. In any and every circumstance, I have learned the secret of facing plenty and hunger, abundance and need. I can do all things through him who strengthens me. (Phil. 4:11–13)

It is through the things Paul learned that he is able to assure the Philippians that 'my God will supply every need of yours according to his riches in glory in Christ Jesus' (Phil. 4:19). Again, looking to the fruit of such training, James calls the church to

[c]ount it all joy, my brothers, when you meet trials of various kinds, for you know that the testing of your faith produces steadfastness. And let steadfastness have its full effect, that you may be perfect and complete, lacking in nothing. (Jas 1:2–4)

To emphasize the point further that training is not necessarily a response to sin, even Jesus, as Hebrews tells us, 'although he was a son, he learned obedience through what he suffered' (Heb. 5:8). It is instructive that it was the Spirit that led Jesus into the wilderness to be tempted by the devil (Matt. 4:1). What the devil meant for evil, God meant for good, for the temptations that Satan designed to bring Jesus to ruin strengthened him. It is noteworthy that this training comes immediately after Jesus' baptism, and before he begins to proclaim that the kingdom of heaven is at hand. Jesus' training did not earn him the status of son, Paul's rejoicing in sufferings was not so that he could earn grace (for grace and peace had been given in Christ, Rom. 5:1), and Israel's training came after she had been redeemed. Rather, in training the Lord fashions a people who will obey him, and in so doing reflect his image faithfully in and throughout the world. The implication of these passages is that the people of God cannot be all that God intends them to be apart from trial and suffering. These are the means by which the Lord trains his people.

In closing this section it is perhaps appropriate to turn to one more passage where the concerns of the wilderness section come together. While not referring specifically to the wilderness, Psalm 46 provides a good example of what God sought to teach Israel, that in knowing God and his presence with them, his people might live without fear, being still and resting in the certain provision of the Lord who claims them as his own, and who will be exalted throughout the nations:

God is our refuge and strength,
   a very present help in trouble.
Therefore we will not fear though the earth gives way,
   though the mountains be moved into the heart of the sea,
though its waters roar and foam,
   though the mountains tremble at its swelling.
                 Selah

There is a river whose streams make glad the city of God,
   the holy habitation of the Most High.
God is in the midst of her; she shall not be moved;
   God will help her when morning dawns.
The nations rage, the kingdoms totter;
   he utters his voice, the earth melts.
The LORD of hosts is with us;
   the God of Jacob is our fortress.
                 Selah

Come behold the works of the LORD,
   how he has brought desolations on the earth.
He makes wars cease to the end of the earth;
   he breaks the bow and shatters the spear;
   he burns the chariots with fire.
'Be still, and know that I am God.
   I will be exalted among the nations,
   I will be exalted in the earth!'
The LORD of hosts is with us;
   the God of Jacob is our fortress.
                 Selah

Chapter Four

The law and the mission of God (Exod. 19 – 24)

Your testimonies are wonderful;
  therefore my soul keeps them.
The unfolding of your words gives light;
  it imparts understanding to the simple.
I open my mouth and pant,
  because I long for your commandments.
Turn to me and be gracious to me,
  as is your way with those who love your name.
Keep steady my steps according to your promise,
  and let no iniquity get dominion over me.
Redeem me from man's oppression,
  that I may keep your precepts.
Make your face shine upon your servant,
  and teach me your statutes.
My eyes shed streams of tears,
  because people do not keep your law.

(Psalm 119:129–136)

What is true for contemporary culture has surely been true since Genesis 3 – humanity carries a deep suspicion, even resentment, for law, particularly God's law. Yet, for the psalmist, the law is wonderful, bringing life, giving light and understanding to the simple, and keeping one from iniquity. The language of desire could not be stronger: 'I open my mouth and pant, / because I long for your commandments.'

Three matters are particularly noteworthy. First, the psalmist loves the LORD, which he articulates in terms of the Lord's name. A reading of Psalm 119 reveals a man who loves the law of the Lord precisely because he loves the Lord, and therefore the Lord's name. Secondly, Psalm 119 suggests no tension between salvation and the law. In fact, the psalmist seeks deliverance so that he might obey the law, for the law for him is freedom. The Lord is both the redeemer and the giver of law, and the psalmist rejoices in both. Finally, for all the joy the psalmist finds in the Lord and his law, all is not well:

> My eyes shed streams of tears,
>   because people do not keep your law.
>
> (Ps. 119:136)

Here the psalmist shares the perspective of the OT itself, which mourns sin and injustice in the earth, and looks forward to the day when all nations will come to Jerusalem, saying:

> Come, let us go up to the mountain of the LORD,
>   to the house of the God of Jacob,
> that he may teach us his ways
>   and that we may walk in his paths.
>
> (Isa. 2:3)

All is not as it should be. Implicit in the psalmist's words is mission.

The problem: law, gospel and the generosity of God

Modern biblical scholarship has not always appreciated the blessing of the law as expressed by the psalmist. An example of this can be found in the work of von Rad. In 1938 von Rad published 'The Problem of the Hexateuch', an enormously influential essay which argued that the Sinai material and the Exodus material were originally independent traditions joined at a later stage in the formation of the Pentateuch.[1] In short, von Rad noted that Deuteronomy 26:5b–9, which he deemed a very ancient creed, briefly summarized Israel's salvation history, with the remarkable omission of Israel's experience at Sinai.[2] This observation, combined with Wellhausen's argument that the Sinai material was later inserted within the Kadesh narratives,[3] became the foundation for von Rad's thesis.

Von Rad's historical hypothesis had important theological impli-

---

[1] The version referred to here is von Rad 1966: 1–78.
[2] Confirming von Rad's hypothesis were Deut. 6:20–24 and Josh. 24:2–13, both likewise summarizing salvation history with no mention of Sinai. See von Rad 1966: 8–13.
[3] See Wellhausen 1885: 343–345.

cations, particularly concerning the relationship between salvation and law. Particularly striking is the following passage:

> Even though the interpenetration of one tradition by the other still fails to achieve complete harmony, the Settlement tradition is theologically enormously enriched by its absorption of the Sinai tradition. The former bears witness to Yahweh's generosity, but over against this, at the very heart of the Sinai tradition, is the demand of Yahweh's righteousness. . . . The blending of the two traditions gives definition to the two fundamental propositions of the whole message of the Bible: Law and Gospel.[4]

Notable in von Rad's theological assessment of the joining of the two traditions is the tension between law and gospel, understood in terms of righteousness and generosity. Even though von Rad finds both the Settlement and Sinai traditions enriched in the relationship, they seem to stand in uneasy tension with one another; hence von Rad's words that the Lord's generosity (of the Settlement tradition) stands *over against* his demand for righteousness (of the Sinai tradition). For von Rad this tension, apparent in the final text of the Hexateuch, runs throughout the Bible in the fundamental propositions of gospel and law.

Von Rad is not alone. To cite one more example of a prominent biblical scholar who seems to see a fundamental distinction between gospel and law, consider the words of James Barr (1973: 45–46):

> Though the Pentateuch contains a number of notable acts of deliverance, and though some of these in some later stages came to be regarded as prime examples of 'salvation,' the inner structure of the Pentateuch is not particularly that of a religion of salvation; it can be read otherwise. In particular, it can be read as the document of a religion of law.

While Barr does not argue that the Pentateuch is exclusively either, by speaking of a 'religion of salvation' and a 'religion of law', he nonetheless seems to view the two perspectives as categorically distinct from one another, perhaps even 'over and against' one another in the manner suggested by von Rad.

---

[4] Von Rad 1966: 54. The 'Settlement tradition' refers to Israel's settlement into the land, from the promises to the patriarchs, to the exodus and finally the conquest.

The analyses of von Rad and Barr raise the question of the relationship between law and gospel in the Pentateuch. Assuming, for the sake of argument, that von Rad's two traditions were originally distinct, does the final form of the Pentateuch support such a *theological* contrast between God's righteousness and his generosity? And is this contrast fundamental, as von Rad implies? The term 'fundamental' implies that something is largely independent and self-sufficient, a basic principle behind which one cannot go. The relationship between God's righteousness and his generosity is not merely an academic question, but one full of personal and pastoral implications. If God is righteous, then how can one stand before him? How can one be sure that he will encounter God's generosity, and not his righteousness? Failure to understand the relationship between righteousness and generosity is in large part behind the common caricature that God in the OT is a God of wrath, while the NT God revealed in Jesus is a God of love. But if God is one, and if Jesus Christ is the same yesterday, today and for ever (Heb. 13:8), then we must press further.

The proximity between the Egyptian deliverance and Sinai make the final form of Exodus a particularly fruitful place to explore this relationship. As Childs (1979: 177) has commented, '[f]or the theologian the book of Exodus provides a classic model by which to understand the proper relation between "gospel and law"'.[5] For the sake of clarity, simple definition is in order. The gospel refers to what God has done for his people; the law refers to what God calls his people to do. In the case of Exodus the gospel is the Lord's delivering Israel from Egyptian slavery, while the law is his call for her to follow his commands. In seeking to understand the relationship between gospel and law, we will take a careful look at the law, and how it serves the Lord's commitment to be known throughout the world. We proceed by asking two questions. First, we will ask *how* the law makes God known to the nations. Secondly, we will ask *what* the law makes known about God. In the end we will discover that the law was given for God's glory and Israel's good, and that the law is not simply an expression of God's righteousness, but his generosity as well.

You shall be holy

In an effort to understand the missionary character of the law, we begin by examining its purpose as given in Exodus. Apart from the

[5] Cf. Clements 1976: 312.

tabernacle instructions and reiteration of certain laws following the golden-calf incident, the law is given in Exodus 20 – 23. Interestingly, the body of law in 20 – 23 is framed by two passages that speak to the law's purpose: the introduction to the law in 19:4–6 and the ratification ceremony after the law was given in 24:3–8. In seeking to understand the purpose of the law, we will address these two passages in order.

The covenant introduction (Exod. 19:4–6)

Our investigation of the purpose of the law for Israel in its canonical context begins with the Lord's initial words to Israel at Sinai:

> You have seen what I did to the Egyptians, how I bore you upon the wings of eagles and brought you to myself. And now, if you listen attentively to my voice and keep my covenant, you will be my treasured possession, distinct from all the peoples, for all the earth is mine. And you shall be for me a priestly kingdom and a holy nation. (Exod. 19:4–6a, my tr.)

The importance of these verses has been long recognized. Durham (1987: 261) sees 19:4–6 as 'a poetic summary of covenant theology', van Zyl (1950) has called 19:4–6 an intentional summary of the entire Pentateuch, Fretheim (1996: 231) has suggested that the entire book of Exodus may be fruitfully approached through these verses, and Brueggemann (1994: 834) has commented that '[t]his speech is likely the most programmatic for Israelite faith that we have in the entire tradition of Moses'. Dumbrell (1994: 80) has gone so far as to argue that 19:4–6 is crucial to understanding the OT as a whole:

> A correct understanding of these verses which summon Israel, as a result of Sinai, to its vocation, is vital. The history of Israel from this point on is in reality merely a commentary upon the degree of fidelity with which Israel adhered to this Sinai-given vocation.

These verses are, in effect, Israel's 'mission statement', defining Israel's purpose as the people of God, and the role of the law in that purpose.[6] We are therefore warranted in taking a close look at these verses.

---

[6] E.g. Paul 1970: 30: '[19:3–6] clearly and unequivocally state the purpose of the forthcoming covenant'. The implication is that studies that seek to understand the

Israel's deliverance

The passage begins with a reminder of what the Lord had done for Israel in delivering them from Egypt. These words are foundational for understanding the Lord's commission to Israel, the presence of 'and now' at the beginning of 19:5 indicating that 19:4 serves as the grounds for what follows. Here the Lord interprets the Exodus experience for Israel. First, the initial phrase 'you have seen what I did to the Egyptians' recalls the Lord's judgment upon Egypt, and in so doing reminds Israel of the incomparable nature of her God. The reminder of the Lord's gracious deliverance of Israel would instil gratitude and trust, as well as fear, as we saw in the implied threat of 15:26 and will see in 20:20, where the terrible theophany on Mount Sinai is given so that '[The Lord's] fear may be before you, that you may not sin' (20:20).[7]

Secondly, the phrase 'I bore you upon wings of eagles' portrays Israel's role in the exodus from Egypt to Sinai as entirely passive. The Lord's statement effectively agrees with Israel's own understanding, as we have seen articulated in Exodus 15, that he alone was responsible for her deliverance, and may also indicate the Lord's care for Israel in the wilderness.[8] That Israel could claim no credit for her deliverance reinforces the message of the exodus: that the Lord is both willing and able to do Israel good. In other words the ensuing call to be a kingdom of priests and a holy nation is given against the background of a great and accomplished deliverance. The Lord delivered Israel from Egypt, and so proved his love and power.

Finally, the Lord brought Israel to himself. While certainly it may refer to the mountain, thereby indicating the fulfilment of the Lord's words to Moses in 3:12,[9] the statement 'I brought you to myself' has a broader significance. The Lord did not deliver Israel for her own sake, henceforth to live independently, but rather for *relationship with him*. In effect, this relationship with the Lord is the goal of the Egyptian deliverance. While this relationship will require roles and definition, and will serve a particular purpose, which will be dealt with in 19:5–6, it bears mention that, while Israel's physical

underlying rationale of the law without reference to 19:4–6 (see e.g. Levenson 1980; Napier 1953) run the risk of missing the central concern of the law, as suggested in its canonical presentation in Exodus.

[7] Nicholson 1977; Childs 1974: 371–373.
[8] Enns 2000: 386–387, in the light of Deut. 32:9–11.
[9] Cassuto 1967: 226–227; Noth 1962: 157.

destination remains the land of Canaan, their ultimate destination is the Lord himself. The Lord's interpretation of the exodus in 19:4 is the ground of this relationship, and thus lays the foundation for the charge given to Israel in 19:5–6.

Israel's calling

Having interpreted the exodus for Israel in 19:4, 19:5–6 goes on to define what it will mean for Israel to be the Lord's people. Israel is spoken of as a treasured possession, a priestly kingdom and a holy nation, each addressing the purposes for which the Lord delivered her and shedding light upon the role of the law in Israel's life. We will examine each in order.

Treasured possession (sĕgullâ). Although appearing only eight times in the OT, *sĕgullâ* has been the least difficult of the three terms to translate (Lipinski 1999: 144–148). Twice referring to a king's personal treasure (Eccl. 2:8; 1 Chr. 29:3), the remainder refer to Israel as the people the Lord has distinguished from the nations (Exod. 19:6; Deut. 7:6; 14:2; 26:18; Ps. 135:4; cf. Mal. 3:17[10]). Well translated 'treasured possession', *sĕgullâ* is most often used of Israel, who occupies a special position among all peoples. This special position is highlighted by the following assertion that all the earth belongs to the Lord (Exod. 9:29), an assertion that in this context is concerned with all peoples.[11] Israel is not the Lord's only possession, but rather a special and treasured possession among all peoples who are his. Dumbrell (1994: 86) has argued that the claim over all peoples renders 'treasured possession' an election term, since it simultaneously sets Israel apart while identifying Israel with the rest of humanity: 'As an election term . . . the note of the specialization from within what is generally available or at the divine disposal, and thus for "private" use, cannot be missed in the word.' The implication is that Israel's status as a treasured possession is not only an end in itself, but also a means to a further end that has in view all peoples of the earth.

Priestly kingdom (mamleket kōhănîm). Of the three terms under discussion, 'priestly kingdom', a hapax legomenon,[12] has been the most difficult to interpret, and has generated a great deal of

---

[10] Mal. 3:17 likewise draws a distinction, *sĕgullâ* referring to 'those who feared the LORD'.

[11] Cf. Exod. 9:29, where the phrase 'all the earth is mine' is intended to establish a claim over not only the land, but over the nation of Egypt, thereby providing the grounds for the Lord's claim to Pharaoh's obedience.

[12] A hapax legomenon is a word or phrase that appears only once in a given work.

discussion.[13] The principal difficulty lies in the ambiguous grammatical structure of the phrase *mamleket kōhănîm*. Steins (2001: 23–24) has argued that the grammar offers five possibilities: a kingdom under the authority of priests, a royal priesthood, a (divine) kingdom over a people of priests, a priestly kingdom, or a kingdom consisting of priests. This grammatical flexibility has led interpreters to appeal to several contexts to adjudicate between the options.[14] Given its singular occurrence in 19:6, the most straightforward solution is to interpret the phrase in its immediate literary context, functioning in parallel with 'holy nation'. The vocabulary of the two constructions has strong associations. *Mamleket* and *gôy* are often used elsewhere synonymously,[15] and priest and holy have obvious parallels with one another.[16] One does not have to claim that the two constructions are strictly synonymous in order to assume that *gôy qādoš* is meant to shed light on *mamleket kōhănîm*. That being the case, the most fitting translation would be 'priestly kingdom', understood as a kingdom with a priestly function.

The question then becomes, what does priestly kingdom say about Israel's role among the nations? As Sarna (1991: 104) writes, 'This concept of priesthood provides the model for Israel's self-image and for her role among the nations of the world.'[17] Therefore, the most natural way to discover what it meant for Israel to be a priestly kingdom is by exploring the analogy Exodus draws and investigating what it meant to be a priest in Israel. In seeking the nature of the priesthood, we look ahead to the tabernacle material in order to make a few broad observations concerning priestly function in the canonical presentation of Exodus.[18]

[13] See e.g. Wells 2000: 50–52; Steins 2001; Schenker 1996; Mosis 1978. For a slightly older but comprehensive survey of approaches to the problem, see Moran 1962.

[14] For instance, Moran (1962) sought to understand the phrase by seeking where else in the OT the terms 'priest' and 'king/kingdom' occur in close proximity to one another, arguing for a royalty of priests. Cf. Levenson 1985: 31. Schenker (1996: 370–372) investigated places where *mamleket* appears in a construct relationship, concluding that 19:6 refers to a kingdom governed by priests.

[15] E.g. 1 Kgs 18:10; 1 Chr. 16:20; 2 Chr. 20:6; 32:15; Pss 46:7; 79:6; 105:13; Isa. 13:4; 60:12; Jer. 1:10; 18:7; Ezek. 29:15, Nah. 3:5. According to Cody (1964: 3–4), the terms 'kingdom' and 'nation' 'belong together naturally as two complements constituting a unity which possesses a land and which, established on that land, enters as a sovereign nation into relations with the world at large'.

[16] The relationship between the terms 'priest' and 'holy' can be seen in the preponderance of both terms in the tabernacle material in Exodus, and will be discussed in more detail in chapter 5.

[17] Cf. Childs 1974: 367.

[18] Although beyond the boundaries of Exodus, Leviticus (10:10–11) and

First, the priest represented the Lord. Exodus illustrates this association through the garments of the high priest. Aaron's garments were made of the same materials, woven in the same manner, as in the Holy of Holies, the specific place in the tabernacle where the Lord dwelt (25:22; 26:34). The unmistakable association between Aaron's garments and the Holy of Holies suggests that Aaron, so dressed, symbolized the Lord's presence. That the word 'glory', *kābôd*, appears in Exodus exclusively in relation to the Lord (16:7, 10; 24:16–17; 28:2, 40; 29:43; 33:18, 22; 40:34–35) makes one exception, the statement that the priestly garments were made 'for glory [*kābôd*] and for beauty' (28:2, 40), all the more striking. In wearing the garments, Aaron effectively represented the Lord as he displayed his glory.

Secondly, the priest represented Israel. Both the garments and the function of Aaron testify to this association. The ephod, worn only by Aaron, contained two stones upon which were engraved the names of the twelve tribes of Israel and was to be worn before the Lord 'for remembrance' (28:12). Similarly, the breastpiece, again worn by Aaron, contained twelve stones, each engraved with the name of a tribe of Israel (28:15–30). The representative function of both these garments is further indicated by the manner in which Aaron is called 'to bear', *nāśā'*, the names of the tribes of Israel (28:12, 29).[19] As Brueggemann (1994: 906) comments concerning the ephod, '[i]n its intention, the ephod serves to bring Israel, with all its generations gathered in a moment, into the holy presence of God'. The function of the priests as bearing the sin of Israel (28:38) and the judgment of Israel (28:30) reinforces the role of the priest as a representative of Israel before the Lord.[20]

Deuteronomy (31:9–13; 33:10; cf. Mic. 3:11; 2 Chr. 15:3) speak of the priest as teacher, a role relevant to the present discussion, particularly given that Israel's obedience to the law, the criteria of her priesthood, would serve to teach the nations of the Lord's wisdom (Deut. 4:6).

[19] Dohmen 2004: 267–268.

[20] Sarna (1991: 184) points out that the phrase *nāśā' 'āwôn* (28:38) may mean either 'to remove sin' or 'to bear sin', and therefore finds the phrase somewhat ambiguous. Without denying a certain ambiguity elsewhere in the OT, the immediate literary context of Exod. 28 suggests that the phrase is best understood as 'to bear sin'. First, Aaron bears (*nāśā'*) the names of the sons of Israel in the breastpiece of judgment upon his heart in 28:29, which serves as the mechanism whereby Aaron bears (*nāśā'*) the judgment of the people of Israel in 28:30. The sentence makes best sense when *nāśā'* is consistently understood as 'to bear'. In 28:43 the linen breeches are required 'so that [the priests] will not bear guilt [*yiś'û 'āwôn*] and die'. To render *nāśā'* in either 28:29 or 28:43 as 'remove' renders each sentence unintelligible. Thus the overall

91

The presence and service of the priest creates the possibility of a relationship between the Lord and Israel, whereby the Lord dwells in Israel's midst: 'And let them make me a sanctuary, that I may dwell in their midst' (25:8). As we will see in the next chapter, the function of the tabernacle depended upon the priesthood. Implied in this verse is that without the mediating function of the priests the Lord could not dwell in Israel's midst. The priests were not set apart and given special access to the Lord for their own sake, but for the purpose of serving both the Lord and the people. Not only were the priests responsible for maintaining the tabernacle so that the Lord would dwell among the people, but there are indicators that the priest secured the Lord's favour towards the people. Having the role of bearing the people's sin, Aaron is commanded to wear the turban plate in order that the Lord might favourably accept them (28:38).

We are now in a better position to understand what it meant for Israel to serve as a priestly kingdom. First, as the priests represented the Lord to Israel, so Israel was to represent him to the nations. As suggested by the priestly garments, Israel was to reflect the likeness of the Lord himself. Israel's presence was to reflect the Lord's own presence. In representing the Lord to the nations, Israel makes him known to the world. Secondly, as the priests represented Israel to the Lord, so was Israel to represent the nations before him. While not developed in Exodus, the analogy suggests that Israel was meant to serve the role of bringing the nations before the Lord 'for remembrance', and may further suggest that in some way Israel was to bear the sin of the nations (28:38). Finally, by representing the Lord to the nations and the nations to the Lord, Israel's presence creates the possibility of a relationship between the Lord and the nations. Noth's understanding is apt: 'Israel is to have the role of the priestly member in the number of earthly states. Israel is to have the special privilege of priests, to be allowed to "draw near" God, and is to do "service" for all the world' (Noth 1962: 157).

Holy nation (gôy qādôš). As with *mamleket kōhănîm*, the term *gôy qādôš* is another hapax legomenon, which appears only here in the OT. The peculiarity of this term lies chiefly in the curious use of *gôy*, 'nation', for Israel, rather than the more common 'people'. In his study of *'ām* and *gôy* Speiser (1960) has argued that the former is generally a more personal term describing a group of people,

---

use of *nāśā'* in Exod. 28 recommends the translation 'to bear'. Cf. Schwartz 1995: 8–10.

whereas the latter refers to an established political entity.[21] Speiser's distinction is important in discerning the Lord's intentions for Israel expressed in the term *gôy qādôš*. Use of the word *'ām* would only serve to reiterate what was already explicit in the use of 'treasured possession' in 19:5, that Israel was the Lord's people. The function of *gôy*, however, explicitly relates Israel to the other nations of the earth by placing her in a similar category.[22] The use of *gôy* reminds Israel that, although set apart, she is still one among many.

Dumbrell (1994: 86–87; cf. 64–68) offers another suggestion for the use of *gôy*. Like Speiser, Dumbrell points out that *'ām* functions as a kinship term, while *gôy* suggests a political entity. However, Dumbrell pushes further, suggesting that the use of *gôy* in 19:6 is an intentional allusion to Genesis 12:2, where *gôy* is used in the Lord's promise to Abram 'I will make of you a great nation.' If so, 19:6 is drawn into the orbit of the Lord's missionary purpose from another angle. It is clear from Genesis 12:1–3 that the great nation the Lord promises to make through Abram is intended to point beyond itself, functioning as the means through which blessing will come to all the families of the earth. For Dumbrell, *gôy* applied to Israel in Genesis 12:2 points to the intention of the Lord to restore, through Abram, the divine purpose of 'kingdom of God rule' in Genesis 1 – 2. Such a notion suggests a political reality, for which *'ām*, as a more personal term, would have been insufficient. Dumbrell (1994: 67) writes:

> Israel as a nation, as a symbol of divine rule manifested within a political framework, was intended itself to be an image of the shape of *final* world government, a symbol pointing beyond itself to the reality yet to be. (Emphasis original)

In other words Israel was to be a picture of the Lord's ultimate intention of governing the world. If Exodus 19:6 refers back to Genesis 12:2, as Dumbrell suggests, then the function of Israel as a *gôy qādôš* is an extension of the Lord's purposes for the families of the earth first given to Abram.[23]

---

[21] Cf. Cody 1964; Wells 2000: 53.

[22] Cf. Cody 1964: 5: 'While *'ām* throughout the Old Testament refers to a people or nation in its aspect of centripetal unity and cohesiveness, *gôy* is linked inseparably with territory and government and what we could today call foreign relations.'

[23] Cf. Paul 1970: 31, who similarly connects 19:6 to Gen. 12: 'For [Exod. 19 – 24] is an integral part of the transformation of the divine promise to Abraham, "I will make of you a great nation" (Gen. 12:2), into reality during the time of Moses.'

Although *gôy* highlights the similarity between Israel and the nations, Israel was to be different, a holy nation. In fact, the use of *gôy* draws out the force of *qādôš*, making distinction between Israel and the nations more vivid (Wells 2000: 54). By stressing Israel's similarity with the nations, *gôy* demonstrates that the difference between Israel and the nations is not firstly a political difference (even if Israel's election has political ramifications). Israel is a nation amongst the other nations of the earth, just as the other nations of the earth are peoples (*hā'ammîm*) like Israel (19:5). Therefore, the difference between Israel and the nations must lie elsewhere. Wherein does this difference lie? First, *qādôš* confirms Israel's priestly function amongst the nations. While the root *qdš* is used frequently in Exodus, it is particularly concentrated in the tabernacle material, which deals in large part with the cultic service of the priests, and therefore *qdš* applied to Israel suggests a priestly function. Secondly, *qdš* suggests that Israel herself reflected the character of the Lord. While not referring specifically to 19:6, von Rad's (1962: 205) words concerning the meaning of holy are instructive here:

> [T]he concept of the holy cannot in any way be deduced from other human standards of value. It is not their elevation to the highest degree, nor is it associated with them by way of addition. The holy could much more aptly be designated the great stranger in the human world, that is, a datum of experience which can never really be co-ordinated into the world in which one is at home, and over against which he initially feels fear rather than trust – it is, in fact, the 'wholly other'.

Von Rad's words help in understanding how Israel was to be distinct, for they suggest that Israel's distinctiveness was not simply being 'better' than other nations, but categorically different. The difference lay not in Israel's nationhood, but in the fact that Israel was the Lord's, and she alone reflected his character. That holiness refers to the Lord's character can be seen in the use of *qdš* throughout Exodus. As Wells (2000: 29–31) notes, with few exceptions the word 'holy' in Exodus is connected to the presence of God, with seventy-eight of the ninety-three occurrences of *qdš* being associated with the Lord's sanctuary. The application of the word to Israel, then, suggests that Israel somehow reflects the Lord's presence.[24]

---

[24] The expectation that Israel is to reflect the Lord's character, implicit in the use of

Summarizing the implications, Wells (2000: 31) writes, 'If the words here were not placed on the lips of YHWH himself, they might sound blasphemous. For this is a statement suggesting that people can, in some way, become like God.' Or, as expressed by Cole (1973: 23), 'Holiness is, in the deepest sense, a definition of God's nature as he expects to find it reflected in his children.' Because Israel was a nation, her holiness would be all the more apparent to other nations that were like her in other respects. What, then, did it mean that Israel was a holy nation? Simply put, Israel was set apart as a nation for the purpose of rendering priestly service in order to reflect the character of God to the nations.[25] In other words, through Israel, God would make himself known to the world.

The covenant ratification (Exod. 24:3–8)

The notion drawn from 19:6, that priestly kingdom and holy nation point to the priestly service of Israel on behalf of the nations, is confirmed in the ratification of the covenant in 24:3–8:

> Moses came and told the people all the words of the LORD and all the rules. And all the people answered with one voice and said, 'All the words that the LORD has spoken we will do.' And Moses wrote down all the words of the LORD. He rose early in the morning and built an altar at the foot of the mountain, and twelve pillars, according to the twelve tribes of Israel. And he sent young men of the people of Israel, who offered burnt offerings and sacrificed peace offerings of oxen to the LORD. And Moses took half of the blood and put it in basins, and half of the blood he threw against the altar. Then he took the Book of the Covenant and read it in the hearing of the people. And they said, 'All that the LORD has spoken we will do, and we will be obedient.' And Moses took the blood and threw it on the people and said, 'Behold the blood of the covenant that the LORD has made with you in accordance with all these words.'

Many have found this passage closely related to 19:3b–8. As Childs (1974: 502–503) comments, 'ch. 24 brings to completion the sealing

---

qdš in Exodus, becomes explicit in Leviticus: 'be holy, for I am holy' (Lev. 11:44–45; cf. 19:2; 20:26; 21:8).
[25] Cf. Deut. 4:5–8.

of the covenant which had been first announced in 19:3. The repetition of the people of the same response (19:8 and 24:3, 7) marks the beginning and end of one great covenant event.'[26] Here we find the same central concern of 19:4–6, sanctification, at the heart of the purpose of the covenant ceremony.

There are several reasons to see 24:3–8 as primarily concerned with sanctification.[27] First, the sprinkling of blood upon the people suggests sanctification. Blood applied to people is highly unusual in the OT. Aside from Exodus 24, the only place where blood is applied to a congregation, there are only two cases where blood is applied directly to a person. The first occurs in the priestly ordination of Aaron and his sons, where blood is directly applied to the tips of their ears, thumbs, and great toes, and sprinkled upon their persons and garments (29:20–21a; cf. Lev. 8:23–24, 30a) in order to sanctify them and their garments (29:21b; cf. Lev. 8:30b). The other instance occurs in the ritual cleansing of a leper, where two applications of blood are applied to a recently healed leper: a sprinkling with blood on the first day when he initially approaches the priest (Lev. 14:7a) and on the eighth day when blood is applied to his ear, thumb and great toe (Lev. 14:14). As a result, the leper is pronounced clean (Lev. 14:7b, 9b, 20b). In both cases, the ordination of priests and the cleansing of the leper, the person to whom the blood is applied moves between realms of sanctity. The priest moves from a common status to his holy status as a priest, while the leper moves from the realm of the unclean to that of the clean.[28] Recognizing the sanctifying purpose of applying blood to people elsewhere, it is appropriate to suggest that the application of blood to the Israelites in Exodus 24 had a similar function of moving Israel between realms of sanctity, from the common realm of all peoples who are the Lord's into the holy realm of those special to him. Exodus 24 is Israel's consecration to her priestly calling.

Secondly, the application of the blood to the people *after* Israel's pledge of obedience supports the notion that the purpose of the blood rite is sanctification. As we have seen, 19:5–6 concerns sanctification, Israel being set apart as a holy nation with a priestly calling that is carried out through obedience. Obedience is likewise central to the blood rite in Exodus 24. Not only does the rite follow Israel's

[26] Cf. Nicholson 1986: 164–178; Baltzer 1971: 28–30.

[27] Cf. Blum 1990: 51; Steins 2001: 28–32; Nicholson 1982: 80–83.

[28] For a general discussion concerning movement between realms of sanctity, see Wenham 1979: 18–25.

pledge to obey the Lord in verses 3 and 7, but Moses declares in the midst of the rite, 'Behold the blood of the covenant that the LORD has made with you in accordance with all these words' (24:8). Whether referring to Moses' reading of the Book of the Covenant or to Israel's pledge of obedience (or both), 'in accordance with all these words' shows that the covenant ceremony cannot be properly understood outside the expectation of obedience. It is therefore inappropriate to posit, as does Schenker (1996: 367), that the foundation of the covenant differs between obedience in Exodus 19 and sacrifice in Exodus 24. Obedience is a central concern for both.

If Israel's sanctification depends upon her obedience in Exodus 19:5–6, and if the ritual of Exodus 24:3–8 is likewise tied to obedience, then it is appropriate for Exodus 24:3–8 to be understood as a rite of sanctification. The words of Nicholson (1986: 173) concerning the relationship between 19:6 and 24:3–8 are worth quoting at length:

> If Exodus 19:3b–8 as a whole is an anticipatory summary and interpretation of the nature and basis of the covenant, it may be suggested that the statement in 19:6a was intended by its author as an interpretation of Exodus 24:3–8; that is, the author of 19:3b–8 understood Israel's status among the nations in a similar way to that of the author of Isaiah 61:6 ('you shall be named priests of the Lord and ministers of our God') and saw Exodus 24:3–8 as a record of Israel's consecration and commissioning as such. Thus, what is set out in programmatic manner in Exodus 19:3b–8 is finally completed in 24:3–8 where Israel gives its pledge of obedience to the words of the covenant and is then, as the author of Exodus 19:3b–8 took it, constituted as Yahweh's 'kingdom of priests and a holy nation'. By such means Exodus 24:3–8 has been interpreted as the solemn commissioning of Israel as a holy nation, obedient to God's will and functioning among the nations in the manner that a priesthood functions in a society – a theologically striking understanding and extension of the ritual described in 24:3–8.

Regardless of how one assesses the direction of influence between 19:3b–8 and 24:3–8, Nicholson's appreciation of the relationship between the two passages is important. In each, sanctification is firmly in view.

Thirdly, understanding Exodus 24:3–8 as a sanctification rite helps explain the connection between 24:3–8 and 24:1–2, 9–11. Scholars have often encountered difficulty in understanding the relationship between the two passages, seeing 24:3–8 and 24:1–2, 9–11 as differing accounts of the same event: the former reporting the ratification of the covenant through sacrifice, the latter through a covenant meal.[29] However, if the emphasis of 24:3–8 is to sanctify Israel, then the relationship between 24:3–8 and 29:1–2, 9–11 can be more easily appreciated. Before partaking of a covenant meal, Israel had to agree to the terms of the covenant and be moved into the realm of sanctity required by the covenant, a covenant that set Israel apart as a priestly kingdom and a holy nation. Such an elevation of sanctity would need to take place before a covenant meal could be shared in the presence of the Lord. That moving between realms of sanctity is at issue in 24:3–8 is further supported by the claim that Moses, Aaron, Nadab, Abihu and the elders saw God (24:10–11), a claim particularly striking when the peaceful scene on the mountain in Exodus 24 is contrasted with the ominous scene at the mountain in Exodus 19. As will be discussed later, access to God was restricted to those priests who had been made ritually holy for the purpose of serving God in the tabernacle. While the observation does not clear up all the difficulties inherent in the notion that the leaders of Israel saw God,[30] it does suggest a plausible relationship between the two sections that allows the canonical form to be understood as it stands.

Fourthly, Israel's designation as a priestly kingdom and a holy nation calls for a rite of sanctification. If Israel's priestly vocation to the nations is analogous to the vocation of the priest to the people, we might expect some type of ceremony to set Israel apart, as was the case for the priesthood within Israel. That both ceremonies included the rare application of blood to people only strengthens this inference. As alluded to above, sanctification is required for one to draw near to God. The priests, unlike the people, were allowed to draw near to God precisely because they were, ceremonially, sanctified to do so. So it must be for God's priestly nation.

---

[29] The notion of two covenant ceremonies explains, in part, the commonly accepted source divisions between 24:3–8 and 24:1–2, 9–11, a division that has, in turn, caused scepticism concerning whether or not 24:3–8 and 24:1–2, 9–11 can be meaningfully related (see e.g. Nicholson 1986: 131). Suggesting a chiastic structure in 24:1–11, Hilber (1996: 177–189) has argued that the literary structure of the passage does not support the separation of the two sections.

[30] For a discussion of the difficulties, see Durham 1987: 344–345, and, for ancient solutions to the problem, Nicholson 1986: 127–130.

Finally, the rite of Exodus 24 serves as a sign of faithful obedience, essential to the sanctification of Israel as the Lord's people. While, as I have argued, there is little by way of theological explanation of the rite in the text, the mention of burnt offerings and peace offerings earlier in Exodus 20 provides an important clue to the significance of the sacrifice. After giving the Decalogue, the Lord tells Moses again to speak to Israel:

> And the LORD said to Moses, 'Thus you shall say to the people of Israel: "You have seen for yourselves that I have talked with you from heaven. You shall not make gods of silver to be with me, nor shall you make for yourselves gods of gold. An altar of earth you shall make for me and sacrifice on it your burnt offerings and your peace offerings, your sheep and your oxen. In every place where I cause my name to be remembered I will come to you and bless you."' (20:22–24)

The reference to the Lord's speaking to Israel from heaven probably points back to the giving of the Decalogue (Nicholson 1977). If so, it is likely that the prohibition of idols functions here in a representative fashion, perhaps as a reiteration of the Decalogue's most pressing concern. The interesting point here is the manner in which the prohibition of idols is contrasted with offering burnt offerings and peace offerings, a contrast suggesting that the sacrifice of burnt offerings and peace offerings is a symbol of the faithful worship of the Lord alone. If this is the case, then the ritual of Exodus 24, involving the offering of burnt offerings and peace offerings, again emphasizes the obedience essential to Israel's consecration as a priestly kingdom and a holy nation, for it moves the expression of faithful worship of the Lord alone to the heart of the covenant-sealing ceremony.[31] In this way Exodus 24 expresses the exclusive worship of the Lord, the foundation of Israel's priestly calling.

Sanctification and the content of the law

The reason for the extended argument that the introduction to the law and the covenant ratification ceremony are principally

---

[31] Interestingly, the only other place in Exodus where sacrificing burnt offerings and peace offerings is mentioned is in connection with Israel's sin with the golden calf, the implications of which will be explored in chapter 6.

concerned with sanctification is to demonstrate that sanctification is at the very heart of the law. Recognizing this, however, raises further questions: How does the law relate to Israel's holiness, and how does Israel's holiness serve the Lord's missionary commitment to be known throughout the world? Here we begin to look directly at the content of the law that Israel is called to obey.

Here it bears mention that, by its very nature, law functions to reveal the character of the lawgiver, since a law code reflects the concerns of the one giving it.[32] Watts (1996: 1) says it this way:

> Speeches always indirectly characterize their speaker by providing readers the basis for inferring what kind of person talks this way. So the law codes voiced directly by God in Exodus, Leviticus, and Numbers provide a powerful impression of the divine character.

The content of the law, therefore, would serve to make the Lord's character known to all who encountered it, whether Israel who heard it from Moses, or the nations who were to see it manifest in the life of Israel. In other words, whether concerning idolatry or the fair treatment of slave girls, specific laws would make a public statement concerning the Lord's character. This recognition again takes us immediately back to the Lord's concern to make his name known, which was, as we have seen, the primary concern of the Egyptian deliverance. Cole (1973: 22) makes this argument explicitly, arguing that the Decalogue, by revealing the Lord's moral nature, is 'a theological explanation of the significance of the name of YHWH'. Cole's insight might well be applied to the entirety of the law, although the connections between the Lord's character and its expression in the law in some instances (e.g. the prohibition of murder) may be more easily understood (at least by a modern mind)

---

[32] Although referring to the 'I am the LORD' formula in Leviticus, the words of Zimmerli (1982: 12) are relevant for the present discussion: 'This repetition [of the 'I am the LORD' formula] pushes these legal statements into the most central position from which the Old Testament can make any statement. Each of these small groups of legal maxims thereby becomes a legal communication out of the heart of the Old Testament revelation of Yahweh. Each one of these small units offers in its own way a bit of explication of the central self-introduction of Yahweh, the God who summons his people – or better, recalling Leviticus 18ff. (and Ezek. 20), the God who sanctifies his people.' Sailhamer (1991: 246–247) goes so far as to argue that the laws of the Pentateuch were not primarily prescriptive, but were rather intended to portray God's divine wisdom and justice.

than in others (e.g. not boiling a kid in its mother's milk). By its very nature, the law makes God known.

This insight takes us to the heart of the Decalogue. The most explicit example of the relationship between holiness and law is the Sabbath, a regular outward and communal expression of Israel's obedience to the Lord. Israel is to sanctify the day (keep it holy), ceasing from her labours on the seventh day as the Lord ceased from his on the seventh day of creation. The Sabbath, then, is observed in imitation of the Lord himself. By taking on the patterns of the Lord, Israel is in effect living according to his likeness and character, a practical expression of the command 'You shall therefore be holy, for I am holy' (Lev. 11:45). The Sabbath serves as a continual reminder that the Lord sanctifies Israel: 'Surely you shall keep my Sabbaths, for it is a sign between me and you throughout your generations, that you may know that I am the LORD, who sanctifies you' (31:13, my tr.). Not only is 'I am the LORD' brought back into view, with the missionary impulse we have observed to this point, but it also brings Israel's missionary calling as a holy nation back into view as the Lord reminds Israel that he sanctifies her.

That the Sabbath is a sign of the covenant between the Lord and Israel suggests further that the Sabbath command represents all of the law. In other words it can be argued that the Sabbath stands as a sign that the whole law is lived in imitation of God. While the Lord's command cited above, 'Be holy, for I am holy,' suggests this in a general fashion, the principle of imitation is also brought out specifically. For example, in Exodus 22:27 the Lord commands the people to return their neighbour's cloak before nightfall, 'for I am compassionate'. The principle of imitation extends throughout the Old Testament into the New. For instance, in teaching his disciples to love their enemies, Jesus holds up the character of God, who is kind to the ungrateful and to the evil, before exhorting them to 'be merciful, even as your Father is merciful' (Luke 6:36). Jesus' parable of the unmerciful servant (Matt. 18:21–35) makes essentially the same point concerning forgiveness – that the disciples are to extend grace to others as God has extended grace to them.

One further example from the Decalogue concerning sanctification warrants mention: the third commandment, the only commandment in the Decalogue explicitly stating its concern with the Lord's name. Popularly understood as referring primarily to speech, the scope of the commandment reaches to include all of Israel's life. Two Hebrew terms warrant attention. The first, *tiśśa'*, from the root *nāśā'*, traditionally translated as 'take', is rendered more literally as 'bear' or 'carry'. The second, *laśśāw'*, 'vain', can also be rendered as 'falsely'. Along these lines, Wagner (1952) has suggested that the verse is a prohibition of 'bearing' the Lord's name falsely, or, in other words, acting in a manner false to the Lord. Not only is the suggestion consistent with the basic meaning of *nāśā'*, but it has significant merit in the canonical context of Exodus. First, it honours the public connection that the Lord has established with Israel in the Egyptian deliverance. Because of this public connection, the question becomes not *whether* Israel will bear the Lord's name, but rather *how* Israel will bear his name. That Israel bears witness to the Lord in both her faithfulness and in her unfaithfulness is apparent throughout the Scriptures, and can be seen in particular clarity in places such as Israel's sin with the golden calf (to be explored later) and the book of Ezekiel. It even becomes the ground from which Paul rebukes the Jews in Romans: 'The name of God is blasphemed among the Gentiles because of you' (Rom. 2:24). Secondly, it honours the sense of purpose for Israel as the Lord's people given in 19:4–6, particularly Israel's function as representing the Lord among the nations. C. J. H. Wright (2006: 92) perceptively speaks of Israel as stewards of the Lord's name. Having learned that there was no one like the Lord, 'They had a sense of stewardship of this knowledge since it was God's purpose that ultimately all nations would come to know the name, the glory, the salvation and the mighty acts of YHWH and worship him alone as God.'

So understood, the missionary impulse behind the law becomes clear – Israel is set apart that she might, in imitation of the Lord himself, live in such a manner that she faithfully represents him to the nations. This means by which the Lord makes himself known is carried forward through the NT. Picking up the language of Exodus 19:4–6, Peter writes, 'You are a chosen race, a royal priesthood, a holy nation, a people for his own possession, that you may proclaim the excellencies of him who called you out of darkness into his marvellous light' (1 Pet. 2:9). Similarly, Jesus told his disciples:

> You are the light of the world. A city set on a hill cannot be hidden. Nor do people light a lamp and put it under a basket, but on a stand, and it gives light to all in the house. In the same way, let your light shine before others, so that they may

see your good works and give glory to your Father who is in heaven. (Matt. 5:14–16)

Both passages above pick up on the missionary impulse of Exodus. The Lord seeks to create a people who follow his laws and walk in his ways, and he plants them in the midst of a world that does not know him. The mission, then, is realized primarily by living as the people of God, which will inevitably draw the attention of those who do not know the Lord, thereby making him known beyond Israel to the rest of the world.

The law and the goodness of God

As we have seen thus far, the primary goal of the Lord in Exodus is to make himself known. To this point, we have sought to demonstrate how the law given to Israel served to make the Lord known to the nations surrounding Israel. The corollary to the Lord's concern to be known is to be known for who he is. In other words the central and obvious point is that the Lord will be known as a particular kind of God. The term 'god' (*'ĕlōhîm*) in the OT may refer to the Lord, or it may refer to something else, such as angels, kings or idols (e.g. Ps. 82 and John 10:34). Similarly, the term 'God' in modern culture often functions as an empty box, a term that suggests little but is rather filled in any number of ways by the one who speaks of God. A name, on the other hand, is specific, suggesting particular contours and definition, speaking to what kind of God the Lord is. As we asked of Israel's deliverance, so now we ask of the commandments: 'What do the commandments reveal about the character of the Lord?'

To this point I have argued that the Lord reveals himself to be good. Yet this is not self-evident to many, particularly in reference to the OT. While the perspective of Richard Dawkins (2006: 51) may be extreme, calling him 'arguably the most unpleasant character in all fiction', many see God as unpleasant at best and evil at worst. One reason is that the Lord gives the law. That God would even give commands suggests to many restriction and control, not freedom and blessing. The intolerance inherent in the cardinal command of the Bible 'You shall have no other gods before me' (Exod. 20:3) only makes matters worse. How, then, is the law an expression of generosity? In order to answer this question we need to look at the actual commands of God. In so doing we will give special attention to the Decalogue.

From a canonical perspective it would be difficult to overestimate the importance of the Decalogue in Exodus.[33] Several items set it apart from the rest of the law: it is the first law code given in the canonical form of Exodus, it is given directly to the people without the mediation of Moses (Exod. 20:22; cf. Deut. 4:36), it is spoken of in different terms (literally, the ten 'words': 20:1; 34:28; cf. Deut. 4:13; 10:4), it alone appeared on the tablets written by the Lord at Sinai (34:28; cf. Deut. 4:13; 5:22) and was specially designated to be placed in the ark (25:16, 21; 31:18). In line with these practical distinctives, interpreters have understood the Decalogue to be special. Cassuto (1967: 205), for instance, calls the Decalogue 'the climax of the entire book, the central and most exalted theme, all that came before being, as it were, a preparation for it, and all that follows, a result of, and supplement to, it'. Importantly for our purposes, Childs (1974: 174) finds its importance in the manner in which it serves to guide the interpretation of subsequent legal material.

The prologue

The reason for speaking to the uniqueness of the Decalogue becomes clear when looking at its content. If the Decalogue occupies a special place at the head of the law, and if it serves in some way as an interpretative guide to the rest of the law, then it follows that the concerns most central to the Decalogue should shed important light on the character of God. Again we are brought to the Lord's concern to be known as God. This concern is immediately apparent in the prologue to the commandments: 'I am the LORD, your God, who brought you out of the land of Egypt' (Exod. 20:2). The prologue functions in several ways. Most often noted among biblical scholars is the manner in which the prologue serves to authorize the Lord's claim over Israel,[34] and to instil in Israel thankfulness to the Lord for her freedom and remind her that she now serves him.[35] However,

---

[33] From a critical perspective, the importance of the Decalogue is not obvious. See e.g. von Rad 1962: 190.

[34] Noth 1962: 161–162. Levenson (1980) argues that an overemphasis on the prologue has led many to assume that Israel's *ethos* (norm) was always rooted in her *mythos* (narrative), a position which he argues strips the law of any independent theological value. Levenson's argument, however, only underlines the point that the law was never intended to have independent value, but was always to be understood as given by the one who redeemed Israel from bondage, who called Israel to live life in reference to him, and who desires to be known for who he is.

[35] Houtman 2000: 16–17. Cf. Clements 1972: 123; Durham 1987: 76, 282–283; Zimmerli 1978: 116.

if 'I am the LORD' is allowed to convey the depth it has acquired to this point in Exodus, several other emphases emerge. The reminder of the Lord's universal supremacy inherent in 'I am the LORD' establishes the Lord's authority over Israel from another direction, and can serve (as we have seen in 15:26 and argued concerning 19:4) as an implied threat for disobedience. Perhaps more importantly, the introduction in 20:2 serves as a reminder of the Lord's central concern in the exodus, that Israel, Egypt and the earth would know 'I am the LORD.' The presence of 'I am the LORD' in the prologue is a reminder of the missionary concern that the phrase has carried to this point. This observation is particularly important, because it brings the Lord's missionary purpose to the head of the law, which has implications for how the rest of the law is understood. As Childs (1974: 401) writes, 'The prologue serves as a preface to the whole law and . . . makes it absolutely clear that the commands which follow are integrally connected to God's act of self-revelation.' The position of the prologue indicates that the ensuing law has a missionary function. This implication is further supported by the observation of Jacob (1992: 545), who connects 20:2 to 19:5, suggesting that 'I am yours' is the complement to 'you are mine', the connection to 19:5–6 reinforcing the missionary thrust of the prologue.

No other Gods

The first commandment, 'You shall have no other gods before me,' is basic to the rest of the Decalogue: 'It sets forth [for the remainder of the Decalogue] an expectation of absolute priority, a first and fundamental requirement of those who desire to enter into the covenant relationship with Yahweh' (Durham 1987: 284).[36] However, due to the difficulty of interpreting the phrase *'al pānāy* (before me), the precise meaning of the command has not been entirely clear. Several options have been put forward.[37] The phrase has been rendered in a spatial sense, such as 'beside me' (Scharbert 1989: 83), 'in front of me' (Cassuto 1967: 241) or, more broadly, 'in my presence' (Jacob 1992: 546), suggesting to some that the command is primarily a cultic prohibition of syncretism in worship.[38] The phrase has also

---

[36] Von Rad (1962: 210) went so far as to say that 'the whole history of Israel's cult is a struggle solely concerned with the validity of the first commandment'.

[37] See Köhler and Baumgartner 1996: 944; Knierim 1965: 20–39; and, particularly, Leibowitz 1976: 315.

[38] E.g. Noth 1962: 162. McConville (2002: 126) illustrates the prohibition with 1 Sam. 5:1–5, the toppling of Dagon in the presence of the ark.

been rendered in a more relational sense, such as 'except me', 'in preference to me' (cf. Albright 1957: 297), 'to my disadvantage' (von Rad 1962: 204), 'in defiance of me' (Köhler 1929: 174), 'over and against me' (MacDonald 2003: 77), or 'during the lifetime' (Jacob 1992: 546–547). Several of the options convey a sense of hostility, a sense consistent with the use of *'al pānāy* elsewhere in the OT.[39]

The varied translations of 20:3 suggest that it cannot be properly interpreted based on linguistic criteria alone. If the first commandment is read in the wider canonical context of Exodus, then the options may be narrowed. What appear to be alternate forms of the first commandment appear elsewhere in Exodus (Knierim 1965: 23–24). The exclusive nature of this commandment in Israel's cultic worship is clear in both 34:14 ('you shall worship no other god') and in 22:20[19] ('Whoever sacrifices to any god, other than the LORD alone, shall be devoted to destruction'). If these verses are allowed to inform 20:3, then worshipping other gods, even if the Lord is acknowledged as supreme, is categorically excluded. The commandment of 23:13, 'make no mention of the names of other gods, nor let it be heard on your lips', likewise affirms a rigid exclusivity, but, significantly, demonstrates that this exclusivity is not limited to cultic worship, for the command is given directly after the Lord's words 'pay attention to all I have said to you'.[40] Given the wide range of laws in the Book of the Covenant, the reference to 'all I have said' rules out the possibility that only cultic concerns are in view. Again, if seen together, 23:13 suggests that the scope of 20:3 is broader than cultic worship. The position of 20:3 at the beginning of the Decalogue suggests the same thing, given that the Decalogue is concerned with far more than cultic law.

There may be no way to translate 20:3 adequately into English. The translation 'before me' speaks to the Lord's intolerance of other gods, but misses the sense of hostility apparent in the term. The suggestions that convey hostility, such as those offered by Knierim ('in defiance of me') or MacDonald ('over and against me') carry the sense of opposition, but are not as clear that all other gods are forbidden to Israel. The problem is that no English term is broad enough to incorporate simultaneously the range of meaning sug-

---

[39] Stamm and Andrew 1967: 79; MacDonald 2003: 77.
[40] Additionally, MacDonald (2003: 75) observes that *'al pānāy* is not common to cultic language.

gested by *'al pānāy*. Patrick's (1985: 42) understanding of 20:3 is sufficient: 'It is safe to say that the force of it is to exclude relations with any other deity.' Brueggemann (1994: 841) gives the positive implication of the commandment: 'The command requires Israel to mobilize all of its life, in every sphere, around one single loyalty.'[41] This loyalty is expressed in loving obedience,[42] implied in the reference to 'those who love me and keep my commands' (20:6), and at the expense of all other idols or images.[43]

Having looked at the meaning and scope of the commandment, we are still left with the question 'How does this rigid exclusivity suggest the goodness of God?' First, the command speaks to the Lord's exclusive love for Israel. Sarna (1991:251) notes that the Hebrew root *hyh*, the root behind 'you shall be' in 19:5, is used for entering a marriage bond (Deut. 24:2, 4; Judg. 14:20; 2 Sam. 20:10; Hos. 3:3; Ruth 1:13), as well as for entering a covenant (Gen. 17:7; Exod. 19:4–5; Lev. 11:45). The exclusivity implied in the picture of marriage fits the strength of the commandment. Jacob (1992: 546, emphasis original) likewise recognizes the image, and draws out the implication:

> At Sinai only God and Israel existed in the world. HE took Israel to His heart – you are mine and belong to no one else! This expression evokes the picture of *marriage*; the wife could belong to only one husband while every other man was an *ish a-her*. They continued to exist, but were not available to her.[44]

Consistent with the notion of marriage is the one stated reason for which the Lord forbids idolatry: 'For I am the LORD your God, a jealous God' (20:5, my tr.).

The picture of marriage implied in the language of the commandment is, of course, made explicit elsewhere in the Scriptures, where

---

[41] Citing the broad range of possible translations of *'al pānāy*, Kaiser (1990: 422) paraphrases 20:3 with Isa. 42:8: 'I will not give my glory to another.'

[42] Kürle (2005: 45) helpfully connects 20:6 to the rest of the law in Exodus: 'The effect [of 20:6] is that the reader perceives the entire legislation in Exodus 20–23 as an expression of a life which befits a God-lover.'

[43] Zimmerli (1950) argues that the prohibition of 20:5 refers to gods, not images. While Zimmerli's contention makes sense of the awkward 'them' of 20:5, the forbidding of making images suggests that both other gods and images are prohibited (cf. Exod. 32 – 34).

[44] Based upon biblical and extra-biblical parallels, Sohn (1999) has likewise argued extensively that the covenant is based upon a marriage formula.

the relationship between the Lord and Israel is described in terms of marriage, whether positively (e.g. 'I remember the devotion of your youth, / your love as a bride,' Jer. 2:2) or negatively (e.g. Hosea's charge to marry a prostitute). The unmistakable point is that the Lord's jealous exclusivity is rooted in love, a love we understand as entirely appropriate between a husband and wife. What has been long recognized as the positive reiteration of the first commandment well fits this context: 'Hear, O Israel: the LORD our God, the LORD is one. You shall love the LORD your God with all your heart and with all your soul and with all your might' (Deut. 6:4–5).

Secondly, the rigid exclusivity of the first commandment reflects the Lord's concern for Israel's welfare. One of the constant refrains of the Bible is that idols are not to be worshipped, not just because idolatry is wrong (or, as suggested above, being unfaithful), but because other gods cannot save. As we have seen, this is one of the major lessons both Israel and Egypt learned, as Pharaoh and Egypt's gods proved unable to save Egypt from destruction. In other words it is not that idolatry is wrong (be that as it may); it is foolish. Isaiah's satire lays bare the folly of idolatry. After asking the question 'Who fashions a god or casts an idol that is profitable for nothing?' Isaiah goes on to lampoon the man who does exactly that:

> No one considers, nor is there knowledge or discernment to say, 'Half of it I burned in the fire; I also baked bread on its coals; I roasted meat and have eaten. And shall I make the rest of it an abomination? Shall I fall down before a block of wood?' (44:10, 19)

Moving away from satire, Isaiah gets right to the point. The folly is serious:

> If one cries to [a false god], it does not answer
> or save him from his trouble.
>
> (46:7)

The problem with idolatry is that it turns one away from the Lord, who alone can save and secure the welfare of his people. The prohibition of idolatry, then, has the dual thrust of calling one *to* the Lord and therefore *away* from idols. Samuel's exhortation to Israel captures the point:

> Do not turn aside from following the LORD, but serve the
> LORD with all your heart. And do not turn aside after empty
> things that cannot profit or deliver, for they are empty. For
> the LORD will not forsake his people, for his great name's
> sake, because it has pleased the LORD to make you a people
> for himself. (1 Sam. 12:20–22)

This dual repudiation of idolatry is carried through the NT,
usually addressed in terms of love of money or covetousness, which
Paul explicitly calls idolatry (Col. 3:5). In the Sermon on the Mount,
for instance, Jesus speaks of the love of money as both foolish, since
'moth and rust destroy' and 'thieves break in and steal' earthly treas-
ures (Matt. 6:19), and as being unfaithful, since 'No one can serve
two masters, for either he will hate the one and love the other, or he
will be devoted to the one and despise the other. You cannot serve
God and money' (Matt. 6:24). John picks up the same dual condem-
nation of idolatry:

> Do not love the world or the things in the world. If anyone
> loves the world, the love of the Father is not in him. For all
> that is in the world – the desires of the flesh and the desires of
> the eyes and pride in possessions – is not from the Father but
> is from the world. And the world is passing away along with
> its desires, but whoever does the will of God abides for ever.
> (1 John 2:15–17)

Here idolatry is both a matter of misplaced love and misplaced trust.
Not only does love of the world squeeze out the love of the Father,
but the world so loved is passing away. The implication is that the
lover of the world will pass away along with the world, while those
who love God and do the will of God will abide. In the end turning
to idols is turning away from the Lord, who alone is able to save. As
Jonah learned:

> Those who pay regard to vain idols
> forsake their hope of steadfast love.
>
> (Jon. 2:8)

By pointing Israel to trust in God, the first commandment, and
indeed the whole law, is a deep expression of God's goodness to
Israel.

Community life and witness

The goodness of God in the law is evident in another way, for an important function of the law was to ensure healthy community life. The actual commands of the law get very specific concerning the manner in which the Israelites are to live with one another. For instance, 'You shall not murder' (20:13; cf. 21:12–14) not only forbids killing the innocent, but also implicitly calls for the community to do what it can to ensure that innocent life is protected (such as ensuring that a dangerous ox is contained, 21:28–32, or that anyone involved in kidnapping is executed, 21:16). Furthermore, the weak and vulnerable are to be dealt with fairly (e.g. 22:21–24; 23:3, 6–9). Fellow Israelites are to deal honestly with one another (e.g. 22:1–4, 7–9; 23:1–2) and to absorb the consequences of negligent behaviour personally (e.g. 21:33–34; 22:5–6, 12). Further than that, the people are commanded to seek the welfare of others (e.g. 23:4–5). The Lord's insistence on goodwill between members of the covenant community extends even to areas where it might seem within the rights of an Israelite to withhold it, such as the call for voluntary kindness to one's enemies (23:5), the injunction to lend without interest (22:25) or the command to return the garment taken in pledge (22:26). Ultimately, all these commands are grounded in love, which is why Paul, quoting Leviticus 19:18, can claim, 'The whole law is fulfilled in one word: "You shall love your neighbour as yourself"' (Gal. 5:14).

The concern for loving one another, incidentally, suggests yet another reason that the Decalogue is introduced with a reminder of Israel's deliverance from slavery. Remembering from whence they came would have the effect of making the Israelites into a particular kind of people, even a kind people, for it would be expected that a people shown kindness would be a people to extend kindness, even the blessing that God intended to extend through Abraham. Hints of this can be found in the Book of the Covenant. In perhaps the most explicit example, the Lord speaks to Israel, 'You shall not oppress a sojourner. You know the heart of a sojourner, for you were sojourners in the land of Egypt' (23:9; cf. 22:21; Deut. 15:12–15). The larger point is that, as Israel has been treated, so they are to treat others, an expectation that spans the Scriptures. This is precisely what gives Jesus' parable of the unforgiving servant in Matthew 18 such power. It is not so much wrong but rather *unthinkable* that the servant who was forgiven much would not forgive another. The impression given by the parable is that the fault of the servant is, at bottom, being unmindful of the grace extended to him.

The Sabbath again provides great help in understanding the essential goodness of the Lord expressed in the law. As we have seen, the Sabbath recalls creation, and particularly the order of creation. God's working for six days and resting on the seventh becomes the order of Israel's week. But the order runs deeper. A striking aspect of creation is the manner in which God orders the heavens and the earth. The land is separated from the seas, the sun and the moon order the days and the seasons, and the animals are created in ordered kinds. What began as chaos in Genesis 1:2 becomes an ordered creation that God deems 'very good' in 1:31. The point is that order begets blessing, and that living according to that created order is the means by which blessing is upheld. In other words it is not simply that God brings a curse upon a world that disobeys his commands (as true as that may be at times), but rather that violating his commands in and of itself violates the blessed order that God intends. Just as violation of the boundary between land and sea brings destruction and chaos, so does violation of the boundary that protects a marriage, or the boundary that protects the life of the vulnerable. This is why God's judgment can be direct, as when he brings the rain in Noah's day or withholds it in Elijah's, or can be indirect, as when Paul describes God's wrath being manifest in God's giving people over to the desires of their hearts (Rom. 1:18–31). Life lived without regard for the order of creation necessarily brings chaos.

The force of the Sabbath, then, is not simply in remembering the fact *that* God created the heavens and the earth, but also in remembering *how* he created the heavens and the earth, through establishing an order that brings blessing and ensures Israel's well-being. That the Sabbath is so closely related to justice bears testimony to this connection between the Sabbath and order. To look at the Sabbath command from the perspective of the Decalogue in Deuteronomy, the rationale for the Sabbath command lies in Israel's deliverance from oppression (Deut. 5:15). This emphasis on freedom and justice can be seen in places as divergent as the Sabbath years when debts would be cleared (Deut. 15), culminating in the year of Jubilee when lands were returned and slaves freed (Lev. 25), the parallel between the Sabbath and extending oneself for the vulnerable in Isaiah 58, and even Jesus' healing on the Sabbath. The point is that the Sabbath is a picture of the way God intends the world to be, a reflection upon the order of creation so formed as to ensure blessing. This is another way that the Sabbath represented the whole of the law.

The implication of the above is that serving the Lord is freedom. As we have seen, Israel was not redeemed from Egypt to be released from all authority, but rather transferred from serving Pharaoh to serving the Lord. Serving the Lord, however, was not destructive or oppressive, but rather the opposite: the means of life. The exhortation to obedience is an exhortation to freedom, to life:

> I call heaven and earth to witness against you today, that I have set before you life and death, blessing and curse. Therefore choose life, that you and your offspring may live, loving the LORD your God, obeying his voice and holding fast to him, for he is your life and length of days, that you may dwell in the land that the LORD swore to your fathers, to Abraham, to Isaac, and to Jacob, to give them. (Deut. 30:19–20)

Even Jesus' words, with their implicit echoes of the Sabbath, speak of service as freedom:

> Come to me, all who labour and are heavy laden, and I will give you rest. Take my yoke upon you, and learn from me, for I am gentle and lowly in heart, and you will find rest for your souls. For my yoke is easy, and my burden is light. (Matt. 11:28–30)

The rest for the weary offered by Jesus is not the throwing off of a yoke, but rather the exchange of a yoke, one that is easy and light and, likewise, carried by Jesus. 'See! The LORD has given you the Sabbath' (Exod. 16:29; cf. Mark 2:27). The Sabbath, then, serves as a testimony of the goodness of God.

Conclusion: law and gospel in Exodus

In chapter 2 we observed that the 'gospel', or the Lord's delivering Israel, was motivated by his desire to communicate to Israel, Egypt and the world that 'I am the LORD' who, unlike Pharaoh or the gods of Egypt, is willing and able to deliver his people. In chapters 19–24 the Lord's concern remains the same, for in Israel's obedience to the law she will represent the Lord, thereby making him known among the nations. The Lord's purpose to be known as God among the nations remains constant; the manner in which that purpose is carried out shifts. In the exodus Israel was largely passive as the Lord manifested himself in the sight of the world through delivering Israel. From Sinai onwards Israel, through her obedience, plays an active role as she makes the Lord known to the nations. As House (1998: 110) writes, 'The covenant's function is to set aside Israel as a special nation that can mediate God's identity to the entire family of nations.' In this way the Sinai material serves the missionary purposes of the Lord. Furthermore, understanding the missionary thrust of the law shows how the wilderness material fits into this larger missionary concern. If the central concern of the law was for the Lord to be known to the nations, then it can safely be said that Israel's preparation to that end shares the same concern.

We now return to the issue with which we began: the relationship between law and gospel in the Pentateuch. Is von Rad's stark dichotomy between law and gospel faithful to their presentation in Exodus? Or, with Barr, must we choose between seeing the Pentateuch as a religion of law or as a religion of salvation? The issue is pressing, for ultimately our understanding of gospel and law gets to the heart of who God is, and who he has made himself known to be.

Exodus firmly brings gospel and law into relationship. For instance, Exodus 19:4–6 begins with what might be called a statement of gospel, 'You yourselves have seen what I did to the Egyptians, and how I bore you on eagles' wings and brought you to myself,' followed by what might be called a statement of law, 'Now, therefore, if you will obey my voice and keep my covenant . . .' Likewise, the Decalogue is introduced in Exodus 20:2 with a reminder of the Egyptian deliverance: 'I am the LORD your God, who brought you out of the land of Egypt, out of the house of slavery.' That the two cardinal passages regarding the purpose and content of the law explicitly bring the Egyptian deliverance into view cautions us against drawing distinctions between the gospel and law that suggest they are either independent of one another or stand over and against one another. The danger of using the term 'fundamental' when speaking of the difference between gospel and law is that it can obscure both the relationship between them and the generosity of God that is foundational to both. In the common usage of the term, fundamental differences are usually irreconcilable. Here the canonical form of Exodus is of great help. To return to Childs (1979: 177), Exodus 'provides a classic model by which to understand the proper relations between "gospel and law"'. How does Exodus shed light on this relationship?

Gospel, then law

Appreciating the order of gospel and law in Exodus is crucial in understanding their relationship. The law in Exodus is given to Israel *after* she has been delivered from slavery. Nowhere does Exodus suggest that Israel was delivered because of her faithfulness to the law (which at that point had not been given). Rather, the reason Exodus gives for Israel's deliverance is that 'God heard their groaning, and God remembered his covenant with Abraham, with Isaac, and with Jacob' (2:24). That Israel is delivered apart from her own power or faithfulness is established in later biblical testimony. For instance, Ezekiel is clear that Israel was not delivered because she was faithful, for in Egypt 'they rebelled against me and were not willing to listen to me. None of them cast away the detestable things their eyes feasted on, nor did they forsake the idols of Egypt' (Ezek. 20:8). Deuteronomy makes plain Israel was not delivered because she was impressive, but due to the Lord's love for her and the promises made to the patriarchs:

> The LORD your God has chosen you to be a people for his treasured possession, out of all the peoples who are on the face of the earth. It was not because you were more in number than any other people that the LORD set his love on you and chose you, for you were the fewest of all peoples, but it is because the LORD loves you and is keeping the oath that he swore to your fathers, that the LORD has brought you out with a mighty hand and redeemed you from the house of slavery, from the hand of Pharaoh king of Egypt. (Deut. 7:6–8)

This passage serves as the ground for the Lord's claim on Israel's obedience. As Deuteronomy has already made plain, Israel is to love God (Deut. 6:4–5). But only because God loved her first. The important point is that Israel is told what to do after she has experienced God's intervention on her behalf. In Exodus gospel precedes law. The deliverance from slavery precedes instructions concerning how to live as a people now free from Egyptian bondage.

This order from Exodus is brought forward into the NT, where gospel again precedes law. The teaching of the NT speaks of the plight of Israel, indeed the plight of all humanity, likewise as slavery. In a particularly stark example, consider Jesus' words to the Jews in John:

So Jesus said to the Jews who had believed in him, 'If you abide in my word, you are truly my disciples, and you will know the truth, and the truth will set you free.' They answered him, 'We are offspring of Abraham and have never been enslaved to anyone. How is it that you say, "You will become free"?' Jesus answered them, 'Truly, truly, I say to you, everyone who commits sin is a slave to sin. The slave does not remain in the house for ever; the son remains forever. So if the Son sets you free, you will be free indeed.' (John 8:31–36)

Speaking to those who held the law in highest regard, Jesus tells them they are enslaved and therefore in need of the deliverance only the Son can bring. The law cannot bring freedom. In fact, misunderstanding the law often obscures the fact that one is enslaved in sin, a recurring theme in John. This is precisely the plight of the Jews Jesus addresses in John. Thinking they would find eternal life in the Scriptures, they missed Jesus, the one to whom the Scriptures pointed, who was able to give life (7:39–40). Rather, the Jews set their hope on a law they did not keep and that therefore condemned them (5:45–47; 7:19). But the law was never meant to be Israel's source of hope. The Lord was. It is this kind of misunderstanding that elsewhere in the Gospels likewise obscures the people's need of Jesus, such as the rich young man who believed he had kept the law (Mark 10:17–22), the elder brother in the parable of the prodigal sons (Luke 15:11–32) or the Pharisee in the temple, who proudly set himself above the tax collector (Luke 18:9–14). Those who hope in the law will never believe they are enslaved to sin, and will therefore never turn to the Son to be delivered.

This is precisely the teaching of Paul. In his letter to the Galatians, most explicitly concerned with the proper understanding between gospel and law, Paul speaks in terms of slavery and freedom: 'For freedom Christ has set us free; stand firm therefore, and do not submit again to a yoke of slavery' (Gal. 5:1; cf. Rom. 7:23). Paul saw as bondage the view that the law was the means by which we are justified before God. Yet, knowing that they are justified by believing in Christ, Paul goes on to exhort the people to do the very thing the law commanded, speaking in terms of freedom:

For you were called to freedom, brothers. Only do not use your freedom as an opportunity for the flesh, but through love serve one another. For the whole law is fulfilled in one word: 'You shall love your neighbour as yourself.' (Gal. 5:13–14)

Or, to look at another example, having declared that man is dead and helpless in sin, unless made alive by Christ, Paul carefully relates faith to works in Ephesians:

> For by grace you have been saved through faith. And this is not your own doing; it is the gift of God, not a result of works, so that no one may boast. For we are his workmanship, created in Christ Jesus for good works, which God prepared beforehand, that we should walk in them. (Eph. 2:8–9)

The salvation Christ brings is the freedom to live as God intended, in conformity with the character of God and according to his ways. This is why Paul can speak in such stark terms about the inability of the law to justify, and yet still give much practical instruction in holy living in his epistles. It is noteworthy that, broadly speaking, Paul's instruction to practical living usually follows an exposition of what God has done in Christ.

The new covenant in Christ

There is, of course, a way in which the law can be seen as preceding the gospel, an emphasis particularly important in Lutheran and Reformed theology, in that the law makes plain the sin from which humanity must be delivered. If it can be said that the law precedes the gospel, it does so by revealing the plight from which man needs deliverance. Nowhere is this better articulated than in Jeremiah 31:31–34, a passage clearly looking ahead to the gospel:

> Behold, the days are coming, declares the LORD, when I will make a new covenant with the house of Israel and the house of Judah, not like the covenant that I made with their fathers on the day when I took them by the hand to bring them out of the land of Egypt, my covenant that they broke, though I was their husband, declares the LORD. But this is the covenant that I will make with the house of Israel after those days, declares the LORD: I will put my law within them, and I will write it on their hearts. And I will be their God, and they shall be my people. And no longer shall each one teach his neighbour and each his brother, saying, 'Know the LORD,' for

116

they shall all know me, from the least of them to the greatest, declares the LORD. For I will forgive their iniquity, and I will remember their sin no more.

Two things warrant attention. First, while the language of slavery is not explicit here (although perhaps implied in the parallel with the former covenant after the Egyptian deliverance, of which more later), Israel's need is twofold. She needs forgiveness, which by definition she is not entitled to. It can only be given. She also needs the renovation of the heart, a condition, as Jeremiah makes plain, that Israel cannot herself correct. What Israel needs she cannot provide for herself. Secondly, the new covenant is given with the law squarely in view, given not so that the law would be done away with, but rather so that Israel would be able to keep the law, now written on the heart. The effect of the law so written on the heart would be that Israel would know the Lord.

It is noteworthy that the promise of the new covenant comes at another moment of redemption in the life of the people of God. The words that introduce the new covenant, 'behold, the days are coming', are words that introduce the promise that the Lord will restore Israel from Babylonian captivity, bringing her back to her own country and cities: 'For behold, days are coming, declares the LORD, when I will restore the fortunes of my people, Israel and Judah, says the LORD, and I will bring them back to the land that I gave to their fathers, and they shall take possession of it' (Jer. 30:3). The parallels between the two covenants are striking. As with the former covenant in Exodus, the new covenant will be established based upon a great deliverance. This is not a work Israel will do for herself, but a work the Lord will do for her. Furthermore, the goals each covenant serves and the relationship each establishes are similar as well. Note the following juxtaposition:

I will take you to be my people, and I will be your God, and you shall know that I am the LORD your God, who has brought you out from under the burdens of the Egyptians. (Exod. 6:7)

And I will be their God, and they shall be my people. And no longer shall each one teach his neighbour and each his brother, saying, 'Know the LORD,' for they shall all know me . . . (Jer. 31:33–34)

The relationship each described between God and Israel is the same, and the purpose of the covenant, that Israel would know the Lord, the same. However, the new covenant presses further than the old covenant ever could, for the deliverance offered in the new covenant is in the end not simply deliverance from Babylonian captivity, but rather from the sin that led her there. It is a promise that lies in the future, of which the return from Babylon is a type. It is a promise that gets to the very heart of the Gospel, fulfilled in the death of Jesus. Jesus' words to his disciples the night before his death make this explicit: 'This cup that is poured out for you is the new covenant in my blood' (Luke 22:20; cf. 1 Cor. 11:25). Everything the new covenant promised in Jeremiah is fulfilled in Jesus – both forgiveness of sins and the renovation of the heart. It is through this covenant, death and subsequent resurrection of Jesus that, in the words of Charles Wesley, 'He breaks the power of cancelled sin.'

Here the relationship between gospel and law becomes clearer. As we have seen, the law is a reflection of the character of God. As Israel is faithful to the law, so she reflects the nature of God who created her, redeemed her and gave her the law so that she might live in the state of blessing that is the lot of those who walk with God and according to his ways. However, she is not willing or able to keep the law, but is rather enslaved by sin. Her need is freedom. She must be delivered from sin. It is only then that living in conformity with the Lord's character becomes possible. After carefully explaining that 'while we were still sinners, Christ died for us' (Rom. 5:8), Paul asks rhetorically 'Are we to continue in sin that grace may abound? By no means! How can we who died to sin still live in it?' (Rom. 6:1–2). In the death of Christ the one in Christ died to sin and is therefore released from its bondage, and, in Christ's resurrection, rose to new life in the Spirit.

Yet freedom in the NT must be qualified, for it does not consist in licence or lawlessness, but rather in placing oneself under another yoke, slavery to Christ.[45] In a parallel passage to his rhetorical question above, and following it, Paul asks:

> Are we to sin because we are not under law but under grace?
> By no means! Do you not know that if you present yourselves

---

[45] For a very helpful and thorough treatment of the issues of slavery and freedom in the NT, see Harris 1999; and, for a more imaginative but theologically rigorous reflection, Card 2009.

to anyone as obedient slaves, you are slaves of the one whom
you obey, either of sin, which leads to death, or of obedience,
which leads to righteousness? (Rom. 6:15–16)

For Paul only two states are variously articulated: slavery and
freedom. Or, said differently, there is slavery to sin and slavery to
righteousness in Christ.[46] The point here is that freedom is defined
as another slavery – this time not to a master that leads to death,
but to a master that brings life. To enter this slavery *in* Christ
requires deliverance *by* Christ. This alternative service is precisely
what Israel was called to – 'You yourselves have seen what I did to
the Egyptians, and how I bore you on eagles' wings and brought
you *to myself*' (Exod. 19:4, my emphasis). With a deliverance *from*
comes a deliverance *to*, in this case, to God. In the end the Egyptian
deliverance (and the release from Babylon) is a type of the gospel,
the freedom through the death and resurrection of Christ from sin
that was the ultimate source of Israel's bondage, and to the ensuing
freedom to love God and one another that makes plain to the
nations that the Lord is God.

Thus we are brought back to Psalm 119. For the psalmist the
law is not bondage, but a delight. He writes as one for whom the
Lord's commands are not burdensome (1 John 5:3), but are rather
a testimony of the goodness of God, and the means by which the
people of God live into the kind of blessing for which God intends
for them. And yet, in his freedom, the psalmist understands himself
to be a slave, an *'ebed*, of the Lord (119: 135). The generosity and
righteousness of God do not exist over and against one another, but
rather characterize the Lord who has made himself known in both
gospel and law.

> The LORD is righteous in all his ways,
> and gracious in all his works.
>
> (Ps. 145:17, my tr.)

---

[46] See the broader discussion of Harris 1999: 69–86.

Chapter Five

The tabernacle instructions (Exod. 25 – 31)

One thing have I asked of the LORD,
    that will I seek after:
that I may dwell in the house of the LORD
    all the days of my life,
to gaze upon the beauty of the LORD
    and to enquire in his temple.

(Psalm 27:4)

For a day in your courts is better
    than a thousand elsewhere.
I would rather be a doorkeeper in the house of my God
    than dwell in the tents of wickedness.

(Psalm 84:10)

One of the great themes running throughout Scripture, particularly evident in the Psalms, is the desire of the people of God to dwell with God, to worship him, to know him. As we will see, the Bible begins in a sanctuary, Adam and Eve walking with God in the cool of the day (Gen. 3:8), and ends in one, as the New Jerusalem descends that she might dwell with the Lord, as a bride with her husband (Rev. 21). The dwelling of God among humanity points to the restoration of *šālôm*, the peace and flourishing that God intended in creation, and which he will again bring about when he restores all things to himself. In effect, these acclamations of praise and desire to dwell in the Lord's house are the fulfilment of the Lord's intention for humanity, even all creation, 'to reconcile to himself all things' (Col. 1:20). Or, said differently, 'This is eternal life, that they know you the only true God, and Jesus Christ whom you have sent' (John 17:3).

Problems with tabernacle interpretation

Given the importance of the Lord's dwelling place in the Bible, we would expect to find great attention given to the tabernacle, the dwelling place of God in Exodus. In this vein Childs (1997: 185–186) writes:

> Because the Bible was traditionally understood as containing the very oracles of God, no word was regarded as superfluous. It was, therefore, thoroughly rational to argue that if Genesis needed only one chapter for the creation of the heavens and the earth but Exodus needed thirteen to describe the tabernacle, the Exodus chapters must contain multitudes of hidden mysteries calling for the most detailed commentary.

What makes Childs's comment so interesting is that theological study of the tabernacle texts of Exodus has often gone in the opposite direction from detailed commentary. For instance, in their respective Exodus commentaries, Fretheim (1991a) gives 19 of 321 pages to the tabernacle material, Enns (2000) gives 54 of 602, Cole (1973) gives 29 of 239, G. H. Davies (1967) 34 of 253, Hyatt (1971) 47 of 345, and, in his explicitly theological commentary, Gowan (1994) 4 of 297. Even Childs (1974), despite the above comment, gives only 54 of his 659 pages to discuss the tabernacle. On a broader level, it is noteworthy that Gerstenberger's (2002) recent OT theology does not discuss the tabernacle, despite the fact that more is written on the tabernacle than any other object in the Pentateuch. While admittedly (and as we will see) not all scholars have comparatively neglected the tabernacle, it is nonetheless common in Exodus commentaries for the amount of space devoted to the tabernacle material to be proportionally less than the amount of space the tabernacle is given in Exodus itself.[1] Further, even where given proportional attention, the tabernacle sections are often uninte-

---

[1] Two comments are relevant here. First, it must be acknowledged that the construction of the tabernacle in 35 – 40 largely repeats the instructions of 25 – 31, which accounts in part for the lack of proportional attention. Secondly, this lack of attention is generally true of Christian, particularly Protestant, commentators. Jewish commentators, as a whole, are far more interested in the cultic sections of Exodus. Cf. Cassuto 1967; Jacob 1992; Sarna 1986; and particularly Haran 1978 and Milgrom 1970. Buber and Rosenzweig (1994: 62) speak of the tabernacle material as 'the climax of the book [of Exodus], which is also perhaps the high point of the whole five books together'.

grated theologically in the rest of the book,[2] either because the tabernacle material can be difficult to assess theologically, or because (in the case of commentaries) the genre of the biblical commentary does not necessarily lend itself to sustained theological integration, since one can comment upon multiple texts without relating them.

Reasons for the general theological neglect of the tabernacle section are several. First, there is the issue of style. For many, the tabernacle sections feel monotonous, calling forth assessments of the material as 'dry history' and 'historical pedantry' (Wellhausen 1885: 337–338), 'ponderous, pedantic, and lacking artistry' (von Rad 1961: 26) and 'long-winded description' (Haran 1978: 150). In a similar vein Klein (1996: 274) writes:

> There is something off-putting about an ancient tent shrine, whose materials include such an enormous quantity of gold and silver, that forms the centre of an elaborate, stylized, and hierarchical camp. The exclusivity of the Aaronic priesthood and the sharp hiatus between clergy and laity are also not in conformity with some current tastes.

Rosenzweig raises the issue of how modern tastes can obscure the force of Hebrew style by way of an interesting example concerning a particular German translation of the tabernacle material. Since the following example is pertinent both here and later in this discussion, it is worth quoting at length:

> The powerful divine speech of chapters 25 through 31, the word concerning the vision vouchsafed to Moses, explaining to what end, to what 'service of labor' his people are to be led after their 'service of bondage,' is in the translation under discussion transposed from its austere, concrete sublimity to a relentlessly chatty idiom that scribbles over all the original clarity of line. It is as if a sergeant attempted in his giving orders to 'explicate' the classical commands of field duty ordinance. An evident example: these chapters are shot through with the word 'made,' which is as it were the theme of this great fugue. The Kautzsch translation, no doubt to keep the reader from boredom, undertakes to render the

---

[2] Although see G. Davies (1999) and Rodríguez (1986).

word in charmingly diverse guises – sometimes as 'erected,' sometimes as 'produced,' sometimes as 'put up,' sometimes as 'worked.' It has not the least suspicion that what happens in consequence is the loss not 'only' of the form but also of the entire meaning of the vision, which in fact looks toward the original model of the 'Dwelling' created on Sinai in the six days of cloudy darkness . . . as a human replica of the divine act of creation. (Buber and Rosenzweig 1994: 62)

Secondly, the general neglect of the tabernacle reflects a noticeable lack of direct theological comment in the text itself, which has influenced the kinds of questions scholars have asked, modern scholarship focusing mainly on the tabernacle's historical authenticity, its construction and the composition of the tabernacle texts. Von Rad (1962: 232–233) described it this way:

> The various pieces of cultic material are to a large extent presented with such bare objectivity, and so much without any addition which gives the theological significance, that the task of interpretation passes over unawares from the hands of the theologian to the biblical archaeologist.

While there may be, in some cases, an appropriate exegetical reserve, not speculating where the text appears silent, there nonetheless appears to be an uncertainty as to the value of the details, which leads many to dismiss their importance. For instance, Klein (1996: 264) writes, 'It is not the details of the tabernacle account that make up its significance, but the underlying notion that God elects to be present with God's people.' Balentine (1999: 137) concurs: 'The focus of the texts themselves is not on cubits and figures, numbers and shapes, but rather on the indwelling presence of God that a sanctuary and its holy accoutrements enables a community to celebrate.' These comments, however, simply beg the question 'Why the details?'[3] The importance of the Lord's dwelling among his people could have been conveyed without the painstaking detail of tabernacle furniture, measurements, types of fabric or priestly garments. The implication is that the details are of small, if any, theological

---

[3] Cf. the refreshing candour of Fretheim (1996: 108): 'the purpose of the sheer volume of detail presented, much of which is repeated in chapters 35–40 is not at all clear'.

importance.[4] The relative silence of much modern scholarship on the tabernacle material suggests a general assent with S. R. Driver (1913: 129) that the priestly writer 'nowhere touches upon the deeper problems of theology'.

Another reason for the comparative neglect of the tabernacle section, particularly in the wider context of Exodus, has to do with Wellhausen's estimation of the tabernacle texts as a postexilic fictional retrojection into Israel's history by the priestly caste for (self-serving) political ends.[5] Not surprisingly, Wellhausen naturally found little of theological worth in the tabernacle material. Although recent scholarship has challenged Wellhausen's position at points, particularly due to archaeological discoveries, Wellhausen's influence has endured.[6] It is not surprising that a general neglect of the tabernacle material, particularly from a theological perspective, has persisted. One of the effects of this perspective is that the tabernacle material has been read in the context of 'P', known by critical scholars as the priestly source, rather than in the context of Exodus. That P is generally considered to be the most easily discernible and definable Pentateuchal source further encourages a search for the theology of P. That P is widely considered postexilic encourages the reading of the tabernacle from a postexilic vantage point, further divorcing the tabernacle from the context of Exodus itself.[7]

Of course, not all interpreters have agreed with the largely negative assessment of the theology of the tabernacle material. Durham (1987: 353) argues that '[the tabernacle] chapters are theological in their origin, theological in their statement, and theological even in their arrangement'. Gorman (1990: 60) suggests that ritual was, for the priests, the primary means for theological reflection.[8] Implicitly responding to Wellhausen's negative view of the priestly material in relationship to the prophets, Jacob (1992: 759, emphasis original) writes, '*The so-called Priestly Code, with its sanctuary, represented*

---

[4] Cf. the new Revised Common Lectionary, where the tabernacle material is absent from the three-year cycle of Sunday readings.

[5] See Wellhausen 1885: 38–51. Arguments for the general historicity of the tabernacle include Sarna 1986; Cross 1981; and Kitchen 2000.

[6] E.g. Klein (1996: 264): 'No critical scholar accepts that the account in Exodus is a literal account of the desert shrine.'

[7] For an argument for P as a complete and separate narrative, in the light of more recent trends in Pentateuchal criticism, see Schwartz 1996.

[8] Cf. the evaluation of Eichrodt (1961, 1: 98–102), that the cult was an integral aspect of spiritual communion with God in the OT.

the crown and noblest expression of prophecy, just as Moses was the greatest of the prophets.' And Longacre (1995: 24) writes:

> Although the surface texture is that of a set of rather detailed and involved instructions, the purpose of the construction, the institution of the regular worship of Yahweh at a central sanctuary – albeit a tent – is presented as something glorious and fraught with deep religious meaning.[9]

Recognizing the theological importance of the tabernacle material does not, of course, indicate that the theological meaning of the details is readily apparent, or even discernible in all cases. But it does mean that it is appropriate to approach the tabernacle material with great theological expectation.[10]

The theology of the tabernacle

What is the tabernacle material of Exodus meant to communicate? Or, since our primary concern is theological, the question may be asked, what does the tabernacle material convey concerning the nature and purposes of God? This chapter concerns the theological significance of the oft-neglected details of the tabernacle. We will focus on three particular aspects of the Lord's nature: the Lord is holy, the Lord is Israel's king, and the Lord is king over the cosmos. The chapter will conclude by examining two direct statements concerning the purpose of the tabernacle.

The Lord is holy: the materials and space of the tabernacle

As mentioned above, the modest amount of theological work done on the tabernacle is in some respects understandable given that the tabernacle material gives little in the way of theological comment. In other words some of the lack of detailed theological work may

---

[9] Although concerning Leviticus, given the exhaustive work he has done in the area of Israel's cult, the words of Milgrom (1991: 42) are relevant: 'Theology is what Leviticus is all about. It pervades every chapter and almost every verse. It is not expressed in pronouncements but embedded in rituals.'

[10] Although generally avoided by modern interpreters, traditionally symbolic interpretation was an important means of seeking the theological significance of the tabernacle details. For a discussion of symbolic interpretation of the tabernacle, and its difficulties, see Childs 1974: 537–539.

reflect exegetical reserve on the part of many interpreters. However, the sheer abundance of technical detail warrants careful investigation. Indeed, it has been argued that the technicalities and repetitions in the tabernacle sections are due to the heightened significance of the tabernacle within Exodus (Haran 1978: 149).

Perhaps the most significant modern work concerning the details of the tabernacle has been done by Menahem Haran. Taking the details concerning the tabernacle construction and the regulations associated with tabernacle worship, Haran has drawn together some important observations concerning the nature of the tabernacle. While not always explicit in drawing out the theology of the tabernacle from his work, it is a short step from many of Haran's observations to their theological implications. The following discussion is largely gleaned from Haran's work.[11]

Many of Haran's observations concerning the materials and workmanship used to construct the tabernacle, as well as the rules concerning access to different areas of the tabernacle, revolve around a dual system: the eastern axis and concentric circles (1978: 164–165). According to the system of eastern axis, as one proceeds from the outside to the inner parts of the tabernacle (all through entrances facing east), the types of fabrics and metals grow more precious. For instance, the outer tent curtains are less magnificent in fabric and workmanship than the outer veil of the tabernacle, which is less magnificent than the inner curtains and, then, the *pārōket* veil, which guards the Holy of Holies. The principle at work in the system of concentric circles is that the closer one moves to the Holy of Holies (containing the ark and the golden cover, or *kippōret*), the more elaborate and magnificent the materials and workmanship involved. Underlying both these observations is the premise that the more precious the materials and the more intricate the workmanship involved, the more important the object, and therefore the greater the level of sanctity assigned to it.[12]

Two factors go into assessing the relative sanctity of fabrics used in the tabernacle: types of thread and types of workmanship. The types of thread used in the tabernacle fabrics (in order of relative

---

[11] See particularly Haran 1978: 149–224. Studies relying largely upon Haran's work include Jenson 1992 and Gorman 1990. Jacob (1992) likewise gives the tabernacle details careful treatment.

[12] Jacob 1992: 760: 'Nobility and distinction were expressed through the value and purity of the material; everything else was subordinate. Mass and proportions, form of thought, execution, purpose, and reason all were matched.'

value) are blue, purple and scarlet-dyed wool, goats' hair and linen. The text also mentions three different types of workmanship (or embroidery): *ḥōšēb*, *rōqēm* and *'ōrēg* workmanship. *Ḥōšēb* workmanship is the most intricate, involves a mixture of threads and includes working with figures, particularly cherubim (26:1, 31; 28:6, 8, 15, 27; 29:5; 31:4; 35:32, 35; 36:8, 35; 38:23; 39:3, 5, 8, 20). *Rōqēm* workmanship is likewise intricate, involving a mixture of threads, but does not work with figures (26:36; 27:16; 28:39; 35:35; 36:37; 38:18, 23; 39:29). *'Ōrēg* workmanship involves only one kind of thread, and does not involve figures (28:32; 35:35; 39:22, 27).

The preciousness of the fabrics corresponds to the relative sanctity of particular zones in the tabernacle. The *pārōket* veil of the Holy of Holies is made of the three dyed wools and linen, with *ḥōšēb* workmanship. Next are the tabernacle curtains, made from the same materials, also of *ḥōšēb* workmanship, although the proportion of expensive wools is less for the tabernacle curtains than in the *pārōket* veil, thereby suggesting a descending level of sanctity.[13] The outer veil of the tabernacle is another step down in sanctity, for although it is made of the same materials in the same order as the *pārōket* veil, the weave is of *rōqēm* workmanship, and therefore does not include cherubim (26:36; 27:16; 36:37; 38:18). Finally, the tent curtains are of (undyed) goats' hair (26:7; 36:14), and the court hangings are made solely of linen (27:9; 38:9).

The same principle of relative sanctity can be seen in the metals used in particular sections of the tabernacle.[14] The pillars of the *pārōket* veil are overlaid with gold, with golden hooks and silver bases. Further out, the pillars of the outer veil are similar with their gold overlay and golden hooks, but have bronze, not silver, bases. Only the inner furniture of the tabernacle and its vessels are specifically to be made of, or overlaid with, 'pure gold' (25:11, 17, 24, 29, 31, 36, 38; 30:3; 37:2, 6, 11, 16, 22, 26). Gold is not found in the court, while bronze, the least precious of the metals mentioned in Exodus, cannot be found in the Holy of Holies (Jenson 1992: 101). Again, the preciousness of the materials corresponds to their proximity to the Holy of Holies.

---

[13] Haran (1978: 162) argues that the difference in proportion is suggested in the respective order of materials mentioned. The finely twisted linen appears first in 26:1 (36:35) concerning the tabernacle curtains, and last in 26:31 (36:8) concerning the *pārōket* veil.

[14] For a helpful table illustrating which metals are used in which zones, see Jenson 1992: 102.

Conforming to the gradations noted above, the priestly vestments exhibit the same pattern of relative sanctity. The garments worn exclusively by Aaron are of a superior quality both in materials and workmanship. The ephod (28:6–12; 39:2–7) and the breastpiece (28:15–20; 39:8–21) are both constructed of the same materials as the *pārōket* veil, with the same *ḥōšēb* workmanship, with the breastpiece being attached to the ephod with rings of gold.[15] In addition, the gold woven into Aaron's garments is likewise 'pure gold', as well as the chains joining the breastpiece to the ephod (28:14, 22; 39:15), the bells (39:25) and the diadem (28:36; 39:30). On the other hand, the garments worn by the rest of the priests (which Aaron also wore) are of inferior quality, both in materials and in workmanship. The regular priestly garments are made of linen, rather than dyed wool. The tunic is made of *'ōrēg* workmanship (Aaron's is distinct in that it only is checkered). Aaron's girdle is of *rōqēm* workmanship, consisting of linen and dyed wools,[16] whereas the priests' girdles are given no such specific comment (28:39–40; 39:29).

The same principles that apply to the materials and workmanship of the tabernacle and the priestly vestments likewise apply to the zones of the tabernacle. Different zones in the tabernacle are associated with differing levels of sanctity. The holy place, the inner furniture and the altar of burnt offering are anointed with the holy anointing oil and are therefore intrinsically holy, thereby communicating holiness to anything that comes into contact with them (the altar, 29:37; the tabernacle, its furniture and its articles, 30:22–29; 40:9–11; cf. Ezek. 44:19). Unlike defilement, this principle of 'contagious holiness' cannot be reversed, which puts those (except priests) who come in contact with the holy things at the risk of death.[17] Therefore, a non-priest may not eat of the ram of ordination (29:33), and death is the penalty for making or using any compound of the holy oil (30:32–33) or holy incense (30:37). It is therefore imperative that no one but the priests, who have been elevated to a like sanctity

---

[15] Haran (1978: 167) notes two differences in that the ephod did not have cherubim worked into it, and that gold was the primary ingredient in the ephod.

[16] The composition and workmanship of Aaron's girdle being similar to that of the tabernacle curtains and the outer veil (Haran 1978: 170).

[17] In explaining the irreversibility of communicated holiness, Haran (1978: 176) uses the example of the censers of Korah and his people, which, having come into contact with the altar (Num. 16:40 [17:5]) and become holy (16:38 [17:3]), had therefore to remain in the holy sphere by being hammered out as plating for the altar by the priests. This also explains the responsibility of the priests to cover the inner furniture before the Kohathites may transport it (Num. 4:5–15).

by being anointed with the holy oil, come into contact with the holy place or the holy furniture. Even the priests, protected by virtue of being anointed with the holy oil and thereby being lifted into the same realm of sanctity (Haran 1978: 177), are in danger of death under certain circumstances (28:42–43).

This careful attention to the details of different fabrics, metals, workmanship, space and ministration communicates the holiness of God. The place where the Lord appeared in the tabernacle (25:22; 30:6, 36), above the *kippōret* in the Holy of Holies, contained the most elaborate materials and workmanship precisely because such was appropriate to the importance of the space. The fact that no other zone in the tabernacle and surrounding area received commensurate materials and workmanship would in effect communicate that there is none like the Lord. The danger associated with the tabernacle, particularly the holy anointing oil, would likewise convey that the Lord is holy. Sarna (1986: 205–206) says it well:

> God's holiness is the very essence of His being, and is intrinsic to Himself. The graduated sequences described above effectuate the gradual distancing from that ultimate Source of absolute holiness. Precisely because the tabernacle was constructed in the first place to give concrete, visual symbolization to the conception of God's indwelling in the community of Israel, that is, to communicate the idea of God's immanence, it was vitally important that His total independence of all materiality, His transcendence, not be compromised. The gradations of holiness are one way of articulating this, of giving voice to God's unapproachable holiness, and of emphasizing His ineffable majesty and the inscrutable mystery that He is.

Although in Exodus the term 'holy' is used predominantly in the tabernacle sections, the concept of holiness is not limited to the cult. The burden of Exodus 1:1 – 15:21 likewise has to do with the Lord's holiness. As we have seen, the manner in which the Lord handled the conflict with Pharaoh was intended to distinguish publicly the Lord from all others, 'that you may know that there is no one like the LORD our God' (8:10[6]; cf. 9:14). The repeated phrase 'that you may know that I am the LORD' carried the implication the Lord was supreme over (and therefore distinct from) all else. In other words holiness is at stake in 1:1 – 15:21, a point made explicit in Israel's song of 15:11:

Who is like you, O LORD, among the gods?
Who is like you, majestic in holiness,
awesome in glorious deeds, doing wonders?

As with the Egyptian deliverance, one of the unmistakable implications of the tabernacle details – from the magnificence of the materials most closely associated with the Lord, to the increasing restrictions of access, to the danger associated with improperly approaching the Lord – is that the Lord is distinct from all else.

The Lord as Israel's king: the tabernacle and Sinai

In addition to communicating that the Lord is holy, the tabernacle communicated that the Lord is Israel's king. The Lord's rule over Israel is expressed by the association between the tabernacle and Sinai, an association suggesting that the tabernacle continues the function of Sinai in Israel's life.

This association between the tabernacle and Sinai can be seen on several levels. First, as many have noted, there are important structural parallels between Sinai and the tabernacle.[18] Mount Sinai appears to be divided into three zones, each with a particular level of sanctity. The first zone is the top of the mountain, where only Moses is permitted to ascend (19:20). The second zone extends upwards from the border of the mountain, but does not include the top of the mountain. Here the select group of Aaron, his sons and the seventy elders are permitted, and only after the covenant sacrifice (19:22). The third zone is the foot of the mountain, which contained an altar for burnt offerings (24:4–5) and was guarded by a border to prevent the common Israelite from ascending the mountain (19:12–13, 21–24). The tabernacle exhibits a similar tripartite structure. The Holy of Holies corresponds to the first zone in that only Moses was permitted within its boundaries.[19] The holy place was off limits to all but a select few, the priests, and thereby corresponds to the second zone. Finally, the outer court (27:9–19), likewise with an altar for burnt offering, is accessible to the common Israelite, and thus corresponds to the third zone of Mount Sinai.

That transgressing the boundary at the foot of the mountain and transgressing the boundaries of the tabernacle both warranted death

---

[18] E.g. Rodríguez 1986: 131–137; Sarna 1991: 105.

[19] Exodus does not explicitly envision Aaron entering the Holy of Holies, unless *haqōdeš* in 28:29, 35 refers to the Holy of Holies, as argued by Milgrom (1975).

further strengthens the parallel between the tabernacle and Mount Sinai. As we have seen, one of the striking features of tabernacle worship is the strict separation between the holy and the common, a separation that, if not honoured, puts the common Israelite in danger of death. The boundaries of Mount Sinai have a similar cultic dimension. Cole (1973: 47) argues that the death penalty at Sinai is essentially cultic in nature – since the mountain was holy, anything that touched the mountain became holy. The nature of contagious holiness, transmitted regardless of the intention, explains why both man *and* beast are subject to death upon contact with the mountain, and also accounts for the Lord's additional warning that the people not transgress the boundary at the foot of the mountain (19:21–24). As Childs (1974: 370) explains:

> The issue at stake is not whether God is a stuffy monarch, who does not think enough honor has been shown him . . . Rather the warning is given for the sake of the people, who have no experience as yet of the dimensions of divine holiness, and lest warned will destroy themselves.

Finally, the language associated with the Lord's descent upon Mount Sinai has strong echoes in the tabernacle chapters. The Lord descended upon Mount Sinai in a cloud (19:9, 16; 24:15–16, 18), just as a cloud covered the tabernacle when the glory of the Lord filled it (40:34–35). Further, according to 24:16 the glory of the Lord dwelt, or tabernacled (qal, *šākan*), upon the mountain covered by the cloud, making the obvious connections with the Lord's dwelling in the tabernacle (*miškān*).[20]

The structural and lexical similarities between Sinai and the tabernacle have led many scholars to see the tabernacle as an extension of Sinai,[21] an association with important theological implications. Mount Sinai is where the Lord gave Israel his law and where Israel pledged to obey (19:8; 24:3, 7). The connection between Sinai and the tabernacle suggests that, despite the lack of direct kingship language in the tabernacle section, the tabernacle is the place where the Lord continued to exercise his reign over Israel. That the tabernacle

---

[20] Clements (1965: 22) finds Sinai 'a literary account of a theophany of Yahweh which continued to be repeated in Israel's cultic life'.

[21] Jacob 1992: 759; Dohmen 2004: 273; Fretheim 1991a: 274; Averbeck 2003: 824; Sarna 1986: 203; Childs 1974: 540; Goldingay 2003: 392.

is associated with the Lord's ruling over Israel is further supported by two considerations: the meetings between Moses and the Lord in the Holy of Holies were for the purpose of the Lord's commanding Israel (25:22),[22] and, more implicitly, the tablets containing the commandments were to be placed in the ark in the Holy of Holies (25:21).[23] Noting that the image of the deity was located in the innermost shrine of temples in other ancient Near Eastern religions, Sarna (1986: 209) writes:

> In Israel, with its uncompromising aniconic, imageless religion, in place of the representation of the deity came the tangible symbol of His Word – the stone tablets of the Covenant. The Ark and its contents became the focus of the collective consciousness of the community. It remained the symbol of the eternal covenant between God and the people, the record of His inescapable demands upon the individual and society in every sphere of life. It was this, not an image, that occupied the center of attention and that was at the core of the religion. This written reminder of God's revealed word constituted the sign of His presence and His indwelling in the midst of Israel. The 'Ark of the Covenant,' therefore, embodied one of the fundamental ideas of the religion: that it is only through His Word that true knowledge of God, the understanding of His essential nature, can be apprehended or at least pursued.

The implication of Sarna's comment is that knowing the Lord could not be separated from obeying his law. As Mount Sinai was the place where the Lord established his authority over Israel as her God, so the tabernacle was the place where he practically extended and perpetuated his authority over Israel.

Sarna's comment also has important implications concerning the nature of Israel's mission. The tabernacle was the means through which the Lord dwelt among his people (25:8), most particularly in the Holy of Holies (25:22; 30:6, 36), the only place in the tabernacle where the Lord would meet with Moses. The fact that the Holy of

---

[22] Cf. 34:34, although it probably refers to the tent of meeting in 33:7–11. Childs (1974: 534) argues that it refers to the tabernacle.

[23] The notion that the Lord's throne was located between the cherubim and that the ark was his footstool, suggested elsewhere in the OT (Pss 99:5; 132:7; 2 Kgs 19:15; 1 Chr. 28:2), likewise supports the notion that the ark was associated with the Lord's rule as king. See Sarna 1986: 209–211.

Holies, the locus of God's presence, was associated with the law suggests that the Lord's presence was inextricably connected with the law. In her obedience to the law Israel would encounter the Lord's presence. To put it another way, seeking the Lord's presence meant living in obedience to his commands. Examples abound in the Scriptures. Expressed positively, the psalmist declares:

> With my whole heart I seek you;
>> let me not wander from your commandments!
>>> (Ps. 119:10; cf. 1:2; 19)

Expressed negatively, consider the words of Jeremiah, standing in the temple gate, as the prophet connects seeking the Lord in his dwelling with their faithfulness to the law:

> Amend your ways and your deeds, and I will let you dwell in this place. Do not trust in these deceptive words: 'This is the temple of the LORD, the temple of the LORD, the temple of the LORD.' For if you truly amend your ways and your deeds, if you truly execute justice one with another, if you do not oppress the sojourner, the fatherless, or the widow, or shed innocent blood in this place, and if you do not go after other gods to your own harm, then I will let you dwell in this place, in the land that I gave of old to your fathers for ever. (Jer. 7:3–7)

If the Lord was sought through obedience to his commands, and obedience to his commands was the means by which Israel fulfilled her intended missionary function among the nations (19:4–6), then Israel's seeking the Lord cannot be separated from her missionary function. As Israel sought the Lord, obeying his law, she fulfilled her missionary function.

This insight is particularly important when the question of the 'method' of mission in the OT is discussed. For example, G. E. Wright (1961: 19) comments that '[a]s to the mission of Israel in the world, the OT, of course, gives no united voice, except on the fact of the mission and on the necessity of becoming and remaining a loyal "people of God"'. This, however, is precisely the point. The method, if it can be so called, consists in faithfulness. Whatever other manifestations of Israel's missionary calling may be present in the OT, they stem from Israel's seeking the Lord and faithfully keeping his law. For Israel to seek the Lord was, necessarily, to participate in her missionary calling.

The Lord as cosmic king: the tabernacle as microcosm of the universe

Thus far we have seen how the tabernacle is the means by which the Lord rules over Israel as her divine king, serving the missionary purpose of 19:4–6 as the place where he continues to give his law (25:22). The tabernacle symbolism presses further, however, suggesting a more cosmic scope to the Lord's reign than that suggested by the parallels between the tabernacle and Sinai. Here we turn to an important parallel between the tabernacle and creation which suggests that the tabernacle represented a microcosm of the universe.

The tabernacle and creation

Significant observations concerning the relationship between creation in Genesis 1:1 – 2:3 and the construction of the tabernacle have been made by many.[24] Often cited are the linguistic similarities in the following table:[25]

Creation of the World	Construction of the Sanctuary
And God saw everything that he had made, and behold, it was very good (Gen. 1:31).	And Moses saw all the work, and behold, they had done it (Exod. 39:43).
Thus the heavens and the earth were finished (Gen. 2:1).	Thus all the work of the tabernacle of the tent of meeting was finished (Exod. 39:32).
On the seventh day God finished his work that he had done (Gen. 2:2).	So Moses finished the work (Exod. 40:33).
So God blessed the seventh day (Gen. 2:3).	Then Moses blessed them (Exod. 39:43).

In addition to the similarities noted above, Blenkinsopp adds two further observations. First, the injunction to observe the Sabbath as a

---

[24] Studies exploring the relationship between Gen. 1:1 – 2:3 and the tabernacle include Blum 1990: 306–311; Buber and Rosenzweig 1994: 18–19; Levenson 1988: 78–99; Gorman 1990: 39–60; Sommer 2001: 42–44; and, focusing on cultic material more generally, Firmage 1999.

[25] The following table, taken from Blenkinsopp (1976: 280) has often been replicated. Levenson (1988: 86) adds Exod. 40:9–11 as another noteworthy parallel to Gen. 2:3.

sign of both the covenant and creation concludes the section of tabernacle instructions. Secondly, the phrase 'Spirit of God' (*rûaḥ 'ĕlōhîm*),
given to Bezalel for the skilled work involved in constructing the tabernacle (Exod. 31:3; 35:31; cf. 28:3), echoes the language prior to creation, where the Spirit of God hovered over the waters (Gen. 1:2).[26]

The number seven likewise forges links between the tabernacle
account and creation. Kearney (1977) observes that the divine instructions in Exodus 25 – 31 fall into seven speeches, set apart by the words
'the LORD said to Moses' or (in two cases) slight variations thereof.
Kearney argues that these instructions, which end with the injunction
to observe the Sabbath, correspond to the seven days of creation.
Concerning the construction of the tabernacle, Kearney (1977: 381)
further observes seven instances of the phrase 'as the LORD had commanded Moses' (40:19, 21, 23, 25, 27, 29, 32), arguing that the phrase
is an intentional allusion back to the seven speeches. While Kearney's
attempt to draw exact correspondences between individual days in
creation and in the construction of the tabernacle seems far-fetched in
places,[27] he appears to be on solid ground in recognizing a structural
similarity between Genesis 1:1 – 2:3 and Exodus 25 – 31.[28] In a similar
vein Gorman notes (1990: 58) that the number seven is important
for the performance of rituals, such as the ordination of the priesthood (Exod. 29:35; cf. Lev. 8:33–35) and the consecration of the altar
(Exod. 29:37), both of which take seven days to perform.[29] Building
upon Rosenzweig's observation concerning its importance in the
tabernacle material quoted above, it is noteworthy that the seemingly
monotonous repetition of the verb 'make' (*'āśâ*) in the tabernacle
material corresponds to its sevenfold occurrence in Gen. 1.[30]

The correspondences between creation and the construction of the

---

[26] The only other occurrence of *rûaḥ 'ĕlōhîm* between Gen. 1:2 and Exod. 31:3 is in
Gen. 41:28, the rarity of the term suggesting an association between the two occurrences. Cf. Levenson 1988: 84; Elnes 1994: 149.

[27] Kearney 1977: 376–377. See the critique of Levenson 1988: 83.

[28] Jacob (1992: 770) draws the parallel between creation and the construction of
the tabernacle in a different manner, suggesting that, in 24:16, Moses was shown the
tabnît (pattern) of the tabernacle during the six days the cloud covered the mountain,
followed by a special seventh.

[29] Gorman notes the importance of seven days in other priestly rituals: the restoration of a leper (Lev. 14:8–9), the cleansing from a discharge (Lev. 15:13, 19, 24, 28),
the purification of the contamination from a corpse (Num. 6:9–10; 19:11, 12, 14, 16;
31:19), and the cleansing after the birth of a boy (Lev. 12:2).

[30] Buber and Rosenzweig 1994: 62. For a more rigorous demonstration of the
importance and pervasiveness of the number seven in Gen. 1:1 – 2:3, see Cassuto
1961: 12–15.

tabernacle point to the intimate association between creation and cult, which warrants a closer look at Genesis 1.[31] In Genesis 1 creation consists primarily of bringing order from chaos, moving from the chaos (*tōhû wābōhû*) of Genesis 1:2 to the satisfied rest of the completed creation. Throughout Genesis 1 this order is achieved through setting boundaries and making distinctions. On days one to four God separates: light from darkness (1:3), the lower waters from the upper waters (1:7), the waters from the land (1:9), and the days from the night (1:14, 18). On the fifth and sixth days the birds and the water creatures, followed by the beasts, are created 'according to their kinds', an expression that implies separation and categorization. The pinnacle of creation, humanity, shows a separation of both nature and function: created as God's image (nature), humanity is charged with naming and exercising authority over the beasts (function).

The connection between speaking and making, or creating, calls forth the recognition of the Lord's power. The Lord commands, and his commands are obeyed,[32] conveyed powerfully in the simple expression 'And it was so' (Gen. 1:7, 9, 11, 15, 24, 30; cf. 1:3). However, the power at work in Genesis 1 is not simply the imposition of the will of the strong upon the weak, who nonetheless had the ability to obey. For instance, a father might command his adolescent son to stand, but would give no such command to his infant son, for the former is able to obey while the latter is not. As Goldingay (2003: 51) has observed, there is no implication that light has the ability to generate itself, that water has the inherent ability to gather itself together, or that the earth has the intrinsic capacity to generate plant life. It is the Lord's command that gives the light, the water and the earth the ability to do the thing required. In other words the Lord's command in creation speaks to his power in a deeper way than simply imposing one's will upon already able subjects. The Lord's ability to bring about his will in the cosmos is due to power inherent in himself, rather than in the materials with which he works. The nuance is important in that it speaks to the extent of the Lord's power over the cosmos. If the Lord's rule of the cosmos

---

[31] Although the treatment here will be limited to Gen. 1, the correspondences between the tabernacle material and creation extend further into Genesis. For connections between the tabernacle and Gen. 2, see Wenham 1994; Beale 2004: 66–80; and for connections to the flood narrative, Weimar 1988: 352–354.

[32] Brueggemann (1982: 30) finds 'command and execution' the central pattern of Gen. 1:1 – 2:4, leading to his conclusion that '[c]reation is in principle obedient to the intent of God'.

is constrained by the ability of the materials to obey, his power is contingent. Genesis 1, on the other hand, gives no indication of limitations upon God's power. By implication, Genesis 1 agrees with the psalmist:

> Our God is in the heavens;
> he does all that he pleases.
>
> (Ps. 115:3)[33]

The connection between creating and separating points to another important inference – establishing boundaries is as important as God's speaking in bringing forth creation. As we have seen, in each day the act of creation involves separation. In fact, it might even be said that establishing boundaries is the same as bringing forth creation.[34] Or, to apply it to God's ruling over creation, his command and his establishing order are both essential in understanding what it means for God to rule. Just as God rules through giving commands, *God rules through establishing order.*[35]

Levenson (1988: 121–127; cf. Balentine 1999: 82–95) finds Genesis 1:1 – 2:3 essentially cultic in nature, arguing that through separating and ordering the Lord constrains and thereby controls evil. The chaos does not disappear. The Lord transforms it. The darkness is not removed, but is given precise boundaries, so that the darkness of night alternates with the light of day. As Levenson (1988: 127) writes, in creation 'God functions like an Israelite priest, making distinctions, assigning things to their proper category and assessing their fitness, and hallowing the Sabbath.' Levenson, however, presses further, suggesting that through the cult the Lord continues to control evil. In a statement that one would expect to refer to explicitly cultic material found in the law, Levenson (1988: 127) comments:

> Among the many messages of Genesis 1:1 – 2:3 is this: it is through the cult that we are enabled to cope with evil, for it

---

[33] Cf. Levenson 1988: 3: 'We can capture the essence of the idea of creation in the Hebrew Bible with the word "mastery." The creation narratives, whatever their length, form, or context, are best seen as dramatic visualizations of the uncompromised mastery of YHWH, God of Israel, over all else.'

[34] Levenson (1988: 122) speaks of 'the process of setting up boundaries and making separations that we have come to call creation'. See also Kapelrud 1979: 164; Goldingay 2003: 90; Sæbø 1998: 160.

[35] The importance of order in creation and in cult prompts Jenson (1992: 215–219) to argue for the concept of order as a possible centre of OT theology.

is the cult that builds and maintains order, transforms chaos into creation, ennobles humanity, and realizes the kingship of the God who has ordained the cult and commanded that it be guarded and practiced.

Not only is creation dependent upon the establishment of order, but order is essential in maintaining the cosmos, for without order, creation collapses back into chaos. Gorman (1990: 42) has gone so far as to argue that maintaining the cultic order serves to maintain the cosmic order, for it is through the cult that sin and defilement, which he argues are the two biggest threats to order in priestly thought, are dealt with and the created order restored. The important point for the present purpose is that creating and maintaining order through making distinctions is an essential aspect of what it means for the Lord to rule over the cosmos.

Particularly with Levenson's comments in mind, we again turn to the construction of the tabernacle. In a manner much like the creation of the cosmos, the construction of the tabernacle both brings out the dual significance of speech (God's commands) and order. As noted above, the tabernacle was constructed according to the Lord's command, a point the narrative takes great pains to convey. Not only are the tabernacle instructions given with very specific detail,[36] but the narrative records that they were carried out precisely as the Lord commanded Moses.[37] Just as the elements obeyed precisely in Genesis 1, so do the Israelites in building the tabernacle. Further, as in creation, Exodus implies that the tabernacle was ultimately the Lord's work. In an allusion to Genesis 1:2 mentioned above, giving the Spirit of God to Bezalel (Exod. 31:1–11; 35:31–35) suggests that constructing the tabernacle and its furnishings required ability given by the Lord in order to be carried out. In other words Israel was no more able to construct the tabernacle according to the Lord's command than the tōhû wābōhû (waste and void) was able to form itself into an ordered creation. As in Genesis 1, the Lord's command carried with it the power for obedience.

---

[36] Despite the detailed description of some aspects of the tabernacle's construction, there are also many essential details left out: 'We are faced with a unique combination of long-winded description on the one hand and total omission of various particulars on the other' (Haran 1978: 150). The omission of important aspects of the construction is another reason that the tabernacle's historical credibility has been questioned (e.g. S. R. Driver 1911: 426).

[37] Exod. 38:22; 39:1, 5, 7, 21, 26, 29, 31, 42; 40:16, 19, 21, 23, 25, 27, 29, 32.

Not just obedience, but order is apparent as well. The effect of Israel's obedience in building the tabernacle was establishing an orderly cultic life. As we have seen above, one of the great characteristics of the tabernacle was the manner in which it expressed order, separating the holy from the common, distinguishing between Aaron, the priests and the people, and distinguishing between kinds of incense and oils, fabrics and spaces. On the most basic level, the tabernacle had the effect of separating the Lord from the people, even as he dwelt in their midst. Just as the Lord rules through establishing order and making distinctions in Genesis 1, so he rules through establishing order and making distinctions in the tabernacle.

The connections between creation and the tabernacle suggest that they are to be understood in the light of one another. For instance, von Rad (1962: 233–234) finds it impossible to understand the tabernacle if divorced from the background of creation:

> The fact that this history of cultic institutions begins with the creation of the world shows the tremendous theological claim made by P. Obviously then the only appropriate way of treating the worship of Israel is to take it in the light of this background – only then is everything set in due proportion. P is utterly serious in wanting to show that the cult which entered history in the people of Israel is the goal of the origin and evolution of the world. Creation itself was designed to lead to this Israel.

Von Rad's quotation raises the important issue of exactly what the connection between creation and the tabernacle is meant to convey. While surely correct that the tabernacle is incomprehensible apart from the background of creation, to suggest that the goal of creation was Israel and its cultic life runs the risk of seeing creation in a manner more Israel-specific than warranted. While von Rad finds the rationale for creation in Israel,[38] it can also be argued that Israel finds its rationale in creation. Knierim's (1995: 181) question is pertinent

---

[38] As mentioned in chapter 4, von Rad found the historical core of the Pentateuch in the credo of Deut. 26:5b–9, in close relationship with Deut. 4:20–24 and Josh. 24:2b–13. Working from the standpoint that these passages encapsulate the core of the Hexateuch, von Rad argues for salvation and election as the central doctrines of Israel's faith, with creation following as a later development, and serving the ancillary function of undergirding those central doctrines. See von Rad's discussions in 1961: 43–44; 1962: 136–153; 1966: 3–8.

here: 'whether the purpose of the creation of the world is the history and existence of Israel, or whether the purpose of Israel's history and existence is to point to and actualize the meaning of creation'.[39] If the latter, the connection between creation and the tabernacle implies that Israel's worship life serves God's original purposes in creation. Seen in such a manner, the universal quality of God's purposes comes to the fore. As Köhler (1957: 87; cf. Goldingay 2003: 100–101) has written, the question 'From where does the history of God's people derive its meaning?' is answered by 'God has given the history of His people its meaning thorough creation.' Raised again are the issues of particularity and universality, and the manner in which they relate to one another. Ultimately, it is probably unwise to press the distinction so far as to choose between the two. The relationship is probably dialectical.[40] However, returning to von Rad's connection between cult and creation, at the very least it must be recognized that failing to see Israel's existence serving God's purposes in creation runs the risk of distorting the meaning of Israel's cultic life, and thus the theological significance of the tabernacle.

While the term 'king' or 'rule' is never used in the tabernacle section, the above parallels between the tabernacle and creation suggest that the tabernacle expressed the Lord's rule over the universe. Just as the cosmos conformed to the Lord's exact specifications ('obeyed') in being brought into order in Genesis 1, so the tabernacle was erected and ordered according to his precise specifications in Exodus 35 – 40. As the above quotations of Levenson and von Rad suggest, the tabernacle serves both as a re-enactment of creation and an extension of the Lord's purposes in creation. This recognition has led many scholars to see the tabernacle as a microcosm of the universe, a miniature world over which the Lord rules as he does over the cosmos.[41] Again, concerning the correspondences

---

[39] Cf. Goldingay 2003: 100–101; Reno 2010: 30–31.

[40] Goldingay (2003: 101) captures well the importance of this dialectic: 'The people of God is always open to overestimating its own significance, and also to underestimating it. When it flourished, it can forget that its raison d'être relates to YHWH's purpose for the world and can begin to think it is important in its own right. When it crashes, too, it can forget its place in YHWH's purpose for the world, and infer from its assumed insignificance that YHWH could let it go out of existence.'

[41] E.g. Fretheim 1991a: 268–271; Leder 1999: 11–35; Goldingay 2003: 395–396; Kline 1980: 35–42; Sarna 1986: 213–215; and particularly Levenson 1988: 78–99. The notion of the tabernacle as a microcosm of the universe goes back at least as far as Philo (*On the Life of Moses* 2, 88, 101–105, 126) and Josephus (*Jewish Antiquities* 3.122–124, 179–187).

between the tabernacle and creation, Levenson (1988: 86) writes:

> Collectively, the function of these correspondences is to underscore the depiction of the sanctuary as a world, that is, an ordered, supportive, and obedient environment, and the depiction of the world as a sanctuary, that is a place in which the reign of God is visible and unchallenged, and his holiness is palpable, unthreatened, and pervasive.[42]

Similarly, Goldingay (2003: 396) comments:

> While the whole world (heaven and earth) is God's home, the sanctuary represents God's home in microcosm. . . . God will dwell in this microcosm of what the cosmos was designed to be and what it therefore is in its essential nature, a place where everything has its place and is in order, in keeping with God's intention for the whole cosmos. Here there is one world, with everyone and everything in their place.

The tabernacle, then, represents all that the cosmos was created to be: the Lord ruling over the universe as king, with all creation in appropriate obedience.

The tabernacle as model of the heavenly dwelling

Related to the notion that the tabernacle was a microcosm of the universe is the notion that the tabernacle was constructed according to the *tabnît* (ESV 'pattern') of the heavenly sanctuary. According to Exodus 25:9, 40 Moses was commanded to build the tabernacle and its furnishings according to the *tabnît* shown him on the mountain:

> According to all that I show you concerning the *tabnît* of the tabernacle and the *tabnît* of all its vessels, thus you shall make it . . . and you shall see and you shall make them in the *tabnît* which is being shown to you on the mountain. (My tr.)

---

[42] See also Fretheim 1991a: 271: 'The tabernacle is the world order as God intended writ small in Israel.' For a more general discussion concerning biblical law as the expression of the laws of nature established in creation, see Levenson 1980: 28–32.

The exact nature of *tabnît* in these verses, however, is not immediately clear. Taken alongside 26:30[43] and 27:8 (cf. Num. 8:4), which likewise refer to what Moses was shown on the mountain (albeit without the word *tabnît*),[44] interpreters have arrived at different understandings of *tabnît*.

In an extended excursus on Exodus 25:40, Davidson (1981: 367–388) finds that attempts to discern the meaning of *tabnît* fall into six categories:

1. A model of the earthly sanctuary.
2. A blueprint of the earthly sanctuary.
3. A copy of the heavenly sanctuary, which serves as a model.
4. A blueprint of the heavenly sanctuary, which serves as a model.
5. The heavenly sanctuary itself, which serves as a model.
6. Subjective inspiration, which serves as the model.

While acknowledging that none of the above suggestions can claim certainty, he argues on the basis of lexical and larger contextual observations that *tabnît* refers to a heavenly sanctuary. Noting that 11 of the 20 uses of *tabnît* (leaving 25:9, 40 aside)[45] refer unambiguously to a solid structure (copies of an original), and that Köhler and Baumgartner categorize the remaining occurrences of *tabnît* under the heading 'model', Davidson rules out blueprint or subjective inspiration (2, 4, 6).[46] Whether *tabnît* refers to a model of the earthly sanctuary, a model of the heavenly sanctuary or the heavenly sanctuary itself (1, 3, 5) depends upon whether the passage suggests a vertical earthly–heavenly correspondence. Davidson argues for a heavenly sanctuary over an earthly sanctuary based on the following considerations. First, as mentioned above, the preponderance of occurrences of *tabnît* suggests an already existing original. Secondly,

---

[43] Weimar (1988: 353–354) sees great theological significance in the vocabulary of 26:30, arguing that the unusual use of the verb *qûm* (stand) rather than *'āśâ* (make) suggests important parallels to the Lord's promises both to Noah (Gen. 6:18; 9:9–11) and to Abraham (Gen. 17:7). These parallels lead Weimar to infer that the tabernacle symbolizes that the people of Israel as a whole stand protected from complete destruction. While it may be questioned whether Weimar places too much weight upon the relatively common verb *qûm*, his suggestion nonetheless becomes extremely interesting when viewed in the light of Israel's experience with the golden calf (discussed below in chapter 6).

[44] 26:30 uses *mišpāṭ* to denote 'plan'. 27:8 does not use a proper noun to describe what Moses saw.

[45] Davidson (1981: 76) mistakenly counts 12.

[46] Davidson 1981: 375–376. Köhler and Baumgartner (1999: 1686–1687) do not categorize the occurrence in 2 Kgs 16:10.

a vision of a heavenly sanctuary is consistent with the immediate literary context of the vision of God beheld by Moses, the priests and the elders in Exodus 24. Thirdly, he cites the common notion in the ancient Near East that an earthly temple replicated an original heavenly temple.[47] Fourthly, he argues that an earthly–heavenly correspondence is common elsewhere throughout the OT.[48] Finally, he sees heavenly–earthly correspondence in the apocryphal and pseudepigraphal literature, rabbinical literature, the LXX use of *typos* and *paradeigma*, and in Philo.[49] Thus Davidson rules out *tabnît* as a model of the earthly sanctuary (1), leaving him with either a model of the heavenly sanctuary or the heavenly sanctuary itself (3, 5). Although Davidson does not find the evidence explicit enough to decide between the final two options, he does argue that *tabnît* must involve a heavenly–earthly correspondence between an original heavenly sanctuary and an earthly replica.[50]

For the present purpose, it is of little importance whether or not *tabnît* in 25:9, 40 is the original heavenly sanctuary or a model of the heavenly original. In either case *tabnît* implies that there is a heavenly sanctuary in which the Lord resides which serves as the structure or pattern for the earthly tabernacle. This correspondence reinforces the notion that the tabernacle functions as a microcosm of the universe. As Rodríguez (1986: 143) notes, a structural correspondence between the heavenly and earthly tabernacles suggests a functional correspondence as well. As demonstrated above, it was from the tabernacle, the 'wandering Sinai', that the Lord ruled over Israel (25:22). The heavenly–earthly correspondence suggests that, as the Lord rules over Israel from the earthly tabernacle, he likewise rules over the cosmos from the heavenly tabernacle. In this way the idea of *tabnît* complements the parallels between the tabernacle

[47] See bibliography in Davidson 1981: 381, n. 1.

[48] Davidson 1981: 382. Davidson cites Gen. 1:27; 28:10–22; Pss 11:4; 18:6[7]; 60:6[8]; 63:2[3]; 68:35[36]; 96:6; 102:19[20]; 150:1; Isa. 6:1; Jon. 2:7[8]; Mic. 1:2; Hab. 2:20.

[49] Davidson 1981: 383–384.

[50] Others who argue for a heavenly original behind an earthly copy include Hamerton-Kelly 1970: 5–6; Jacob 1992: 770; Cassuto 1967: 322; McNeile 1908: 158; Eichrodt 1961: 423; G. H. Davies 1967: 201; Weimar 1988: 350, 285. For the same argument from a wider biblical perspective, and particularly concerning the temple, see Clements 1965: 63–78. Dohmen (2004: 247) sees the significance of the 'model' not in Moses' seeing a heavenly original, but in the manner in which the 'model' alerts the reader to Moses' indispensable function as the one through whom the Lord communicates to Israel. Houtman 2000: 345–346 is unconvinced that the tabernacle replicates a heavenly original.

and creation, likewise suggesting for the tabernacle a more cosmic scope.

Direct theological statements: Exodus 25:8 and 29:45–46

Finally, although rare, there are a few direct theological statements in the tabernacle material to consider. While not the only theological statements in the tabernacle material – indeed I have argued that the details of the tabernacle are theologically rich – 25:8 and 29:42b–46 are arguably the most explicit, and are widely recognized as particularly important.[51] Of particular interest is that both directly address the Lord's purpose for the tabernacle. What does the Lord's intention to dwell among his people reveal about his character and purposes?

Exodus 25:8. 'Let them make me a sanctuary, that I may dwell in their midst' (Exod. 25:8). The purpose statement is straightforward enough, so much so that it is not given much attention in several commentaries. There are two aspects of this statement, however, that deserve particular attention: the desire of the Lord to dwell among his people, and the necessity of the tabernacle to that end.

The desire for the Lord to dwell among his people brings us to another important connection between the tabernacle and creation. Wenham has observed striking parallels between the tabernacle and the Garden of Eden.[52] For instance, the entrance to Eden faced east, guarded by cherubim, while tabernacle entrances likewise faced east, the Holy of Holies symbolically guarded by the cherubim woven into the *pārōket* veil. Gold and precious stones, specifically mentioned in Eden, both appear in the Holy of Holies. Of particular interest is the *šōham* (ESV 'onyx') stone. Appearing specifically in Eden (Gen. 2:12), all other appearances of the *šōham* stone, with one exception, are connected either with Eden or the tabernacle.[53] Furthermore, Wenham notices that God's walking 'to and fro' in Eden (Gen. 3:8, hithpael of *hālak*), appears again as God walks 'to and fro' in the tabernacle (Lev. 26:12; Deut. 23:15; 2 Sam. 7:6–7; all hithpael of *hālak*). He also sees a priestly role for Adam in the garden, noting that the same verbs 'to till and to keep' used of Adam's charge in the

---

[51] E.g. Clements (1965: 115) argues that 25:8–9 and 29:45–46 are 'the motive clauses for the entire cult and worship of Israel'.

[52] Wenham 1994: 399–404. For a full-length treatment of the correspondences between the tabernacle and creation, and their theological implications, see Beale 2004.

[53] Exod. 25:7; 28:9, 20; 35:9, 27; 39:6, 13; 1 Chr. 29:2; Ezek. 28:13. The exception is Job 28:16.

garden are used again (only) in reference to the Levites in the sanctuary (Num. 3:7–8; 8:26; 18:5–6).[54]

The implication of the above is that the Garden of Eden is an archetypical sanctuary. If this is the case, there are two important inferences that we can make concerning the character of the Lord and his purposes towards his people. First, Eden affirms the goodness of God. One of the striking features of Eden is its lavish abundance. Beauty in the form of gold, rivers and trees pleasant to the sight, provision in the trees 'good for food', meaningful purpose in tilling and keeping the garden, marital intimacy and the ability to know and be known without shame, and access to God – all suggest that not only were Adam and Eve's needs met, but also the desires of their hearts. The acclamation of the psalmist, apparently referring to the temple, captures the delight brought forth by such abundance:

> How lovely is your dwelling place,
>   O Lord of hosts!
> My soul longs, yes, faints
>   for the courts of the Lord;
> my heart and flesh sing for joy
>   to the living God.
>
> (Ps. 84:1–2)

The blessing of Eden testifies to the generosity of God and his purpose to do good to his people.

Furthermore, the Lord desires fellowship with his people. Immediately after Adam and Eve eat of the forbidden tree, the Lord is walking in the cool of the day and calls to the man, 'Where are you?' (Gen. 3:8–9). While the reason for the Lord's question has been much discussed (e.g. perhaps he was giving Adam the opportunity to confess), one unmistakable implication of the question is that *he expected Adam and Eve to be with him*. In other words life in the Garden of Eden is a picture of the fellowship that God intended and desired with humanity. Eating of the tree in effect severed that fellowship. As Amos says (in language that curiously hints at the tabernacle):[55]

---

[54] Beale (2004: 66–70) provides further support for Adam as priest in Eden, particularly in arguing that Adam's role included guarding the sanctuary.

[55] Here *hālak*, as we have seen, is the same as used of the Lord's walking in the sanctuary, and the root for 'meet' (*y'd*) is as used in the 'tent of meeting', an alternate name of the tabernacle that speaks to its purpose.

Do two walk together,
unless they have agreed to meet?

(Amos 3:3)

That the Lord desires to dwell among his people in the tabernacle, then, suggests a restoration of the purpose for which he created humanity.

The tabernacle is also *necessary* if the Lord is to dwell among his people. As has been discussed above, the Lord's holiness was a cause of potential danger for Israel. The restricted access to the Holy of Holies and the severe penalties for transgressing the boundaries of the tabernacle (or mountain) all testify to the danger of God's holiness: 'for man shall not see me and live' (33:20).[56] Therefore, if the Lord were to dwell in the midst of his people, there must be a mechanism whereby he could simultaneously be present and yet protect the people from his holiness. The tabernacle, with its carefully guarded boundaries, provided a place where the Lord could dwell in Israel's midst, and yet still remain distinct. The fact that the Lord needed to remain distinct indicates that, while the tabernacle does allow the Lord to dwell among the Israelites, a level of separation must be maintained.

Exodus 29:45–46. The statement of 25:8 begs a further question. *Why* does the Lord desire to dwell among his people? The answer to that question is made clearer in a second theological statement, 29:45–46, a text many interpreters find the high point of the entire tabernacle material:[57]

I will dwell among the people of Israel and will be their God. And they shall know that I am the LORD their God, who brought them out of the land of Egypt that I might dwell among them. I am the LORD their God.

According to these verses, the Lord delivered Israel from Egypt so that he might dwell in Israel's midst, in effect a reiteration of 19:5, 'I . . . brought you to myself'. However, the appearance of 'I am the

---

[56] Although cf. 24:11 and 33:11, which stand in tension with 33:20. For a discussion of the delicate and mysterious matter of seeing the Lord in Exodus, see Moberly 1983: 79–83.

[57] E.g. 'the highpoint of Yahweh's words' (Weimar 1988: 346), 'the heart of P's tabernacle theology' (Elnes 1994: 152), 'the sum and crown of all that has gone before' (Cole 1973: 205). Klein (1996: 271) calls 'I am the LORD' in 29:46 the theological summary of the entire book of Exodus.

LORD,' particularly given that the context of the Egyptian deliverance is reintroduced, points back to the purposes of 1 – 15, and functions to connect the purpose of the tabernacle with the purpose of the exodus. Concerning 29:46 Brueggemann (1994: 914) comments:

> The final statement of the chapter is especially remarkable. It not only refers to the exodus, but also reasserts the formula of acknowledgment. Remarkably, the old liberation formulas are joined to an affirmation concerning the abiding, dwelling presence of God. By bringing together 'brought out' (יצא *yāṣā'*) and 'know' (ידע *yāda'*) with 'dwell' (*šākan*), this verse joins together liberation with presence and historical event with ritual stability . . . and in a canonical mode joins chaps. 1 – 15 and 25 – 31.

Brueggemann's observation has important implications for the interpretation of 29:45–46. Perhaps due to the repetition of the Lord's dwelling among his people (cf. 25:8) many commentators find the end goal of the tabernacle as the Lord's fellowship with Israel.[58] If the tabernacle sections are treated in isolation from the context of Exodus as a whole, such a deduction might be warranted. However, to conclude that the Lord's ultimate goal in the tabernacle was fellowship with Israel can obscure the fact that Israel was called for a specific purpose. Houtman's (2000: 553) comment on 29:46 provides a good example:

> Not the settlement in Canaan (3:8, 17; 6:8), but YHWH's residence in the midst of Israel is here mentioned as the goal of the exodus out of Egypt. When YHWH dwells in the midst of Israel (29:45) and takes up contact with the Israelites (29:42b, 43a), then they will understand that the purpose of the exodus was YHWH's fellowship with Israel (cf. 19:5 and see Lev. 26:11, 12).

Surely Houtman is correct to note the Lord's purpose of fellowship with Israel. However, to suggest that fellowship with Israel is *the* purpose of the exodus misses the thrust of 'I am the LORD' in 29:46.

---

[58] Cf. Hyatt 1971: 264; Blum 1990: 297; S. R. Driver 1913: 129; and particularly Klein 1996: 271 and Longacre 1995: 25, who both explicitly refer to the Lord's dwelling among Israel as the 'ultimate purpose' of the tabernacle.

The issue here is somewhat delicate, and has to do with assessing the canonical weight of the text.[59] While the nations are not explicitly mentioned in the tabernacle material, the reappearance of 'I am the LORD,' which has had international implications to this point in Exodus, again brings the Lord's purposes for the nations into view. It is interesting that Houtman supports his comment by citing 19:5, concerning Israel's status as a treasured possession among all peoples of the earth, but does not cite 19:6, which concerns Israel's function as a priestly kingdom and holy nation.[60] The splitting of 19:5 from 19:6, which Houtman neglects to defend, is dubious, for it subtly misrepresents the nature of the covenant, implying that Israel was a treasured people without regard to her specific calling. However, it is precisely this split that appears, at least implicitly, in many theological treatments of the purpose of the tabernacle.[61]

From a canonical perspective, better is the handling of Jacob (1992: 863), who, commenting on the conceptual setting from which to understand the tabernacle, writes:

> Israel, which had stood at the mountain of revelation before its heavenly king, would not remain at Sinai; therefore God wished to move with His people. In order that they constitute a priestly kingdom, they shall prepare a place appropriate to His being, so that HE could dwell in their midst as their king and they could constitute a priestly kingdom.

[59] It might be objected that the above suggestion reads too much into the phrase 'I am the LORD,' treating the phrase as a lexical unit that carries independent meaning. Such an objection has been voiced emphatically by Barr (1961: 274) as a common methodological flaw of much Biblical Theology: 'It seems to me clear that the insistence on a synthetic approach, on "seeing the Bible as a unity", on overcoming the divisions which literary criticism and religious history caused to appear throughout the Bible, has been much to blame for the exaggerations and misuse of the interpretation of words.' Such a comment points out what is undoubtedly a danger, particularly for the present work. Barr's contention that the sentence, not the word, is the 'linguistic bearer of the usual theological statement' (1961: 263) is sound, and calls into question any exegesis that relies too heavily on 'general' meanings of words outside the contexts of sentences. It is, of course, a corresponding (and somewhat circular) truth that sentences are made up of words, which carry independent meaning (or range of meaning) that must be appreciated in order for a sentence to be intelligible. Discerning appropriate literary boundaries is, of course, essential in careful interpretation. The present point suggests that 'I am the LORD' is best understood in the wider context of Exodus, where the phrase has to this point been so important, and in a manner consistent with what the phrase has communicated to this point.

[60] S. R. Driver (1911: 362) makes the same move.

[61] Enns 2000: 536; Hyatt 1971: 291, 294; Cassuto 1967: 388–389; Blum 1990: 297.

Understanding the tabernacle in the context of Israel's calling as a priestly kingdom brings Israel's broader purposes in view, a perspective hinted at by the reappearance of 'I am the LORD' in 29:45–46. To be clear, the above argument does not suggest that God's dwelling with Israel was not an end in itself.[62] Rather, it simply recognizes that the purpose of the tabernacle was not *limited* to Israel, by virtue of the fact that Israel herself was called for the nations. As Fretheim (1991a: 271) remarks concerning the tabernacle, 'This microcosm of creation is the beginning of a macrocosmic effort on God's part.'

In line with the concerns above, Beale (2004: 81–121) has made a compelling case that, as the tabernacle represents God's dwelling with his people, the purpose of Israel was to expand the boundaries of the tabernacle to include all nations. Noting the connection between the Lord's promise to multiply Abraham and to make him a blessing to all the families of the earth, Beale demonstrates how the multiplication of Israel is linked not only with Israel's missionary call, but also with temple building. For example, in response to his dream where God promises Jacob offspring 'like the dust of the earth' and 'in you and your offspring shall all the families of the earth be blessed' (Gen. 28:14), Jacob calls the place the house of God, setting a stone as a memorial, which Beale suggests is the equivalent of building an altar.[63] Beale argues this coincidence of themes suggests that the mission of God to the nations is to be understood as the expansion of God's tabernacle throughout the earth. Making much of the parallels between the tabernacle and Eden discussed above, Beale sees the connection between the blessing of the world and the temple as an extension of the missionary mandate implicit in Genesis 1 – 2. As Adam and Eve are fruitful and multiply, their descendants increasing in number and filling the earth, the Garden of Eden, the arena of God's presence, is expanded accordingly. While Adam failed in his charge to 'guard' and 'keep' the garden, the commission is passed on to Abraham and his descendants. In the end the missionary mandate first given to Adam, and then to Israel, is given so that the Lord's presence would extend throughout the earth, bringing blessing to all its families. While failure will continue until the 'Last Adam' will fulfil the mandate on behalf of

---

[62] What is at stake when speaking of ultimate goals will be further explored in the conclusion.

[63] For further examples, which include Noah, Abraham, Israel, David and Solomon, and postexilic and end-time Israel, see Beale 2004: 100–112.

all, the extension of the Lord's presence is conceived in terms of the dwelling of God.

While we have explored much of the theology of the tabernacle, it must be remembered at this point that the theology of the tabernacle cannot be understood in its fullness apart from the golden-calf narrative and apart from the account of the tabernacle construction in 35 – 40. It is to the narrative of the golden calf that we now turn.

Chapter Six

The golden calf (Exod. 32 – 34)

> The LORD, the LORD, a God merciful and gracious, slow to anger, and abounding in steadfast love and faithfulness, keeping steadfast love for thousands, forgiving iniquity and transgression and sin, but who will by no means clear the guilty, visiting the iniquity of the fathers on the children and the children's children, to the third and the fourth generation.
>
> (Exodus 34:6–7)

It is difficult to overestimate the importance of the above verses. They are the longest and most complete description of the Lord's character to be found in the Scriptures, and canonically later Scriptures frequently return to them. When Moses pleads for the Lord to pardon Israel for refusing to enter the land, he quotes Exodus 34:6–7 as the grounds for his appeal (Num. 14:18). In calling Israel to repent, Joel gives Israel ample assurance that she will be received:

> Return to the LORD, your God,
>   for he is gracious and merciful,
> slow to anger, and abounding in steadfast love;
>   and he relents over disaster.
>
> (Joel 2:13)

Yet there is no place for presumption, for as Nahum proclaims in reference to Assyria:

> The LORD is slow to anger and great in power,
>   and the LORD will by no means clear the guilty.
>
> (Nah. 1:3)

In a rather awkward twist Jonah flees from the Lord's call to preach to Nineveh, mourning that he cannot count on the Lord's judgment falling there, precisely because 'I knew that you are a gracious

God and merciful, slow to anger and abounding in steadfast love, and relenting from disaster' (Jon. 4:2). In particular, David seems to have deeply ingested the implications of the Lord's character as made known in Exodus 34:6–7. 'The LORD is gracious and merciful, / slow to anger and abounding in steadfast love' (Ps. 145:8) is the lesson David draws from the mighty deeds of the Lord. That '[t]he LORD is merciful and gracious, / slow to anger and abounding in steadfast love' is the ground upon which David blesses the Lord's holy name (Ps. 103:8). He appeals for deliverance from his enemies by praying:

> But you, O Lord, are a God merciful and gracious,
> slow to anger and abounding in steadfast love and
>   faithfulness.
>
> (Ps. 86:15)

Even David's cry to the Lord for forgiveness regarding his sin with Bathsheba is grounded here as he calls upon the steadfast love and mercy of the Lord to forgive his transgressions, iniquity and sin (Ps. 51:1–2).

The manner in which the character confession of Exodus 34:6–7 informs Israel's prayers, praises and preaching suggests that these verses are of paramount importance in knowing the Lord not only in Exodus, but throughout the Scriptures. However, before we can appreciate the merciful and gracious character of God more broadly, we must examine what it meant in Exodus. For here again, the Lord makes known his name, and this time in a way deeper than has to this point been possible.

The theological problem of Exodus 34:6–7

Despite its importance in Exodus and in Israel's later reflection upon the character of God, Exodus 34:6–7 poses a theological difficulty. How are the Lord's mercy and grace to be understood alongside his declaration that he will judge the guilty? Does not the Lord have *either* to forgive the iniquity of sinners *or* visit iniquity upon sinners? Or, as it is commonly expressed, what is the relationship between mercy and judgment?

In turning to Exodus 32 – 34, Israel's sin with the golden calf, there are several reasons for concentrating on 34:6–7. First, as Goldingay (2003: 37) comments, 'Exodus 34:6–7 constitutes a retrospective systematic theological reflection on the narrative beginning in Exodus 32.'[1] If this is the case, then 34:6–7 provides a good lens through which to view the golden-calf chapters theologically. Secondly, the importance of the canonical context is particularly apparent in the interpretation of 34:6–7. As we shall see, the ability to wrestle meaningfully with the theological difficulties raised in the confession is closely related to the context in which it is interpreted. This is particularly important for the present thesis, for any unified reading of Exodus must wrestle with the theological tensions in the book. Thus 34:6–7 provides a good test case for the hermeneutical concerns I have raised to this point. Thirdly, 34:6–7 raises an issue, indeed *the* issue, that has been at stake throughout Exodus: the Lord's name, and the character of God who bears it. In other words a major concern throughout Exodus has been to demonstrate what kind of God the Lord is. As we shall see, in these chapters the Lord makes himself known to Israel at a depth that to this point has not been possible.

We begin by looking at how others have dealt with the theological tension of 34:6–7. Interpretation, biblical or otherwise, is in large part a matter of deciding upon context. We will take particular note of how the interpreter's chosen context affects his ability to wrestle with the theological difficulties of the passage. After a return to Exodus 20:3–6, for reasons that will become apparent, we will then take a careful look at 32 – 34 as a whole, asking how Moses' intercession apparently moved the Lord from his declared intent to destroy Israel to granting her full forgiveness. I will end by arguing that an appreciation of what I have called the Lord's missionary commitment to be known among the nations is of great help in understanding the apparent tension between mercy and judgment inherent in Exodus 34:6–7.

Exodus 34:6–7 in other contexts

Those who interpret 34:6–7 apart from its canonical context in Exodus include Dentan, Wright, Andersen, Raitt and Laney. Dentan (1963), in an effort to understand its theology better, is primarily concerned with the origin of Exodus 34:6–7. Lacking confidence in the literary integrity of chapters 32 – 34,[2] Dentan examines

---

[1] See also Moberly 1983: 130, who argues that, along with 33:19, 34:6–7 constitutes 'the highpoint upon which the surrounding narrative is dependent and up to which it leads'.

[2] The general assessment that 32 – 34 has a particularly complicated and fragmented compositional history is shared by many, causing scepticism concerning the

the confession apart from its canonical context in Exodus, instead working within an alternative context of recognized bodies of Hebrew literature (Deuteronomic, Wisdom, Priestly and Prophetic). Dentan's treatment is essentially an effort to locate the words and phrases of 34:6–7 within a distinct body of literature. For instance, Dentan finds *ḥannun* (gracious) uncharacteristic of Deuteronomic language, but common in Wisdom literature. As he moves through each lexical unit, Dentan finds strong affinities with Wisdom literature in almost every case, while finding no affinities with other biblical corpora. Dentan therefore suggests that 34:6–7 has its origin in Wisdom literature. He further supports his claim by drawing attention to thematic similarities between 34:6–7 and Wisdom literature, such as a concern for moral behaviour and a 'universalistic' character concerned not primarily with Israel specifically, but more broadly with humanity in general. Dentan concludes that 34:6–7 was a later addition by the Wisdom writers, a 'calm, rational, and generous spirit' added to balance the 'fanatical intensity' of much of the OT literature (1963: 51). In addition, Dentan considers the confession to be concerned only with individuals, not with nations or other social groups.

Dentan's work provides a particularly interesting example of how the decision to lift the character confession from its canonical context in Exodus affects interpretation. First, his comment that the description was added later to soften an otherwise harsh conception of God shows that he actually sees the confession working *against* the canonical context in which it is set. Secondly, even though Exodus 32 – 34 is concerned primarily with the fate of Israel as a *nation*, Dentan finds the confession only to concern individual people. While it may have implications concerning individuals, any sense that the confession concerns Israel as a nation is lost.

G. E. Wright (1971) shares Dentan's scepticism concerning the literary integrity of 32 – 34, which undermines his confidence that the confession should be evaluated in that context. With the exception of his comment that 34:6–7 is given in response to Moses' request of 33:18, Wright gives little discussion to the wider narrative context of 32 – 34. Rather, Wright sets his discussion of the confession in the context of sources, specifically other revelations of the Lord's name in Exodus, where he argues that J (34:6–7) is more concerned

usefulness of 32 – 34 as a context. For a counter argument that 32 – 34 is a structural unity, see Davis 1982.

about making a theological statement concerning God's character than either E (3:13–15) or P (6:2–9), who are more concerned with what the Lord is called. After making several source-critical observations, Wright focuses upon brief lexical studies of *ḥesed* (steadfast love) and *nāśā'* (forgive) in an effort to draw out the theology of the passage. Wright's discussion is largely his theological reflection on 34:6–7 as it stands by itself. Although he speaks of both the mercy and judgment aspects of the confession, he does not discuss their relationship.

Andersen (1986: 45) is aware of the passage's difficulties, stating at the outset that 34:6–7 contains 'paradoxes, contradictions, mysteries'. With the particular concern that exegesis is compromised when interpreters rely on lexicons at the expense of interpreting words in their immediate literary contexts, Andersen addresses 34:6–7 through a study of *ḥesed*, which he claims has often been misinterpreted, therefore leading the exegesis of *ḥesed* texts in the wrong direction. Rather than the immediate literary context, Andersen employs similar statements concerning God's character in the Pentateuch as his controlling context in his treatment of 34:6–7. In his 'synoptic study' Andersen interprets the confession primarily in relation to Exodus 20:5–6, Numbers 14:18–19 and Deuteronomy 7:9–10. Aside from the comment that the Lord was justified in his anger towards Israel after the calf, the context of Exodus (as well as Deuteronomy and Numbers) is absent from his discussion. His exegesis of the passage, while helpful in illuminating the relationship between the texts with which he works, nonetheless does not wrestle with the difficulties he poses. Ultimately, Andersen (1986: 51) concludes, 'there is no justification for his compassion and kindness, and his *ḥesed* is completely incomprehensible'. Given his emphasis on firmly locating individual words within their immediate narrative contexts, it is curious that Andersen largely ignores the narrative context of 34:6–7.

Finding 34:6–7 to be the most important OT text bearing upon the issue of forgiveness, Raitt (1991) examines the character confession in an effort to answer the question posed in his title 'Why Does God Forgive?' Raitt (1991: 47) is also aware of the difficulties: 'Exod. 34:6–7 is a hard saying. Both ancient and modern interpreters of it back away from taking the whole thing, in all its stresses, seriously.' Largely ignoring the wider literary context, Raitt instead focuses his discussion upon the passage itself, particularly the apparent poles of mercy and judgment, while broadening his discussion to include other OT passages that address the topic of forgiveness.

While Raitt's discussion contains helpful insights, his (1991: 46) conclusions concerning 34:6–7 seem to leave his initial question unanswered:

> Why, in Exod 34:6–7 does God forgive? Because it is not true to God to see him only as a punishing God. Because the Sinai Covenant carries the dialectic of forgiveness and punishment alternatives. Because the forgiveness and punishment alternative are always held in tension. Within the mystery of God's holiness forgiveness and punishment are not mutually contradictory.

He goes on (1991: 55) to make four further observations:

> Looked at as a whole, Exod 34:6–7 makes these four affirmations: 1) Sin is taken completely seriously, 2) God is just, 3) God has such depth and richness of love that he can overcome sin with forgiveness, and 4) God also will punish sin wherever and whenever it occurs.

While each of these statements may be true, none of Raitt's reasons or affirmations actually answers the question he asks of the text. Further, the tensions raised by Raitt's own observations (such as the relationship between 3 and 4 above) are left unaddressed.

The concern Laney (2001) brings to the text in his treatment of 34:6–7 is simply a desire to know more clearly the nature of God as revealed in the confession, and does not raise any of the text's difficulties. To include Laney alongside other interpreters who have interpreted the confession out of its canonical context may seem strange considering that Laney's article begins with a two-page treatment of 32 – 33. While he gives more than passing comments, however, it is unclear how this treatment informs his exegesis of 34:6–7, which consists primarily of general lexical studies seemingly unrelated to his discussion of 32 – 33. In effect, Laney likewise lifts the confession out of its canonical context. Laney's conclusion is simply an observation of Moses' response of worship, and he does not draw any conclusions concerning some of the difficulties inherent in the passage.

One curious similarity shared by the above interpreters is a difficulty in grappling with the confession's tensions at any depth. Neither Dentan nor Wright makes any attempt to wrestle with the tensions within the confession. Raitt leaves unanswered the great question he poses in his title. Andersen accepts the tension as mystery, with the affirmation that ultimately the reasons for God's *ḥesed* are unknowable. Laney leaves the theological tensions unaddressed. Taking the findings (or lack thereof) of these interpreters together, one gets the impression that the problem is methodological. Whatever fruit may be gleaned from lexical studies and comparative analysis with other OT texts, interpreting 34:6–7 outside its narrative context leaves important difficulties unanswered.

Exodus 34:6–7 in its canonical context

Those who interpret 34:6–7 within the narrative context of 32 – 34 include Freedman, Moberly, Gowan and Brueggemann. Freedman (1955) is concerned with the theological issues raised by the confession: the problem of divine immanence and transcendence, the problem of election, and the problem of divine justice and mercy. While Freedman gives much broad theological reflection on the confession, often ranging beyond the immediate context, it is clear that he roots his discussion in the context of 32 – 34. For Freedman (1955: 7) the confession is given by God 'in order to clarify and explain his role in the tragic incident of the golden calf'.

Freedman's conclusions, which he gives throughout his essay, demonstrate that he wrestles with the deep theological issues raised in the confession. For instance, concerning the difficulty of mercy versus judgment, Freedman (1955: 14) writes:

> At first sight, this may seem a strange contradiction. But the Israelite did not regard it as a paradox at all. . . . The establishment of the moral order of the universe, and the principle of justice in human affairs, were acts of grace. They exemplified the compassion and loyalty of God. At the same time, forgiveness was itself part of the process of justice. In the Bible, justice is not conceived as a rigid system of retribution for wrong-doing, but a flexible process by which good is promoted and evil restrained. On the other hand, mercy and forgiveness do not proceed from indifference to questions of right and wrong, but are invariably conditioned by moral considerations.

Freedman (1955: 15) goes on to explain the relationship between forgiveness and judgment in the following manner: 'Forgiveness does not contradict judgment; it is based upon it. Only when the issue of right and wrong has been settled, and the verdict rendered, does mercy have its role.'

While Moberly clearly roots his discussion of 34:6–7 firmly in the context of 32 – 34, his most valuable theological reflections on the confession may occur with reference to 20:5–6. Commenting that critical scholarship has generally viewed 20:5 as dependent upon 34:6–7, Moberly draws out several theological observations that arise if 34:6–7 is read in the light of 20:5, according to the narrative order in Exodus. From this perspective, Moberly observes that the sequence of judgment and mercy is reversed from 20:5 to 34:6–7, and that the statement of mercy in 20:6 is greatly expanded in 34:6–7. Most helpful is his observation that, in 34:6–7, *ḥesed* being shown to those keeping the commandments is absent, an observation from which Moberly infers that the Lord's *ḥesed* is shown to Israel *independently* of her obedience. The theological fruit of Moberly's exegesis is found not only in the words of 34:6–7 itself, but in the movement from 20:5–6 to 34:6–7. In this way Moberly's approach is different from Andersen's. While Andersen also treats 20:5–6 in his discussion of similar passages, he examines the two passages largely independently. Moberly, on the other hand, explores how 20:5–6 and 34:6–7 function together in the canonical movement of Exodus.[3]

Like Moberly, Gowan (1994: 219–243) discusses 34:6–7 in both its immediate and its wider literary context. Most helpful is his discussion of the Decalogue in relationship to Israel's sin with the golden calf, which 'provides the essential context for the dialogue between Moses and God' (1994: 221). Regarding theological reflection on the character confession, Gowan is chiefly concerned with the mystery of how God can both be just and forgive sin. He does not seek to resolve any of the tensions in the confession, but is rather content to speak of the mystery of undeserved forgiveness. He does mention that God forgives because of an 'unwavering intention to save' (1994: 226), although how he reconciles this 'unwavering intention' with the part of the confession that speaks of judgment is unclear. He goes on to speak of how later biblical writers used the allusion

---

[3] It is interesting, however, that Moberly does not give much attention to the apparent mercy–judgment paradox of 34:6–7. This may be due to Moberly's understanding (1983: 33) of paradoxical language as a means of communicating mystery: 'Such is the inherently mysterious nature of God and his ways with men that it is often difficult to make a statement in a theologically reflective way without wishing to qualify it, sometimes by the assertion of an apparently opposite truth.'

in such a manner that gave Israel confidence that the Lord would persist with them, despite their sinfulness.

Of the interpreters cited above, Brueggemann (1994: 943–949; 1997: 213–228) may be the most aware of the theological difficulties 34:6–7 poses. Among the difficulties he cites are the tension (or, in his words, contradiction), between mercy and judgment, and, more fundamentally, the tension between God's inclination to be for Israel and to be for himself. Brueggemann (1997: 227) writes concerning the latter:

> The tension or contradiction is that Yahweh is for Israel (or more generally 'for us,' *pro nobis*) in fidelity, and at the same time Yahweh is intensely and fiercely *for Yahweh's own self*. These two inclinations of Yahweh are not fully harmonized here, and perhaps never are anywhere in the Old Testament. This reading of the statement entails the conclusion that there is a profound, unresolved ambiguity in Yahweh's life. As a consequence, in any moment of Yahweh's life with Israel, Yahweh has available more than one alternative response to Israel, and Israel is never fully, finally certain of Yahweh's inclination toward it.

That Brueggemann sees such tensions suggests that his thought is firmly rooted in the canonical context of Exodus. While the tension between mercy and judgment is apparent when 34:6–7 is read in isolation, the seemingly paradoxical tension between the Lord's concern for Israel and his concern for himself is not obvious in 34:6–7, and can be made only in the broader context of Exodus. Despite his observations, however, Brueggemann does not adequately wrestle with the confession's tensions. Distancing himself from any attempt to harmonize or otherwise relate the tensions in the confession, Brueggemann opts instead to move the ambiguities and contradictions he finds into the Lord's own character, suggesting an instability in the Lord that ultimately left Israel unsure of who he was and what she could expect from him.

Can any conclusions be drawn from the manner in which these interpreters handle the difficulties raised in the confession? While they offer different theological reflections, their general confidence in the immediate literary context allows them to press more deeply into the mysteries and difficulties inherent in the description of the Lord's character than those who do not. Freedman directly addresses the relationship between justice and mercy, and offers some helpful insights. While not directly addressing some of the tensions in the confession, Moberly's insistence on interpreting it in its canonical context, both in terms of 32 – 34 and 20:5–6, has nonetheless allowed him to offer some very suggestive theological reflections. While Brueggemann does not adequately wrestle with the tensions in the confession, he nonetheless has identified important issues at stake in 34:6–7 as a result of attending to the larger canonical context of Exodus. It would seem, in the survey of interpreters cited above, that those who have sought to understand 34:6–7 in the context of Exodus (at least 32 – 34) show greater ability to wrestle with the theological issues the confession raises.

The point of the above survey is to suggest that interpreting Exodus 34:6–7 in its canonical context has proven to be more fruitful theologically than interpreting it outside that context. Moberly (1983: 32) explains:

> In the exegesis of Ex. 32–34 it is proposed that frequently sense may best be made on the assumption of a knowledge of the preceding narrative in Ex. 19–24; (25–31); and more generally Ex. 1–18. The point is a corollary of the importance of context for exegesis. The more a writer assumes that the context makes his meaning clear, the less he need specify individual points. It is hardly surprising, therefore, that the less the context is taken into account, the wider the range of interpretations of any given unit that becomes available.

The following argument will therefore explore 34:6–7 firmly within the canonical context of Exodus. In so doing I will again argue that the Lord's commitment to be known throughout the earth drives how the Lord responds to Israel after her idolatry, and that an appreciation of the Lord's missionary commitment helps make sense of the apparent tension between mercy and judgment in the description of the Lord's character.

Exodus 20:2–6

Before looking at 34:6–7, we return again to 20:2–6, for two reasons. First, the sin in 32 – 34 is a direct repudiation of the command forbidding idols, and therefore the command warrants another look in order to understand the nature of the sin. Aaron himself seems to try to incorporate the calf within the worship of the Lord by making an altar before it and proclaiming, 'Tomorrow shall be a feast to the LORD' (32:5), a perspective shared by some interpreters.[4] Yet, as is clear from the Lord's own response, and the difficulty with which the covenant is restored, the worship of the calf is a direct repudiation of the Lord. A look at the commandment helps us understand why this would be so. Secondly, 34:6–7 contains an almost verbatim quotation of 20:5, suggesting that an understanding of 20:2–6 is essential for making sense of the Lord's character revealed therein. In looking back at 20:2–6 we will focus upon the explicit reason why the Lord forbids idols: 'For I am the LORD your God, a jealous God' (20:5, my tr.).

I am the LORD

Noteworthy is the reappearance of 'I am the LORD,' easily missed in English translations that render 20:5 'I the LORD your God am a jealous God.' To render it in the precise form it is given in Hebrew draws to mind not only what we have observed of 'I am the LORD' to this point, but in particular its appearance in the introduction to the Decalogue in 20:2: 'I am the LORD your God, who brought you out of the land of Egypt.' In other words 20:2 sets an important context in which the commandment against idolatry is to be read.

The purpose of 20:2, as we have seen, is to remind Israel, before giving her the law, of what the Lord did for her in delivering her from Egypt. In other words Israel was reminded that she was a people redeemed by her God, one both willing and able to do her good. As we have seen, for Israel to know the Lord meant she knew him as her redeemer. It is in this context that the law is given to Israel.

The commandments, then, begin by forbidding other gods, which naturally flows out of what has come before. In Miller's (2009: 16) paraphrase, 'I am the LORD your God, so you shall not have other gods.' Having just been reminded that 'I am the LORD your God, who brought you out of the land of Egypt, out of the house of slavery,' the repetition suggests that to worship another god, or image,[5] is in effect a repudiation of the Lord who has made himself

---

[4] E.g. Sarna (1986: 217–218) finds Israel's action with the golden calf 'perfectly natural and understandable', arguing that in demanding a 'god' Israel 'intended nothing more than an appropriate object emblematic of the Divine Presence' and that no rejection of the Lord is implied. See also Albright (1957: 202–203, 265–266), who argues that the calf was not a rival god, but a pedestal for the Lord himself.

[5] The command forbids both (Stamm and Andrew 1967: 80).

known to Israel as her redeemer. This repudiation is precisely what we see in Israel's idolatry in Exodus 32, when Israel worships the calf with the words 'These are your gods, O Israel, who brought you up out of the land of Egypt!' (32:8). Not only is the credit for the Egyptian deliverance given to idols, but it is done in the precise language with which the Lord calls Israel to remember him in 20:2. In her idolatry Israel repudiates the Lord as her redeemer.

Not only does Israel's idolatry repudiate the Lord as her redeemer in the past, but she also looks to the calf as a redeemer for the future: 'Up, make us gods who shall go before us' (32:1). Nervous that Moses' absence will mean that they will go into the land unaccompanied, the people seek a presence that will ensure that they will arrive in the land safely. The concern is real, and justified, for the land is not only occupied, but it is occupied by peoples whom the Israelites cannot drive out on their own. The only way for Israel to enter the land is to be assured that they will be strengthened and protected as they enter. As we have seen, these were the precise concerns of Moses (and apparently Israel) when the Lord called Moses to lead Israel out of Egypt, prompting the Lord's promise 'I am with you.' This is precisely the issue in Numbers 13 – 14. Responding to Israel's anxiety concerning the strength of the inhabitants of Canaan, Joshua and Caleb speak to the people: 'If the Lord delights in us, he will bring us into this land and give it to us . . . the Lord is with us; do not fear them' (14:8–9). Before entering the land, Israel knows she needs a redeemer. The extent to which people look to the Lord is the extent to which they remember what the Lord has done for them. In the words of Moses to the people, 'The Lord your God who goes before you will himself fight for you, just as he did for you in Egypt before your eyes' (Deut. 1:30).

The implication of Israel's idolatry, and the reasons behind it, suggest that idolatry is principally about redemption, understood as seeking one's welfare apart from God. This is consistent with the broader witness of Scripture, which often casts idolatry in these terms. For instance, in Isaiah 43, 'I am the Lord' is spoken of in terms of redemption: 'I am the Lord your God, / the Holy One of Israel, your Saviour' (43:3), 'I, I am the Lord, / and besides me there is no saviour' (43:11). The point is twofold: the Lord is Israel's redeemer, and therefore nothing else is. As we noted earlier, Isaiah goes on to lampoon the notion that other gods can redeem. Having a tree, the idolater uses half to cook and warm himself, while 'the rest of it he makes into a god, his idol, and falls down to it and wor-

ships it. He prays to it and says, "Deliver me, for you are my god!"'
(44:17). In this vein C. J. H. Wright (2006: 169) writes:

> We tend to idolize the things (or people or systems) that we
> place our trust in to deliver us from the things we fear. The
> idolatrous dimension emerges when we place ultimate faith in
> such things, when we believe all the promises that are made
> or implied in them, and when we make all the sacrifices that
> they demand in exchange for what they speciously offer . . .
> Ultimately, it seems, we never learn that false gods never
> fail to fail. That is the only thing about a false god you can
> depend on.

Other gods can never redeem, for they are 'the work of human
hands, that neither see, nor hear, nor eat, nor smell' (Deut. 4:28).

A jealous God

The Lord's commitment to be known as God is further strengthened
by the appositive, a jealous God. Concerning the word 'jealous',
qannā', two particular items warrant mention, both of which flow
from my discussion in chapter 3 concerning the Lord's jealousy.
First, the Lord's jealousy is personal. Von Rad (1962: 207) is surely
right in seeing the Lord's jealousy as 'springing from the very depths
of personality', so much so that the Lord defines his name as jealous
in 34:14. Secondly, the Lord's jealousy is intolerant of rivals. Always
appearing in the context of false worship when speaking of God,[6]
qannā' suggests that the Lord will not share his claim to exclusive
love and worship with anyone or anything else, suggesting, as we
have seen, the relationship between a husband and a wife.[7] Clements
(1972: 124) writes concerning the Lord's jealousy:

> The title [a jealous God] does not imply unworthy feelings of
> envy or suspicion in God but his determination to uphold his
> honour in the face of evil and falsehood, and his refusal to
> allow himself to be displaced by any rival.

[6] Exod. 20:5; 34:14; Deut. 4:24; 5:9; 6:15. In each of these instances, God's jealousy
is the grounds for the prohibition of idolatry. See Reuter 2003: 47–58.

[7] Noting that the primitive meaning of qannā' is 'to become intensely red', Sarna
(1991: 110) argues that qannā' lends itself to the implied metaphor of marriage being
the nature of the covenant. For a sustained argument in this direction, see Sohn 1999.

Or, in Houtman's (2000: 31) succinct definition, the Lord's jealousy means that 'he claims all honour for himself'. The Lord is honoured when he is known for who he is.

Although the Lord's jealousy is often conceived in terms of judgment due to false worship,[8] it is equally important to note that his jealousy is also expressed in showing *hesed* to those who love him. Helpful in this vein is Goitein's (1956: 2) definition of *qannā'* as

> the strength of an emotion and the exclusiveness of its direction. It denotes complete devotion either to one's own aims or to another person. Therefore, the word can stand parallel either to Love, as in the Song of Songs viii 6, or to Hatred and Anger, as in Deuteronomy xxix 19.

Both outworkings of jealousy articulated by Goitein, love and anger, are apparent in 20:5–6. The manner in which 20:5–6 is phrased has the effect of dividing the people into two categories: those who love the Lord and those who hate him. Those who love the Lord are treated with *hesed*, while those who hate him are visited with anger. Important to observe is that both the Lord's responses, of love and judgment, are rooted in his jealousy. The implication is that all the Lord's dealings with Israel, whether in love or judgment, are rooted in his jealous commitment to being known as God, an implication that will become particularly important later in our discussion of 34:6–7.

Forsaking God

Later biblical reflection on the sin of the golden calf confirms that, in making and worshipping the calf, the people rejected God. Particularly poignant is the reflection of Psalm 106:

> They made a calf in Horeb
>   and worshipped a metal image.
> They exchanged the glory of God
>   for the image of an ox that eats grass.
> They forgot God, their Saviour,
>   who had done great things in Egypt,
> wondrous works in the land of Ham,
>   and awesome deeds by the Red Sea.

---

[8] E.g. Freedman (1955: 155–156) connects the jealousy of God only with judgment, but not mercy.

Therefore he said he would destroy them –
   had not Moses, his chosen one,
stood in the breach before him,
   to turn away his wrath from destroying them.

(106:19–23)

The sin is described in terms of forgetting God, their Saviour, and exchanging his glory for another. The clear implication is that, in worshipping the calf, Israel forsook the Lord. While not rooted explicitly in Exodus 32, Jeremiah rebukes Israel in the same language of exchange:

Has a nation changed its gods,
   even though they are no gods?
But my people have changed their glory
   for that which does not profit.

(Jer. 2:11)

The sin, then, is the forsaking of God and embracing gods who, in the end, cannot benefit those who worship them. As we saw in the Egyptian deliverance, here again the folly of idolatry is brought to the fore. Jeremiah goes on to speak of idolatry in precisely those terms:

[T]hey have forsaken me,
   the fountain of living waters,
and hewed out cisterns for themselves,
   broken cisterns that can hold no water.

(2:13)

The exchange of living water for a dry cistern is foolish in the extreme.

In the end this exchange of the glory of God for an idol is the essence of sin, as Paul makes clear in what is perhaps the most foundational teaching about sin in all of the Scriptures:

Although they knew God, they did not honour him as God or give thanks to him, but they became futile in their thinking, and their foolish hearts were darkened. Claiming to be wise, they became fools, and exchanged the glory of the immortal God for images resembling mortal man and birds and animals and creeping things. (Rom. 1:21–23)

Paul's description of the nature of sin well describes Israel's sin in Exodus 32. In failing to glorify God and give thanks to him ('These are your gods, O Israel, who brought you up out of the land of Egypt!', v. 4), they exchange God's glory for an image. Like Jeremiah, Paul frames sin here in terms of folly.

I close my comments concerning idolatry with a comment from C. J. H. Wright (2006: 160), who draws together the notions of jealousy, futility and the folly of idolatry:

> To say that the gods are the work of human hands is to prick human hubris and to invite fierce repudiation. Paul saying it in Ephesus was enough to start a riot (Acts 19:23–41). For if it is indeed true that the gods we exalt so highly are resplendent products of our own creativity, then it is not surprising that we defend them so belligerently. And in our jealous protectiveness of the gods we created for ourselves, we display a parody of the true jealousy that is the prerogative of the only true God whom we did not create. We invest so much of ourselves in our gods, spend so much on them and blend our identity and significance with theirs that it simply will not do for us to have them unmasked, mocked or toppled. And yet, of course, topple they must before the living God. For that is the destiny of all human effort that is not for the glory of God or offered to be redeemed by him.

From (near) ruin to restoration: the theology of Exodus 32 – 34

The following will seek to account for the movement between the Lord's declaration to destroy Israel in 32:10 to his restoration of the covenant in 34:10, focusing on the roles of Moses' intercession, Moses' character and Israel's repentance in Israel's restoration.

Moses' intercession for the Lord

Exodus 32 begins by describing Israel's sin concerning the golden calf, which serves as the context of the ensuing narrative. Uncertain of what has become of Moses due to his extended absence on the mountain, the people gather against Aaron and demand that he make for them gods who will go before them. Taking the golden earrings of the Israelites, Aaron fashions a molten calf, whereupon the people proclaim, 'These are your gods, O Israel, who brought you up out of the land of Egypt!' (32:4b). Seeing the people's response, Aaron builds an altar and calls for a feast to the Lord the next day, a celebration, with burnt offerings and peace offerings, food, drink and merriment.

With regard to the seriousness of the sin, two comments are particularly pertinent. First, in words that echo 20:2, which explicitly credits the Lord with the exodus from Egypt, Israel's acclamation of 32:4b credits the calf. As argued above, the position of 20:2 at the head of the law suggests that Israel's acknowledgment of the Lord as her deliverer is foundational for the ensuing law. By denying that the Lord delivered them, the people in effect undermine that foundation, an inference confirmed as Moses shatters the tablets containing the Decalogue (32:19). Secondly, the offering of burnt offerings and peace offerings serves as an ironic comment on Israel's sin. As mentioned in chapter 4 concerning 20:22–24, sacrificing burnt offerings and peace offerings was an expression of the pure worship of the Lord, understood over and against the worship of idols. Further, the only place in Exodus where burnt offerings and peace offerings are offered is the covenant ratification ceremony of Exodus 24, where Israel (after her pledge of obedience) is consecrated as a people holy to the Lord and set apart for his purposes. By offering burnt offerings and peace offerings in the context of idolatry, Israel has perverted the pure worship of the Lord and thereby repudiated her holy calling. In other words Israel's actions have reverted her from the holy to the common. Yet, as we have seen in the tabernacle material immediately preceding, while the common can be moved into the realm of the holy, there is no mechanism whereby the holy can be translated back into the realm of the common. Anything withdrawn from the holy must be destroyed, an implication entirely consistent with the Lord's response, a declared intent to destroy Israel.

First petition (Exod. 32:11–13)

The Lord responds to Israel's sin with hot anger. Having ordered Moses to descend the mountain, the Lord speaks to the gravity of Israel's sin in two ways. First, he describes Israel's sin in terms of the commandment forbidding idolatry. Not only does the Lord say that people 'have turned aside quickly out of the way that I commanded them', but he uses the language of 20:4–5: they have made for themselves and worshipped a molten calf. Secondly, he relates to Moses that Israel has credited the molten calf with delivering them from Egypt, another reference to the Decalogue (20:2). Calling them a stiff-necked people, the Lord commands Moses, 'Let me alone, that my wrath may burn hot against them and I may consume them, in order that I may make a great nation of you' (32:10).

Moses immediately intercedes:

> O LORD, why does your wrath burn hot against your people, whom you have brought out of the land of Egypt with great power and with a mighty hand? Why should the Egyptians say, 'With evil intent did he bring them out, to kill them in the mountains and to consume them from the face of the earth?' Turn from our burning anger and relent from this disaster against your people. Remember Abraham, Isaac, and Israel, your servants, to whom you swore by your own self, and said to them, 'I will multiply your offspring as the stars of heaven, and all this land that I have promised I will give to your off-spring, and they shall inherit it for ever.' (32:11–13)

Moses opens his intercession with a reminder of Israel's relationship to the Lord. The question *why* is rhetorical. Moses is not asking the reasons for the Lord's anger (he has already been told), nor is he simply reminding him of what he has done for Israel. Rather, Moses' description of Israel in 32:11 as the people the Lord brought out with great power (*běkoah gādōl*) and a mighty hand serve to remind the Lord of his purposes in the plagues, 'to show [Pharaoh] my power [*kōah*], that my name may be declared throughout the earth' (9:16, my tr.).[9] This connection back to 9:16 also helps explain Moses' reference to 'your people'. Unwilling for the Lord to forsake Israel, as implied when the Lord referred to 'your [Moses'] people' (32:7) and 'this people' (32:9), Moses reminds the Lord that they are the Lord's people. While some have taken 'your people' to refer to the Lord's love for Israel,[10] that Moses describes 'your people' as those the Lord delivered in such a spectacular and public manner points to the visible association between the Lord and Israel forged in the plagues. In other words the connection with Israel wrought in the plagues makes Israel the Lord's concern. Buber's (1994: 144) paraphrase captures the sense well: 'You cannot assign this people

---

[9] That the word *kōah* appears only one other time in Exodus, again in connection with the display of the Lord's power in the plagues (15:6), suggests that 32:11 may refer back to 9:16.

[10] E.g. Cassuto 1967: 416.

to me, nor seek to replace it by me; this concerns not me but you, this is *your* people, you are the one who brought it here!' (emphasis original). The effect of Moses' reference to Israel as the Lord's people is meant to suggest that the Lord has publicly bound himself to Israel.

Having established the connection between the Lord and Israel, Moses follows with two direct appeals. First, he invokes the Lord's reputation, suggesting that the destruction of Israel will disparage the Lord's character in the eyes of the Egyptians. At stake here is exactly how the Lord wants to be known to Egypt. The implication of Moses' comment is that Egypt will continue to recognize the Lord as powerful, but also as evil. In other words, as we have seen earlier, the Lord is not only concerned to display his power, but is also concerned to make known what kind of God he is. Moses' appeal is based upon the premise that the Lord seeks to make himself known as a God who is both powerful *and* good. Margaliot (1994: 44), therefore, does not go too far when he suggests (in the imaginary words of Moses) that nothing less than the Lord's recognition as God amongst the nations is at stake: 'Your very divinity, your recognition as a God by other nations and Israel is here most seriously endangered.'

Secondly, Moses invokes the Lord's promises to the patriarchs. The ground of this second appeal has been debated. A common Jewish reading suggests that Moses appeals to the merit of the patriarchs.[11] While Moses does describe the patriarchs as the Lord's servants, he goes on to describe them as those to whom the Lord swore by himself, thereby laying the emphasis on the *promises* he made to the patriarchs. By emphasizing the promises, Moses brings the Lord's integrity to the fore. Again, the issue is bound to the Lord's honour, this time as one who keeps his word.

The appeal to the patriarchal promises may also have a wider scope. First, as Jacob points out, the reference to Abraham, Isaac and *Israel* (rather than Jacob) suggests the bond between the Lord and the people in a way that would not be so apparent if Moses had just mentioned Jacob.[12] By speaking of Israel, Moses reminds the Lord that he has bound himself to this people. Secondly, the

---

[11] See e.g. Cassuto 1967: 416 and Brichto 1983: 9. Jacob (1992: 946) places the emphasis on the promises to the patriarchs.

[12] Jacob (1992: 946) points out further that the only other time 'Abraham, Isaac and Israel' is mentioned is 1 Kgs 18:36, a similar circumstance where Israel's future is in jeopardy.

reference to the patriarchal promises calls to mind Genesis 12:1–3, the place where those promises were first articulated.[13] While Genesis 12:1–3 does not explicitly speak of the Lord's honour, it clearly has the nations in view: that all the families of the earth would find blessing through Abraham. So, while appealing to the Lord's integrity, it is quite possible that Moses in 32:13 also appeals to the Lord's purposes in calling the patriarchs. If this is the case, the reasons of integrity and worldwide purposes in 32:13 should not be separated too sharply, particularly given that they both deal with the Lord's honour. The reason that Moses' appeal in 32:13 is so compelling, then, is not only that a broken word dishonours God, but that failure to follow through with his promises brings into jeopardy his purpose to make himself known to the nations.

That Moses' concerns were compelling is suggested in the Lord's response: 'And the LORD relented from the disaster that he had spoken of bringing on his people' (32:14). At this point it is important to be clear about the reasons why the Lord relented. Albeit in slightly different ways, both of Moses' appeals are grounded in the Lord's commitment to be known as God amongst the nations. In 32:12 Moses appeals to the Lord's international reputation (specifically Egypt). In 32:13 Moses appeals both to the Lord's integrity and to his purposes for blessing the nations inaugurated in Genesis 12. It is noteworthy that in neither case does Moses ground his appeal in Israel. He does not make light of her sin, nor does he appeal to any special love the Lord may have for her. The reminder that Israel is 'your people' (32:11) is the most Moses will say of Israel. Durham's statements (1987: 429) that 'Moses' whole concern is with the people' and that the Lord repented because he was 'moved with pity for Israel under such a threat as he had made' therefore miss the primary issue at stake. The grounds of Moses' appeal are concerned solely with the Lord's commitment to make himself known: as one who has a reputation to uphold, as one who has made promises he has sworn to keep, and as one who has embarked upon a plan to make himself known to the nations. In other words Moses grounds his plea for Israel *in the interests of the Lord himself*. This must not be missed, for it is crucial for understanding what is at stake in the Lord's response to Israel. Rather than defending the people before

---

[13] Childs (1974: 567) argues that the Lord himself suggests the link to Gen. 12:1–3 by using the term 'great nation' in 32:10.

the Lord,[14] Moses defends *the Lord* before the Lord. On these grounds, the Lord reverses his decision to destroy Israel.

Second petition (Exod. 32:31b–32)

After the first intercession, Moses descends from the mountain and sees Israel's idolatry for himself. After smashing the tablets in hot anger, destroying the calf and forcing Israel to drink its dust, confronting Aaron and ordering the slaughter of three thousand Israelites, Moses returns to the Lord with the following request: 'Alas, this people has sinned a great sin. They have made for themselves gods of gold. But now, if you will forgive their sin – but if not, please blot me out of your book that you have written' (32:31b–32). Here Moses presses further than in 32:11–13. Rather than asking that the Lord not destroy Israel (which has been granted), Moses asks for the Lord to forgive Israel,[15] offering to assume Israel's fate should the Lord not forgive.[16] In so doing Moses unequivocally asserts his solidarity with Israel.[17]

Moses' request is denied. The Lord will not allow Moses to assume Israel's punishment, and pledges to punish the guilty (32:33–34).

---

[14] See Krašovec 1999: 91.

[15] Contra Childs (1974: 558, 571), at this point the Lord has not forgiven Israel. The Lord's threat in 32:10 was to destroy Israel, which is therefore what he relented of in 32:14. In addition, Moses does not ask for forgiveness in 32:11–13, as he does in 32:32 and 34:9. To suggest that 32:14 grants forgiveness removes the rationale for Moses' petition in 32:30–34. Interpreting 32:14 as indicating forgiveness causes Childs problems later in the chapter: 'The forgiveness for which Moses interceded in vv. 11ff. and which he received in v. 14 does not tally well with the punishment in vv. 25ff., nor the refusal of forgiveness in vv. 33ff.' Childs cites these as inconsistencies, and uses them as grounds for arguing that 32:7–14 is a Deuteronomic addition. However, if it is recognized that forgiveness has not been granted (or even asked for) in 32:7–14, the apparent inconsistency fades and with it the need to invoke another source to explain it.

[16] It is unclear from the grammar whether or not Moses is suggesting he take Israel's place in punishment (Childs 1974: 571) or that he simply share Israel's punishment (Cassuto 1967: 423; cf. Moberly 1983: 199; Hafemann 1995: 205). However, Moses' concerns in 32 – 34 suggest the former, given that Moses' sharing Israel's punishment would not solve the problem of the Lord's honour with which Moses is so concerned, whereas Moses' taking Israel's punishment upon himself (and thereby sparing Israel) would. It is noteworthy that the interpreters cited above who reject the notion of Moses' offering himself as a substitute for the people do not argue for the point, but simply assert it.

[17] It is interesting to note that the Lord himself, at times, seems to assume Moses' solidarity with the people as well. For instance, when some went to gather manna on the Sabbath, the Lord identifies Moses with the guilty: 'How long will you [pl.] refuse to keep my commandments and my laws?' (16:28). This may be implied in the Lord's reference to Israel as Moses' people in 32:7.

The question arises: Why did the Lord deny Moses' request here after granting his request earlier in 32:14? The text is not explicit. However, it is worth noting that, unlike 32:11–13, where Moses offers a carefully reasoned request grounded in the Lord's commitment to be honoured amongst the nations, here Moses gives no reasons why the Lord should forgive Israel, a point to which we will return later. Moses simply makes the request, and is apparently denied.[18]

Third petition (Exod. 33:12–18)

Moses' third intercession of 33:12–18 comes as a response to a further problem: although the Lord has agreed not to destroy Israel, he refuses to accompany Israel into Canaan. This sets up the central issue of chapter 33, the problem of the Lord's presence with Israel. This third intercession is both complicated and extremely important.[19] As Brueggemann (1979: 48) has written, 'There can be little doubt that Exodus 33 is the most sustained and delicate attempt to deal with the problem of Yahweh's presence/absence in Israel.'

In investigating Moses' intercession, it is important to be clear about the nature of the problem. While the Lord has declared he will withhold his presence, he nonetheless promises Israel safe passage to the land (33:2) and an abundant land ('flowing with milk and honey', 33:3). Furthermore, the Lord's withholding his presence is an act of mercy, since his going with Israel would mean their destruction (33:3b). Yet, despite the promise of safe passage and abundant land, the news is received as a 'disastrous word' (33:4). Why the word is thus received by the people is never stated. However, the recognition that life would be good in the land despite the Lord's absence is important, for it suggests that, both for Moses and for Israel, something deeper is at stake than Israel's welfare, a point to which we will return below.

---

[18] Hafemann (1995: 205) suggests that Moses appeals to the existence of a 'faithful remnant', embodied in himself, as the basis for the Lord's mercy. This is unlikely for at least two reasons. First, Hafemann's argument that only the most guilty were slaughtered (cf. Jacob 1992: 956; Brichto 1983: 16–17) is not explicit in the text, and is difficult to reconcile with the ensuing plague. Secondly, if Moses were petitioning on behalf of a faithful remnant, it is unclear why he would ask for forgiveness, given that forgiveness need only be granted to the unfaithful (cf. 32:33 and Gen. 18:22–33, where Abraham petitions for justice for the righteous, rather than for forgiveness for the wicked). A more straightforward reading suggests that the Lord denies Moses' request to bear, or to share in, Israel's punishment.

[19] Aside from the commentaries, extended discussions of the issues at stake in Exod. 33:12–23 include Brueggemann 1979; Muilenburg 1968; Piper 1979; and Irwin 1997.

After a recounting of Israel's reaction to the Lord's word, Moses offers a third petition, given in two parts. The first is as follows:

> Moses said to the LORD, 'See, you say to me, "Bring up this people," but you have not let me know whom you will send with me. Yet you have said, "I know you by name, and you have also found favour in my sight." Now therefore, if I have found favour in your sight, please show me now your ways, that I may know you in order to find favour in your sight. Consider too that this nation is your people.' (33:12–13)

Although indirectly, Moses expresses his dissatisfaction with the Lord's declared absence from Israel, particularly given the special favour Moses has found in his sight.[20] Moses' recognition of the Lord's favour is particularly important, for Moses uses it as leverage as he continues to intercede.[21] Based on this special favour, Moses makes two further petitions: that he would know the Lord's ways and that the Lord would reinstate Israel as his people.[22]

Moses' request that the Lord acknowledge Israel as his people is particularly significant. First, Moses reaffirms his solidarity with Israel. If the Lord wants to show favour to Moses (who already has found favour in his sight), then the Lord must show favour to Israel as well. Knowing that he cannot appeal to anything in Israel, for she has 'sinned a great sin' (32:30, 31), Moses uses *his own* favour with the Lord as leverage in order to restore Israel to a position of similar favour in the Lord's sight. Secondly, the reference to Israel as a nation (*gôy*) in 33:13 is probably another reference to a holy nation in 19:6 (*gôy qādôš*). As discussed in chapter 3, the term *gôy* is most often used for non-Israelite nations, and rarely for Israel herself. In Exodus, applied to Israel, *gôy* occurs only here and in

---

[20] Often observed, Moses' charge that the Lord had not revealed who would accompany Israel is curious in the light of 33:2, and is often interpreted as suggesting dissatisfaction.

[21] For a range of possible meanings of the phrase, see Moberly 1983: 70.

[22] Childs (1974: 594) does not see this final phrase as a petition, but rather as the grounds for Moses' plea, arguing that Moses appeals to the covenant, which he regards as still operative despite Israel's sin. This seems unlikely for two reasons. First, the symbolic import of Moses' shattering the tablets suggests that he understood the covenant to be broken (a point Childs himself makes on p. 569). Secondly, all that the Lord has granted Israel to this point has been continued existence. At this point the relationship between Israel and the Lord is still severely impaired. Neither forgiveness nor the Lord's presence has been granted. Hence it is more likely that Moses appeals for the restoration of the covenant.

19:6, suggesting the possibility that Moses is reminding the Lord of Israel's purpose given in 19:4–6.[23]

The Lord's response in 33:14 is somewhat enigmatic, in a manner often obscured by English translations: 'My face will go, and I will give you [sing.] rest' (my tr.). Suggestions as to the meaning of the Lord's response have varied. Some have argued that he grants Moses' request in full.[24] Others have suggested that he offers only a partial concession to Moses,[25] while some argue that the Lord offers Moses nothing at all.[26] Given Moses' continued intercession, both in 33:15–16 and 34:9, it is unlikely that Moses is completely satisfied. Particularly significant is that the Lord's promise of rest is singular, directed to Moses alone (Moberly 1983: 74). Despite Moses' efforts to get the Lord to include Israel in the favour he has towards Moses, Israel has not been fully restored. The Lord's response drives Moses to intercede again.

Moses' second intercession pushes further than the first. Whereas in 33:13 Moses requests a reinstatement of Israel as the Lord's people, only tentatively broaching the subject of the Lord's presence, this time Moses boldly seeks for the Lord to reverse his intention of 33:5, 7 not to accompany Israel into the land:

> If your presence will not go, do not bring us up from here. For how will it be known that I have found favour in your sight, I and your people? Is it not in your going with us, so that we are distinct, I and your people, from all the people upon the face of the earth? (33:15–16, my tr.)

Moses appeals to the Lord in two ways. First, he again reminds the Lord of the favour he has in the Lord's sight. Then Moses asks, 'How will it be known?', a question that suggests the Lord's favour towards Moses is something that should be, to a certain extent, public knowledge. Probably in response to the Lord's promise to Moses alone in 33:14, Moses goes on to include Israel in that favour, again carrying the unmistakable implication that he stands in soli-

---

[23] See also Gen. 12:2, the cardinal missionary text, where *gôy* is used of Abram's descendants.

[24] E.g. McNeile 1908: 214: 'It is a complete and final response, exhibiting full forgiveness and reconciliation.' Cf. Cassuto 1967: 434; Durham 1987: 447.

[25] Childs 1974: 594–595; Terrien 1978: 142.

[26] Brueggemann 1979: 50; Gowan 1994: 231.

darity with Israel.[27] Moses then presses further, declaring that Israel will not be distinct among all peoples should the Lord withhold his presence.[28]

This final argument proves the clinching argument, for in 33:17 the Lord responds unambiguously, 'This very thing that you have spoken I will do.' The argument's effectiveness again lies in its appeal to the Lord's purposes with Israel.[29] As in 33:13, there is a subtle allusion to 19:6. While the word 'holy' (*qādôš*) is not used, as in 19:6, the idea is clearly the same – Israel is intended to be a people distinct from all others. In Janzen's (1997: 246) words, 'Moses implicitly appeals to God's original intent that this people should be a "distinct" people, "a priestly kingdom and a holy nation" (19:3–6).'[30] Moses thereby brings the Lord's missionary purpose for Israel back into view. In other words Moses' successful appeal in 33:15–16 is based upon the same foundation as his successful appeal 32:11–13: the Lord's honour among the nations.

This understanding helps explain Moses' dissatisfaction with the Lord's absence, despite the promise of protection and abundance. That Moses is not interested in enjoying a good life with Israel if it

---

[27] Contra Fretheim (1991a: 297), it is not that Moses is trying to change the Lord's thinking concerning Israel, but rather Moses is asserting that he will not be separated from them.

[28] According to Muilenburg (1968: 180), 33:16 implies that Israel is the object of knowing, that only through the Lord's going with Israel will *Israel* know she is distinct. There are, however, several reasons for understanding 33:16 to refer to non-Israelite nations. First, non-Israelite nations recognizing Israel's distinctiveness is consistent with Moses' appeal to the Lord's reputation among the nations in 32:12. Secondly, as suggested above, the word *gôy* in 33:13 may point back to 19:6, which clearly has the nations in view. Finally, the same root, *plh*, is used three other times in Exodus (8:22[18]; 9:4; 11:7), each time to show *Egypt* that Israel is distinct. See Buber and Rosenzweig 1994: 146.

[29] Moberly (1983: 72) finds Moses' favour in God's sight as the reason for Moses' successful intercession. While certainly the favour Moses enjoys is vital, the *content* of his intercession is necessary as well, as illustrated by the development of Moses' prayer in 33:12–16. Moses in 33:12–13 had already grounded his appeal in the Lord's favour towards him, yet had not received the answer he sought. The reference to the Lord's plan for Israel in 33:16 is the new element in 33:15–16, suggesting that this is the argument that clinches the response Moses seeks. Both Moses' favour in the Lord's sight *and* the content of his intercession are of vital importance in Moses' success.

[30] Cf. Hammer 1978: 347; Hafemann 1995: 214; Terrien 1978: 144. Blum (1990: 63) sees 33:16 referring to 19:5, but not to 19:6. While it may be granted that Moses has 19:5 in mind, there is no reason to assume that, in the canonical presentation, Moses would have understood 19:5 apart from 19:6, a point made previously in the discussion of 29:46. Indeed, it is the appeal to the purposes of 19:5–6 that gives 33:16 its force.

does not include the Lord's presence indicates a desire for relationship, to know him. This desire is probably behind Moses' following request, 'show me your glory' (33:18).[31] Furthermore, and as importantly, Moses is not content to live well in the land if it will not further the missionary purposes of Israel as given in 19:4–6. While Moses' desire to know the Lord is clear in this intercession, it is interesting to note that the only specific reason that Moses insists upon the Lord's presence among Israel concerns his purposes in regard to the nations. In other words while the intercession certainly concerns Israel's fate, Moses again focuses the issue on the Lord's commitment to be known and honoured as God.

Fourth petition (Exod. 34:9)

In response to Moses' final petition to 'show me your glory', the Lord reveals his character in Exodus 34:6–7,[32] which serves, finally, as the declaration of forgiveness for which Moses petitioned in 32:31b–32. Here is the theological climax of the section, and the ultimate fulfilment of all that Moses has sought for the Lord and Israel. Now the covenant can be restored. While technically the covenant is not reinstated in 34:6–7, Moses can now appeal to the Lord's revealed character and once more petition for Israel's forgiveness. Whereas in 32:32 he did not offer any grounds for his appeal, in 34:9 Moses offers a fourth and final petition: 'If now I have found favour in your sight, O Lord, please let the Lord go in the midst of us, for it is a stiff-necked people, and pardon our iniquity and our sin, and take us for your inheritance.' Again appealing for Israel's forgiveness, Moses now grounds his appeal both in the favour he enjoys with the Lord and in the revelation of the Lord's character he has just been given.[33] The Lord's response of 34:10 follows naturally: 'Behold, I am making a covenant.'

---

[31] Exactly what Moses is asking for has generated much discussion, and will be addressed below.

[32] The Hebrew wording of 34:5 allows for either Moses or the Lord as the speaker. Based on the Lord's promise to proclaim his name in 33:19 and the manner in which Moses appeals to 34:6 in his intercession of 34:9 (supported by Num. 14:17–18), it is likely the speaker is the Lord. For possible renderings of 34:6, see Scharbert 1957: 131.

[33] Piper (1979: 208–209) makes the interesting suggestion that Moses also appeals to Israel's stiff-necked nature. Rather than as a concessive, Piper interprets *kî* (for) in 34:9 as the grounds of Moses' appeal, Moses being confident of forgiveness for Israel based upon the Lord's merciful nature just revealed in 34:6–7. If this is the case, the petition of Moses is all the more bold in that Israel's stiff-necked nature was previously the grounds behind the Lord's stated intention both to destroy Israel (32:9) and to withhold his presence (33:3, 5).

The reinstatement of the covenant in 34:10 effectively ends Moses' intercession. Moses has been successful in moving the Lord from his stated intention to destroy Israel to forgiving Israel and reinstating the covenant. In short, Moses' success was due to the manner in which he grounded his petitions in the Lord's own purpose to be known as God amongst the nations. Each time Moses appealed to the Lord's honour or reputation in some manner, the request was granted. The only time Moses did not appeal in such a way, the request was apparently denied (32:32). In fact, Moses did not even appeal to the Lord's grace until 34:9, *after* the Lord had revealed himself as merciful and gracious, and the forgiver of sins. In other words the content of Moses' appeals, grounded in the Lord's concern for his honour, was effective in his intercessions with the Lord.[34] Thus, while perhaps legitimate to see Moses defending Israel in 32 – 34, it is closer to the text to see that, in his concern for the Lord's reputation and purposes, Moses is defending the Lord.

Moses' character

A further matter concerning Moses' successful intercession remains to be addressed. As important as the content of Moses' intercession is in the Lord's decision to reinstate the covenant with Israel, 33:17 suggests an additional reason for the Lord's change of heart: Moses' favour in his sight. This raises the question 'What about Moses causes him to find favour in the Lord's sight to the point that he exerts such influence over the Lord's dealings with Israel?' Although the answer, it must be acknowledged, is nowhere explicitly given in Exodus, inferences based upon Moses' prayers and actions may indicate that, at least in part, Moses found favour with the Lord due to Moses' own concern for the Lord's honour.[35]

The first indication that Moses is primarily concerned with the Lord's honour is Moses' rejection of personal privilege at the expense of the Lord's reputation. It is quite possible that the Lord's stated intention to destroy Israel and make a great nation of Moses

---

[34] For an excellent argument along similar lines, see Hafemann 1995: 189–231.

[35] Hafemann (1995: 212) argues, 'It is not Moses' merit or character that should motivate YHWH to act in the future, but the evidence of God's own bestowal of his "favour/grace" on Moses in the past.' While he does not explain his assertion, it seems that the issue turns on whether or not *ḥēn* (favour/grace) signifies a favour that is always undeserved. While certainly the Lord's grace to Israel in 32 – 34 is undeserved, other places in the OT suggest that *ḥēn* may be given in response to obedience or humility (e.g. Ps. 84:11[12]; Prov. 3:4, 34). See Freedman 1986: 30–33. Such a sense may well be at work in the Lord's favour towards Moses.

(32:10) carries a subtle appeal to Moses' self-interest. In effect, by calling Moses to stand aside as Israel is destroyed, the Lord offers Moses the opportunity to assume the place of an Abraham as the patriarch of a new people. Despite what appeal this might have had, Moses rejects the proposal outright. As discussed above, the Lord's honour is at stake, and Moses' reaction to the Lord's stated intention reveals that he is more concerned with the Lord's reputation among the Egyptians than his personal aggrandizement.[36] If 32:10 in any way served to appeal to Moses' self-interest, his ensuing intercession in 32:11–13 makes it clear that the Lord's honour is more important to Moses than personal ambition.

The second episode that sheds light on Moses' character is his reaction to Israel's idolatry. Commentators have often argued that Moses' hearing of Israel's idolatry on the mountain is inconsistent with his fierce reaction in seeing it himself, leading some scholars to suggest a source-critical problem.[37] It is not obvious, however, that such a solution is necessary. It is common to human experience that hearing about something and seeing it with one's own eyes can often be far different experiences, for it is often in the direct encounter that the weight of a particular circumstance is felt. Along these lines, Driver suggests that seeing the spectacle of Israel's idolatry caused Moses to realize the gravity of the offence in a way he had not before, thereby triggering the fierce reaction and destruction of the tablets.[38] If Driver is right, moving too quickly to a source-critical solution to Moses' reaction misses the human element, and in effect obscures the rather important implication that not only is Israel's idolatry an offence to the Lord, but it is an offence to Moses. Further, it is noteworthy in this light that the same language of burning anger is used to describe Moses' reaction in 32:19 (*wayyiḥar 'ap*) and the Lord's reaction previously in 32:10 (*wĕyiḥar 'appî*). The similarity between the Lord's reaction and Moses' suggests that Moses shares the zeal that the Lord has for his honour and reputation.

The slaughter of the three thousand at the hands of the Levites

---

[36] The Hebrew root *ḥlh*, translated 'besought', may also carry the sense of 'to be ill', which could suggest a certain revulsion at the idea. See Seybold 1981: 399–409 for the semantic range of *ḥlh* and the difficulties in precisely identifying the root.

[37] Cf. Coats 1977: 98, who shares the common view that the account assumes Moses had no prior knowledge of Israel's sin.

[38] S. R. Driver 1911: 350; cf. Houtman 2000: 614. This need not conflict with the idea that the shattering of the tablets is symbolic of the broken covenant (Sarna 1986: 216).

is a third episode that shows Moses' zeal for the Lord's reputation. The slaughter by the Levites is typically taken to be the punishment for the sin of the calf. To be sure, the action has a strong element of punishment in it, but the immediate reason for the slaughter may lie elsewhere. A hint as to the reason is found in 32:25–26:

> And when Moses saw that the people had broken loose [*pārua'*] Aaron had let them break loose [*pĕrā'ōh*], to their shame [*lĕšimṣāh*] among their enemies – then Moses stood in the gate of the camp, and said, 'Who is on the LORD's side? Come to me.' (My tr.)

Interpretation of the above passage has proven difficult, particularly given the uncertainty of the words 'broken loose', Hebrew root *pr'*, and 'derision', *šimṣâ*. Better attested, *pr'* has been rendered 'to let free', 'to leave unattended' or 'to run wild',[39] but can also be understood in the more profound sense of departing from that which is true and right.[40] A hapax legomenon, *šimṣâ* has understandably been more difficult to interpret, as can be seen in the divergence of suggestions. Modern English Bibles have translated the phrase as 'derision' (ESV, NASB, NRSV), 'shame' (AV, RSV), 'laughingstock' (NIV) and 'menace' (NJPS). Sarna (1991: 208) follows the NJPS and translates *lĕšimṣāh* as 'so that they were a menace', suggesting that their activities were designed to generate fear amongst their enemies. Houtman (2000: 663–664) takes the opposite view, translating *lĕšimṣāh* as 'so that they were not concerned', suggesting that Israel's worship left them defenceless against their enemies. Recognizing that the exact meaning is elusive, Childs (1974: 570) translates *lĕšimṣāh* as 'to the delight'.

The interpretation of the passage can, therefore, take several directions. Interpretations of 32:25 include sexual revelry (Cassuto 1967: 420), ecstatic behaviour (Knight 1976: 189) or a repudiation of the Lord's rule over Israel (Janzen 1990: 607). Exactly what Israel was engaged in is perhaps not too consequential for the present purpose. Significantly, the different interpretations share the recognition that Israel's behaviour had public ramifications in the eyes of

---

[39] Köhler and Baumgartner 1996: 970.

[40] Janzen (1990: 604) has argued this point in depth, writing that the 'consistent connotation [of *pr'*] is of the relaxing and disregard for, or flouting of and rebellion against, structures and constraints considered (rightly or wrongly) to be foundational to true and life-giving order'.

her enemies. This raises the possibility that, rather than punishment, the immediate issue for Moses is the shame that Israel is bringing upon the Lord in the sight of her enemies. In fact, the presence of the passive participle *pārua'* allows for the possibility that Israel was acting *at that time* in a manner that would publicly dishonour the Lord in the sight of the nations. If so, the urgency and immediacy of the slaughter would be better viewed not primarily as a vehicle for retribution, but rather as an extreme measure to stop the public disgrace Israel was bringing upon the Lord.[41] As Durham (1987: 431) writes, 32:25–29 serves simply 'as the report of how the out-of-control Israelites were brought under control again'.

This interpretation sheds important light on Moses' character, particularly when compared to his reaction to the Lord's declared intention to destroy Israel in 32:10. Unlike his response to 32:10, there is no record in 32:25–26 of Moses' interceding on Israel's behalf. On the contrary, Moses does not seem to flinch in obeying

---

[41] This interpretation also offers possible solutions to two other problems connected with the slaughter. First, it may explain why there are apparently two accounts of the Lord's punishing Israel, the slaughter of the three thousand and the plague of 32:35 (some include Israel's drinking the water as a third). The seeming presence of two accounts has led some scholars to suggest that the two punishment accounts come from different sources (cf. Noth 1962: 245, who judges 32:25–29 to be an addition concerned with why the Levites were entrusted with the priestly office). Rather than attributing each to different sources, the above interpretation suggests that the reasons for the two disasters were different. The plague was the Lord's punishment, while the slaughter was an immediate measure to preserve the Lord's reputation. That the slaughter of the three thousand was not primarily a vehicle of punishment is further supported by Moses' words to Israel following the slaughter: 'You have sinned a great sin. And now I will go up to the LORD; perhaps I can make atonement for your sin' (32:30). The mention of atonement for Israel and Moses' subsequent petition to the Lord indicate that Moses himself did not think the slaughter adequately served the purpose of punishing Israel for her sin. Secondly, the above interpretation offers a possibility concerning the identity of the three thousand killed. Often it is assumed that those who were killed were the ringleaders of the rebellion (e.g. Brichto 1983: 15). While certainly plausible, it is nowhere suggested in the text. Another interpretation suggests that the drinking of the dust of the tablets functioned to distinguish the guilty from the innocent, in a manner comparable to the water of bitterness in Num. 5 (cf. Noth 1962: 249–250). Again, while possible, it is unsupported in Exodus. An alternative possibility is that the three thousand were those publicly engaging in the shameful behaviour. Besides being an inference more directly connected to the text, such behaviour would be publicly and immediately recognizable, thereby distinguishing those participating from those not in the midst of the people. Hence the need to move further beyond the text and surmise some kind of special discernment on the part of the Levites or any special properties of the water diminishes. The observation of Walzer (1968: 2–3) that the slaughter is the only instance in the wilderness where the Lord does not directly punish the Israelites himself may also suggest that something other than punishment is at work here.

the Lord's call to order such a brutal command. The explanation plausibly lies in the fact that, in contrast to his proposed wholesale destruction of Israel in 32:10, the patriarchal promises and the Lord's international reputation (the grounds of 32:11–13) would not be compromised by the partial destruction of the unfaithful (those not on the Lord's side) in this instance. Because the Lord's integrity and reputation are not compromised in killing the unfaithful Israelites, and because the people are engaged publicly in shameful activities, Moses can act in a swift and decisive manner. Moses' actions in calling for the slaughter of the three thousand and his steadfast intercession in 32:11–13 that the Lord not completely destroy the nation of Israel are therefore consistent. If the above interpretation is valid, then it suggests that Moses dealt with Israel in the matter of the three thousand in an effort to preserve the Lord's honour, again revealing a zeal for the Lord's honour that drives his actions.[42]

Moses' offer of himself in place of the Israelites in 32:32 is a fourth instance where his zeal for the Lord's honour is apparent. One thing made clear about Moses in 32:32 is that Israel's restoration is more important to Moses than his own life. Exactly why Moses offered himself in place of Israel is less certain. Was it Moses' love for Israel? Or was it Moses' love for the Lord? Both? While it must be acknowledged that the text is not explicit, given that nowhere in Exodus 32 does the text comment on Moses' love for Israel, the evidence in Exodus suggests that Moses' offer is based primarily upon his zeal for the Lord, even if Moses did have a corresponding zeal for Israel.[43] Buber (1958: 135–136) captures it well: 'To be sure, [Moses] is not concerned with the soul of man, he is concerned with Israel; but he is concerned with Israel for the sake of YHVH.' If this is correct, 32:32 provides strong support for the notion that

---

[42] Whybray (1996: 119) sees Moses in two distinct roles in Exod. 32: the bold and merciful intercessor who bravely stands against the Lord on behalf of the people, and the wrathful Moses who slaughters the three thousand as 'the ruthless opponent of the people'. In the end he finds the two pictures theologically incongruous, and attributes them to different traditions both of which a final redactor deemed to be so important that he held them together despite the different pictures they give of Moses. Holding these passages together, however, sheds much light on what it means for Moses to be the mediator. By dismissing an important tension as a compositional problem, the nature of Moses' solidarity with *both* the Lord *and* Israel is missed, as well as the recognition that both actions are driven by the same motivation that the Lord be known and honoured as God among the nations.

[43] Thus the comment of Krašovec (1999: 91) that 'Moses reacts so forcefully because his love for his people is so extreme' needs to be qualified.

Moses' favour in the Lord's eyes has to do with the Lord's favour in Moses' eyes. This suggests that, in offering himself, Moses is not only asserting his solidarity with Israel, as argued above, but is more fundamentally asserting his solidarity with the Lord himself.

Finally, Moses' favour in the Lord's eyes has a strong connection with his desire to know God, a desire most clearly manifest in his request for the Lord to 'show me your glory' (33:18). The exact nature of the request has been debated. Terrien (1978: 144), for instance, finds Moses' request egocentric and arrogant, driven by 'the lure of infinity' and 'the lust for absolute knowledge'. It is difficult, however, to reconcile egotism with Moses' declaration that he would die in place of Israel (32:32) and his refusal to take Abraham's place at the head of a new people (32:10–13). It is also difficult to reconcile egotism with the Lord's positive response, giving Moses, at least in part, what he asks for. Piper, Moberly and others suggest that Moses' request is for assurance regarding the Lord's promise of his presence with Israel given in 33:17. Piper argues that Moses' request is driven by the staggering nature of his larger petition, that the Lord take an idolatrous and rebellious people, whose stiff-necked nature cannot abide the Lord's presence (33:5), and grant them his special favour as his own people. As Piper (1979: 207–208) writes,

> the magnitude of his request drives Moses to probe into the very heart of God, as it were, to assure himself that God is in his deepest nature the kind of God who could 'pardon our iniquity and take us for [his] inheritance'. . . . The request to see God's glory should be understood in this context as a desire to have God confirm his astonishing willingness to show his favour to a stiffnecked, idolatrous people.

Moberly (1983: 68) concurs, arguing that Moses presses further into the Lord's character because the fundamental issue of Israel's sinfulness remains unresolved. If the Lord were to come into the midst of the people, it would again mean judgment. Therefore, Moses needs assurance that forgiveness is grounded in the character of God himself.

A further possibility is that the request comes from Moses' desire to know God, particularly triggered by the staggering nature of the mercy the Lord had just granted in 33:17. Curiously, this aspect of Moses' intercession has received little attention in the commentaries.[44] Margaliot (1994: 46), noting the audacity of this request, states that seeing the Lord's face 'is to be equated with an intimate knowledge of his personality, the way a person looks at the face of his fellow-man, enabling him to know to a large extent his thoughts and intentions'. While there are probably other factors at work in Moses' request, such as those suggested above by Piper and Moberly, there is no reason to rule out the straightforward and simple suggestion that Moses' request reveals a desire to know the Lord: 'Show me now your ways, that I may know you' (33:13). Given that the central concern of the book of Exodus is the Lord's desire to be known, it is entirely possible that Moses' request is, at least in part, based on a desire to know the Lord as the Lord desires to be known. Piper sees this, commenting (1979: 214) that 'what was clearly at the heart of Moses' request was a longing to know the glory of God's character from which flowed the mercy that he had just been promised'.[45] If so, there is a personal element at work in Moses' request, but of a nature different from the egotistical sense Terrien posits. Such a desire on Moses' part would also explain his concern for the Lord's glory demonstrated throughout his intercessions.[46]

Israel's repentance

One more consideration is relevant in seeking why the Lord reinstates the covenant with Israel: Israel's repentance. To this point we have looked upon Moses' intercessions, particularly the manner in which Moses appealed to the Lord's honour and worldwide purposes. Never does Moses appeal to anything in Israel, except in calling her the Lord's people. Several interpreters, however, have suggested that Israel's repentance may be the reason for restoring the covenant. For instance, Milgrom finds Israel's stripping off her ornaments in 33:4 to be a demonstration of her contrition, which calls forth the renewal of the covenant in 34:10.[47] While it goes too

[44] Although see Brichto 1983: 28, who translates 33:18 as 'Show Yourself to me, now!', and Cassuto 1967: 435, who renders 33:18 as 'grant me, pray, the privilege of Thy manifesting Thyself to me'.

[45] Although, curiously, he writes elsewhere that 'it is impossible to construe Moses' request in 33:18 as an expression of a desire mystically to enjoy God's essence' (1983: 60). There does not seem to be a reason to choose between the two.

[46] If the above interpretation is correct, it calls into question the comment of Van Seters (1994: 323) that 33:18–23 is 'so entirely out of character with [33:12–17] and with what follows in 34:1–10 that it must be judged as an addition'. Cf. Noth 1962: 257.

[47] Milgrom 1990: 395. Cf. Noth 1962: 254; Krašovec 1999: 96–97; Kaiser 1990: 482.

far to say, as does Jacob (1992: 960), that '[t]hrough this act [of humbly putting off their garments] they designated themselves as the true *b'nei yis-ra-el* and "saved" themselves',[48] it would nevertheless be wrong to rule out Israel's repentance as having significant relevance. Therefore a brief investigation of Israel's repentance and its role in her restoration is warranted.

To understand the nature of Israel's repentance, we must begin with the declaration of the Lord's absence that triggers Israel's response:

> Depart; go up from here, you and the people whom you have brought up out of the land of Egypt, to the land of which I swore to Abraham, Isaac, and Jacob, saying, 'To your offspring I will give it.' I will send an angel before you, and I will drive out the Canaanites, the Amorites, the Hittites, the Perizzites, the Hivites, and the Jebusites. Go up to a land flowing with milk and honey; but I will not go up among you, lest I consume you on the way, for you are a stiff-necked people. (33:1–3)

It is particularly important to note what is granted. Guidance and safe passage are promised. The land is described as 'flowing with milk and honey', indicating that a life of abundance and prosperity lies before Israel. Further, they will travel without the danger of utter destruction, which may come upon them if the Lord were to go with them. The language 'lest I consume you on the way' suggests that the Lord's absence, rather than being a curse, is actually a blessing for Israel, given their stiff-necked nature.[49]

Recognizing what the Lord grants Israel focuses the issue of Israel's repentance. Despite all that is granted, Israel takes the declaration of the Lord's absence as a 'disastrous word' (33:4) and

---

[48] Not only does the text not support this directly, but we have seen that Israel's 'salvation' (or, to this point, non-destruction) has been effected by Moses' intercession, which has not appealed to Israel, but to the Lord himself.

[49] It should be noted here that we need to look no further than Moses' petition of 32:13 to explain the Lord's concessions to Israel. As has been argued above, the Lord relented, in part, based on his concern to be faithful to his prior promises to the patriarchs (reiterated to Israel in 6:8). Faithfulness to those promises required that they should actually enter the land and that that land should be of the (abundant) kind promised. The Lord's sending the angel (to guide and protect) and his refusal to go himself ensures the former, while the reiteration of the phrase 'a land flowing with milk and honey' ensures the latter.

mourns. The implication is that Israel is not primarily interested in the Lord's gifts, but rather in the Lord himself. Israel is not content to enjoy an abundant life in the land if it involves separation from her God. The contrast with 32:1 could not be stronger. In 32:1 Israel charges Aaron to 'make us gods who shall go before us'. The text records no lamenting or mourning for absence of Moses, but rather an aggressive attempt to secure someone to accompany the people into the land. It is apparently not important to Israel who that someone is, as long as they are escorted safely into the land. Israel's response of mourning in 33:4, however, demonstrates a change of heart. No longer is Israel content to be accompanied to the land by just anyone. The people have been granted an angel to take them in safely and are unsatisfied. It must be the Lord. The promise of safety and abundance does not appeal to Israel outside the presence of the Lord in her midst.

This narrative hints further that this change of heart is accompanied by a willingness to obey. Many scholars have pointed to an awkwardness, or for some a contradiction (Jacob 1992: 959), in the relationship between 33:4, where Israel put off her ornaments, and 33:5, where the text records that the Lord told Israel to put off her ornaments. A common critical solution, taken by Childs and others, is to attribute the two verses to different traditions.[50] It is not at all obvious, however, that such a move is required. It is, of course, well within the possible range of Hebrew grammar for the waw at the beginning of 33:5 to introduce an explanation. The text in 33:4 does not demand that Israel's putting off her ornaments be a spontaneous response; it records only that Israel mourned and put off her ornaments. The explanation follows immediately in 33:5 – the Lord commanded Israel to remove her ornaments. The translation adopted by many English Bibles reflects this sense of explanation: 'For the LORD had said to Moses . . .'[51] Israel's putting off her ornaments in response to the Lord's command need not suggest that her mourning was not genuine, nor her repentance artificial. In fact, it may do the opposite. The sin of making and worshipping the golden calf was one of disobedience. 33:4–5 is an instance of Israel's *obedience*. At this point, the text may well be hinting that Israel is now willing

---

[50] Childs (1974: 589) cites several other reasons for assuming different traditions: the appearance of Horeb, rather than Sinai, in 33:6, the plural address of 33:5 (compared to the singular of 33:4), and the form of address of 33:5, which Childs finds common to P.

[51] E.g. ESV, RSV, NRSV, AV, NKJV, NIV, NASB.

to obey the Lord. As we have seen, Israel's obedience is essential to her position as a priestly kingdom and a holy nation. Israel's existence as the Lord's people is unintelligible outside her obedience. Israel's repentance, then, must involve obedience. It would not be unusual, or far-fetched, to see in Israel's putting off her ornaments an example not only of mourning but of a repentant heart willing to obey.[52]

That Israel genuinely repented of her sin is further indicated in her response to the Lord's presence in 33:7–11. The Decalogue, as we have seen, explicitly called for Israel to worship no god but the Lord. As we have seen, the sin of the golden calf was an explicit repudiation of the Lord's command not to worship a graven image (20:5). In 33:7–11, however, Israel worships appropriately. Responding to the Lord's presence, visible in the pillar of cloud, Israel worships (33:10). Furthermore, the text takes pains to qualify the extent of this repentance: 'when *all* the people saw the pillar of cloud . . . *all* the people would rise up and worship' (33:10, my emphases). Israel's repentance is not partial, but corporate.

Does suggesting that Israel's repentance plays a part in the Lord's restoration of Israel somehow provide an exception to the trajectory we have seen thus far in Exodus, that the Lord acts as he does for the sake of his name? There are two reasons why the Lord's responding to Israel's repentance is entirely consistent with, and even grounded by, the commitment to his universal honour. First, as indicated above, Israel's repentance is necessary for her to be reinstated as the Lord's treasured possession, and to function as a priestly kingdom and a holy nation, for her calling is dependent upon her obedience. In other words Israel's repentance is necessary if she is to function within her missionary calling. Secondly, Israel's repentance indicates a *desire* for the Lord that she did not have previously. Again, 32:1 indicated that Israel was primarily interested in the gifts or benefits the Lord had offered: safe passage to the land, and presumably the abundant life associated with it. On the other hand 33:4–11 indicates that Israel is not content with safe passage or the promise of an abundant life in the land apart from the presence of her God. She

---

[52] Several interpreters (e.g. Krašovec 1999: 95; Cassuto 1967: 427) have suggested that Israel's stripping herself of her ornaments is not only a gesture of remorse, but also a repudiation of the very objects which she used to create the calf, a gesture of devotion to the Lord that further supports the notion of Israel's repentance. That Israel's repentance involves practical obedience is confirmed in the tabernacle section following, to be discussed in chapter 7.

is not primarily concerned with the Lord's gifts, or even his threats. She will be content with nothing but the Lord himself. This is a very deep expression of honour, to esteem the presence of a person more than the gifts that person affords. And such an expression of honour by the people whom the Lord has called to be his treasured possession among the nations is entirely consistent with his commitment to make himself known throughout the world.

Conclusion: a proposal for Exodus 34:6–7

The foregoing discussion has suggested that the success of Moses' intercession is grounded in his appeal to the Lord's commitment to be known amongst the nations. Both times Moses appealed to the Lord's commitment to his honour among the nations in 32:11–13 and in 33:12–17 (particularly 33:16) his prayer was granted. The one time Moses did not (32:34) his request was apparently denied. This leads to the conclusion that the Lord restored Israel due to his commitment to being known for who he is throughout the world. On a broader level this suggests that, in Piper's (1983: 90) words concerning God's righteousness in the OT, 'The most fundamental characteristic of God's righteousness is his allegiance to his own name, that is, to his honor and glory.' In other words the Lord's allegiance to himself, here expressed in his purpose to be honoured as God amongst the nations, is the standard by which he makes decisions.

We are now in a position to look at Exodus 34:6–7 and explore some of the theological tensions inherent in the confession. As indicated above, the tension between judgment and mercy has perplexed some interpreters. Yet, having seen how the Lord's commitment to his glory motivates his dealings with Israel in Exodus 32 – 34, the relationship between mercy and judgment becomes more apparent. As is clear from 20:4–6, the Lord must punish idolatry. Failure to do so would not only go against his word of 20:5, but would also implicitly suggest that idolatry was not overly serious. Such a suggestion would, of course, dishonour the Lord himself. Yet as we have seen, idolatry is serious. By trusting in gods that cannot save or satisfy, Israel spurns the Lord who created her for himself. Therefore, the Lord must punish Israel, lest his glory be diminished and his purposes undermined. On the other hand, the Lord must extend mercy in order to uphold his honour,[53] for failure to do so would

---

[53] That the Lord's mercy is grounded in his concern for his honour is abundantly

compromise both his reputation in the eyes of the surrounding nations and his mission to those nations through Israel.[54] In other words the reason that the Lord must punish Israel and the reason that he must extend mercy towards her are the same: to uphold his honour and maintain his purpose to be known. To do one and not the other would be to compromise that honour and thereby undermine that purpose. The Lord must do both. This is exactly what we find in 34:6–7, a statement concerning the Lord's character that explicitly states that he is merciful, forgiving sin, yet will also punish sin. This characterization is entirely consistent with the Lord's dealings with Israel in 32 – 34, both forgiving Israel and renewing the covenant, and punishing her for her idolatry. In both forgiving and punishing Israel, the Lord maintains his honour and preserves his missionary purpose amongst the nations.

Rather than seeing the coexistence of mercy and judgment as a manifestation of the conflicted inner nature of God, as Brueggemann suggests, the above interpretation suggests the opposite: both judgment and mercy flow from the Lord's settled commitment to be honoured as God amongst the nations. This understanding does not, of course, solve all the mysteries in the confession. For instance, although there may be hints in Israel's repentance, Exodus is nowhere explicit concerning who will be punished and who will be shown mercy. In fact, the Lord's words of 33:19, 'I extend grace to whom I will extend grace, and I show mercy to whom I will show mercy' (my tr.), explicitly hide those decisions within the counsel of the Lord alone.[55] However, it does allow the reader to understand that mercy and judgment are not at odds with one another, but are both the logical outworking of the Lord's commitment to be honoured as God. Thus the Lord's 'unwavering commitment to save' (Gowan 1994: 221) can be understood alongside his judgment, for

clear in the OT. Cf. e.g. Deut. 32:26–27; Ezek. 20:8b–9; cf. Josh. 7:8–9; 1 Sam. 12:22; Ps. 25:11; Isa. 43:25; 48:9–11; Dan. 9:18–19.

[54] Abraham's intercession for Sodom (Gen. 18:22–33) is instructive here, for Abraham's petition for the Lord to act justly towards Sodom was based upon the righteousness of the people. The Lord's right to slay the wicked is never questioned. Although he significantly reduced the number of righteous needed to save the city (and the text may imply that the Lord might have made further concessions), Abraham's petition did not save Sodom. On the contrary, Moses appealed to the Lord in an entirely different manner, grounding his requests not in the righteousness of the people, but in the interests of the Lord himself. That the Lord had already forged a public connection with Israel, and not with Sodom, may explain the difference in the Lord's response in each case.

[55] Piper 1979: 210; cf. Childs 1974: 596.

the Lord makes himself known in both. In answer to Raitt's question concerning why God forgives, he forgives that he might be known among the nations. The above argument would suggest that Andersen (1986: 51) overstates his case when he asserts that 'there is no justification for his compassion and kindness, and his *hesed* is completely incomprehensible'. Even though mystery concerning the Lord's *hesed* remains (33:19), the incident with the golden calf suggests that the Lord's *hesed* is not completely incomprehensible, but can, at some level, be understood. That mercy is undeserved and given freely does not mean that the Lord has no discernible reasons for extending it. Likewise, Dentan's suggestion that 34:6–7 was added to balance out an otherwise unattractive picture of the Lord becomes unnecessary, for the Lord's exercise of judgment and his extension of mercy flow from the same settled commitment. It is the same Lord who does both. Exodus 34:6–7 simply reflects the manner in which the Lord has acted all along.

Here we return to the fundamental tension ('contradiction') Brueggemann sees between the Lord's commitment to Israel and his commitment to himself. According to Brueggemann, these two commitments 'are not fully harmonized here, and perhaps never are anywhere in the Old Testament' (1997: 227). The emphasis on the Lord's concern to be honoured as God amongst the nations could leave the impression that the Lord is self-serving, with no genuine concern for Israel or the nations.[56] Such a reading would, of course, be false to Exodus. The Lord does exhibit genuine concern for the people. Remembering the covenant, which as I have argued is bound up with his missionary concern to bless the nations in Genesis 12, is triggered by the cries of his oppressed people (2:23–25; 3:7–8; 6:5), and the land promised to Israel is an abundant land (3:8; 33:3). The law, as we have seen, is meant for Israel's blessing, for the instruction concerning peaceful life together is an expression of the Lord's generosity. The plain sense of 34:6 speaks of the Lord's grace, mercy and willingness to forgive. The character of the Lord so made known works itself in real mercy – Israel is not destroyed, but is in fact fully reinstated into her covenant relationship with the Lord (34:10). The above reading of 32 – 34 suggests that the Lord's commitment to his glory and Israel's good are not at odds with one another, but in fact fit naturally together: *the Lord is for Israel precisely because he is for*

---

[56] This is the impression left by Eslinger (1991), who argues that the Lord's actions in the exodus are rooted in himself, with little or no appreciable concern for Israel.

himself – that he might be known for who he is, and his purposes realized. Perhaps the most striking thing to be learned from Moses' intercession is that the Lord moves in mercy towards Israel on the grounds of his commitment to himself – his reputation and his purposes. The relationship between the Lord's mercy and his concern for himself expressed in Exodus is similarly expressed by Ezekiel, later reflecting upon the Lord's response to Israel in the wilderness:

> But the house of Israel rebelled against me in the wilderness. They did not walk in my statutes but rejected my rules, by which, if a person does them, he shall live; and my Sabbaths they greatly profaned.
> Then I said I would pour out my wrath upon them in the wilderness, to make a full end of them. But I acted for the sake of my name, that it should not be profaned in the sight of the nations, in whose sight I had brought them out. Moreover, I swore to them in the wilderness that I would not bring them into the land that I had given them, a land flowing with milk and honey, the most glorious of all lands, because they rejected my rules and did not walk in my statutes, and profaned my Sabbaths; for their heart went after their idols. Nevertheless, my eye spared them, and I did not destroy them or make a full end of them in the wilderness. (Ezek. 20:13–17)

One of the central messages of Exodus 32 – 34 is that it is precisely because the Lord is for himself that he is for Israel.

Exodus 34:6–7 leaves us with one other problem that, in its context in Exodus, is unresolved. In Exodus mercy and grace have been extended as complete forgiveness is offered, the covenant is restored and the Lord's presence is again promised to Israel. That being the case, how are we to understand the Lord's declaration that he will not clear the guilty?

The answer to this question is not given in Exodus, and is only made known as the Lord continues to make himself known through the Scriptures, revealing ultimately in Jesus what was previously seen only in shadows (e.g. Heb. 10:1; Col. 2:17). Here we come to yet another allusion to Exodus 34:6–7, this time in the NT, the prologue of John's Gospel: 'And the Word became flesh and dwelt among us, and we have seen his glory, glory as of the only Son from the Father, full of grace and truth' (John 1:14).

There are several reasons to see John 1:14 as a direct allusion to

Exodus 34:6–7.[57] First, the language of 'grace and truth' takes the reader back to the 'steadfast love and faithfulness' of Exodus 34:6.[58] Secondly, the collusion in John 1:14–18 of 'dwelling', 'glory', Moses, law and God being made known is likewise found in Exodus 32 – 34, where all these terms are at stake. In Exodus, as we have seen, God's glory is revealed precisely in declaring his character, including his abounding steadfast love and faithfulness. The Lord's glory is his goodness in both Exodus (33:18–19) and John (1:14). The Word that 'dwelt among us' brings to mind the precise issue at stake in Exodus 33 – 34: How can the Lord be present among his people who have rejected him, having exchanged his glory for another? The mention of Moses and the law both draw the reader back to Exodus, for Exodus is where the law, initially, is both given and broken. Finally, as we have seen, the issues of seeing (and not seeing) God and of the Lord's making himself known are central to Exodus 33 in particular. In short, it is not just the language but the thrust of these chapters that call together John 1:14–18 and Exodus 32 – 34.

But where does this take us? John claims, 'we have seen his glory . . . full of grace and truth'. The glory of God is central throughout the Gospel of John. As we have seen above, the Lord's revealing his glory in Exodus indicates that he makes himself known for who he is. The same is true of glory in John. When Jesus makes his glory manifest, he makes known who he is (e.g. John 2:11; 11:4). When he makes manifest the Father's glory, he makes the Father known for who he is (e.g. 17:4, 6). With this in mind, the moment in which the Father and the Son are glorified becomes of unspeakable importance:

'The hour has come for the Son of Man to be glorified. Truly, truly, I say to you, unless a grain of wheat falls into the earth and dies, it remains alone; but if it dies, it bears much fruit. . . .

'Now is my soul troubled. And what shall I say? "Father, save me from this hour"? But for this purpose I have come to this hour. Father, glorify your name.' Then a voice came from heaven: 'I have glorified it, and I will glorify it again.'

---

[57] For a lengthy and detailed case establishing this connection, see Tsutserov 2009.

[58] This is despite the fact that John uses *charis*, where the LXX translates *ḥesed* in Exod. 34:6 with *polyeleos*. Tsutserov (2009: 141–145) observes that *charis* brings the reader back to Exod. 33, in that the concentration of *charis* four times in John 1:14–18 corresponds to its sixfold occurrence in Exod. 33:12 – 34:10. In this way John's use of *charis* suggests an even stronger allusion to Exod. 34:6 than *eleos* might have suggested.

The crowd that stood there and heard it said that it had thundered. Others said, 'An angel has spoken to him.' Jesus answered, 'This voice has come for your sake, not mine. Now is the judgment of this world; now will the ruler of this world be cast out. And I, when I am lifted up from the earth, will draw all people to myself.' He said this to show by what kind of death he was going to die. (John 12:23–24, 27–33)

Here we have the moment that God is most completely known, as the Father and the Son are both to be glorified in the crucifixion of Jesus. This hour is the hour in which the glory of Christ, who is the Word who was God and with God, is manifest in grace and truth. This grace and truth, however, is expressed in the carrying out of *judgment*, as the ruler of this world is cast out, and as Jesus, as the Lamb of God, bears the sin of the world (John 1:29). In other words the moment when God is most completely made known, in the Father and the Son, is the moment when, simultaneously, mercy is extended and judgment is executed.

How does this address the question that Exodus 34:6–7 leaves us? Did not God in effect clear the guilty by forgiving Israel? Yes, but only because he did not clear the guilty. Simply put, the guilty are not cleared, but are in fact judged – in Christ. 'Now is the judgment of this world' clearly indicates that the world is judged, in (at least) two ways. First, the evil of the world is shown for what it is: 'And this is the judgment: the light has come into the world, and people loved the darkness rather than the light because their deeds were evil' (John 3:19). Secondly, as declared by John the Baptist, Jesus is 'the Lamb of God, who bears the sin of the world!' (John 1:29, my tr.). The glory of God is again the goodness of God, as Jesus himself bears the sin of the world, exposing sin for what it is, and yet taking it upon himself so that 'I, when I am lifted up from the earth, will draw all people to myself' (John 12:32). In Christ the presence of God is again available to humanity, the world the Son came to save (3:16–17). In this way Jesus manifests the name of God (John 17:6). It is no coincidence that the most complete description of the Lord's character to be found in the Scriptures is precisely that which is revealed in Jesus, where God is most fully made known.

Looking at Jesus to address the issue of judgment posed by Exodus 34:6–7 raises one more issue that must be handled carefully, lest we read the New Testament back into the Old. How are we to understand Moses' offer to take Israel's judgment upon himself?

There are at least two reasons to see Moses' offer as akin to Jesus' death on the cross. First, according to the flow of Moses' petitions, his death would have served the purpose of sparing both the people and the Lord's honour. In other words should the Lord visit the sin of the people upon Moses, the people would have been spared and the promises could proceed without injury to the Lord's reputation or his purposes. Clear from the NT, and particularly evident in John 12 (discussed above), is that Jesus' death served both the glory of God and the good of his people.

Secondly, here Moses is showing his solidarity with both the Lord and the people. As we have seen, Moses will not allow himself to be separated from Israel, but rather insists that any favour the Lord grants him also be granted to Israel (33:13, 15–16). Yet Moses also demonstrates solidarity with the Lord in that he will not allow the Lord's honour or purposes to be compromised in the sight of the nations. Here Moses shows himself truly to be a high priest. He represents God to the people, shattering the tablets before Israel in hot anger, carrying out the Lord's command to kill the unfaithful in the camp, speaking the word of the Lord to the people. He represents the people before God, petitioning fervently and repeatedly that they not only be spared, but also be forgiven and restored fully to the covenant and promise of the land. Yet Moses presses even further, representing *God* before God in the manner in which he seeks to persuade the Lord to act for the sake of his own name.

Jesus likewise demonstrates solidarity with both the Lord and with his people. In what has become known as his high priestly prayer, Jesus (praying to the Father before his death) emphasizes both his oneness with the Father, and his oneness with his disciples and those who would believe through them.

> I do not ask for these only, but also for those who will believe in me through their word, that they may all be one, just as you, Father, are in me, and I in you, that they also may be in us, so that the world may believe that you have sent me. The glory that you have given me I have given to them, that they may be one even as we are one, I in them and you in me, that they may become perfectly one, so that the world may know that you sent me and loved them even as you loved me. Father, I desire that they also, whom you have given me, may be with me where I am, to see my glory that you have given me because you loved me before the foundation of the world.

> O righteous Father, even though the world does not know
> you, I know you, and these know that you have sent me. I
> made known to them your name, and I will continue to make
> it known, that the love with which you have loved me may be
> in them, and I in them. (John 17:20–26)

It is precisely this oneness with the Father, and his oneness with his disciples, that takes Jesus to the cross.

If the above reasoning is faithful to the text, then an important question is raised: Why did the Lord reject Moses' offer to take upon himself the sin of the people? In other words why Jesus and not Moses? While Exodus is silent on the matter, we might well infer, based on numerous passages in the NT, that Moses was *insufficient* for such a task. It is the 'Lamb of God', the 'Word made flesh and [who] dwelt among us', who is able to bear the sin of the world. Or, to quote Paul, 'For our sake he made him to be sin *who knew no sin*, so that in him we might become the righteousness of God' (2 Cor. 5:21, my emphasis). Again, nowhere is this suggested in Exodus. Rather, having read the Lord's refusal for Moses to take the place of the people in Exodus, the reader of the NT, seeing Jesus doing that exact thing, may well look back at Exodus and ask why Jesus would be sufficient when Moses apparently was not. To ask such a question raises the central question in the NT: 'Who do you say that I am?' (Matt. 16:15). In the end Jesus cannot be known for who he is apart from the cross.

We return a final time to Brueggemann. The Lord's glory is being known for who he is. To the extent that the Lord is, in Brueggemann's words, for his own self, it bears remembering that the Lord's commitment to his own glory is manifest precisely in his graciousness, his goodness. Or to say it differently, God's selfishness is manifest in his *selflessness*, shown most supremely in the Son's pouring himself out for the glory of God and for the blessing of the world. What we saw in Exodus 1 – 15 remains true in Exodus 32 – 34, even if taken a step deeper: to know the Name of the Lord is to know him as redeemer.

Chapter Seven

The tabernacle construction (Exod. 35 – 40)

The glory of God is man fully alive. If the revelation of God through creation already brings life to all living beings on the earth, how much more will the manifestation of the Father by the Word bring life to those who see God.

(Irenaeus, *Against Heresies* 20.7)

This quote from Irenaeus, the famous second-century bishop of Lyons, is often quoted, for it speaks to something profound concerning the will of God for his people. God is glorified when man lives life to the full, a sentiment echoing Jesus' own desire for his people: 'I came that they may have life and have it abundantly' (John 10:10).

Irenaeus' words, so quoted, of course beg a question: What does it mean to be fully alive? Irenaeus defines life as that which is brought to those who see God, the Father being made known through the Son, the Word of God. Life lived to the full is not therefore a life of fun and adventure (although it may be), but rather a life lived in reference to God, given to those who see him. Yet, as we have seen in the last chapters, although the Lord may dwell among his people, his glory remains hidden. In response to Moses' request 'Please show me your glory,' the Lord says:

'[Y]ou cannot see my face, for man shall not see me and live.' And the LORD said, 'Behold, there is a place by me where you shall stand on the rock, and while my glory passes by I will put you in a cleft of the rock, and I will cover you with my hand until I have passed by. Then I will take away my hand, and you shall see my back, but my face shall not be seen.' (Exod. 33:20–23)

According to Irenaeus, life is given to those who see God. And yet the glory of God remains hidden, at least in part, even for Moses.[1]

The problem: tabernacle theology and canonical order

The problem I will address in this final section is rather a tendency. As previously observed, treatments of the tabernacle material in Exodus tend to address the two sections together. Enns (2000), for instance, discusses the two sections jointly, giving a separate treatment of 40:34–38 at the end. Similarly, Childs (1974) focuses his discussion on 25 – 31, and gives fewer than five pages of commentary to 35 – 40. The reason for such is understandable, given that 35 – 40 largely repeat verbatim 25 – 31.[2] And, to a certain extent, I have followed that practice, particularly in my observations concerning the tabernacle and creation in chapter 5, where I included 35 – 40 in the discussion.[3] However, the practice of treating the tabernacle sections together can also stem from a lack of appreciation of the canonical form of Exodus. One modern expression of this tendency, alluded to earlier, is the impulse to read the tabernacle material in the context of P, whether in an effort to discern the 'theology of P' or to seek to understand Israel's cultic worship. That such critical scholars do not consider 32 – 34 to be part of P has led to the practice of treating the tabernacle material without reference to 32 – 34.[4] That 32 – 34

---

[1] Although cf. 24:11 and 33:11, which stand in tension with 33:20. For a discussion of the delicate and mysterious matter of seeing the Lord in Exodus, see Moberly 1983: 79–83.

[2] There are differences between 25 – 31 and 35 – 40 as well, both in the details and in the order of construction. See Childs 1974: 633–634. The differences are more acute in the LXX, prompting some to suggest that 25 – 31 and 35 – 40 were translated by different hands. See Wade 2003.

[3] Many of the theological insights concerning the tabernacle discussed in reference to 25 – 31 are equally appropriate here. For example, as discussed in chapter 5, the tabernacle functioned as a microcosm of the universe, with the Lord ruling and all creation being in compliance. One of the ways in which this microcosm is apparent in Exodus is the connection between the creation account in Gen. 1 and the completion of the construction of the tabernacle in Exod. 39 – 40. Because of the creation themes apparent in 25 – 31, and because of the close relationship between 25 – 31 and 35 – 40, I have already discussed this connection between the tabernacle and creation, and will therefore not revisit the discussion here. It bears mention here, however, since the connection between Gen. 1 and the tabernacle material is not brought out fully until 35 – 40. As in the case of many treatments of the tabernacle, approaching the tabernacle material as such accounts for the brevity of this chapter compared to chapter 5.

[4] E.g. Van Seters 1994: 291.

is in the midst of the tabernacle material, however, is actually of great significance in understanding important theological aspects of the tabernacle. Relevant here is the simple principle, articulated by Rosenzweig and others, that 'it is impossible to transmit the content without at the same time transmitting the form. How something is said is not peripheral to what is said.'[5] Likewise, commenting on the first tabernacle section, Knierim (1995: 115) writes:

> This structure [of 25:1 – 30:10] demands much more than our usual recognition of the redactional or compositional technique of the writers. It especially prevents us from quickly setting aside the 'redactional framework' as a mere shell for the important essence of the text, as if we possessed any essence without this framework!

To the extent that Rosenzweig or Knierim's comments are true, to discuss the tabernacle while neglecting 32 – 34 necessarily diminishes its theological impact.

This chapter will seek to demonstrate how the position of the golden-calf narrative in the midst of the tabernacle material is crucial in understanding the theological importance of both sections. Therefore, the scope will be brief, resulting in a shorter treatment of 35 – 40 than of 25 – 31. Rather than revisiting many of the theological discussions of chapter 5 concerning the details and function of the tabernacle, this section will focus on two important ways that the theology of the tabernacle is impacted by the golden-calf narrative.

The priority of presence in the Lord's mission

The Lord's presence is crucial throughout the book of Exodus. The Egyptian deliverance was accomplished because the Lord fulfilled his promise to Moses that 'I am with you' (3:12). The Lord trained Israel in the wilderness so that Israel would trust the Lord's presence with her, as her protector and provider. And, as we saw in chapter 5, two of the most important theological statements in the tabernacle material have to do with the Lord's presence:

> Let them make me a sanctuary, that I may dwell in their midst. (25:8)

[5] Buber and Rosenzweig 1994: 61.

I will dwell among the people of Israel and will be their God.
And they shall know that I am the LORD their God, who
brought them out from the land of Egypt that I might dwell
among them. I am the LORD their God. (29:45–46)

As suggested by the above verses, the tabernacle material of 25 – 31
indicates both the Lord's desire to dwell among Israel and the means
by which he might do so.

The golden-calf section brings the issue of presence into particularly sharp focus, making plain the necessity of the Lord's presence
both for Israel's life and her mission. It is the issue of the Lord's
presence that drives the people to approach Aaron: 'Up, make
us gods who shall go before us. As for this Moses, the man who
brought us up out of the land of Egypt, we do not know what has
become of him' (32:1). It is not necessarily dissatisfaction with the
Lord or with Moses that leads Israel to seek other gods, but rather
the people's need for someone to lead them into the land.[6] The
people are not faulted for their anxiety over Moses' absence, nor
for their desire for a discernible presence, but rather for seeking
that presence apart from the Lord and outside the boundaries that
he established explicitly in the Decalogue. In fact, their desire for
a discernible presence is entirely appropriate, as suggested by the
fact that the Lord was instituting the tabernacle precisely so that he
could dwell in Israel's midst. One of the ironies here is that, at the
very time that the Lord is instructing Moses concerning the practical means by which he would be present to Israel, Israel was seeking
the presence of other gods. In so doing, Israel rejects the Lord. As
Childs (1974: 564) notes, in demanding a calf 'the people demand a
substitute for Yahweh himself'.

As we have seen, without his presence with Israel, the Lord's plans
for Israel are brought to an end. This is evident from two perspectives. From Israel's perspective, the people have been consciously
dependent on the Lord from the beginning. In fact, it was precisely
the promise of the Lord's presence that encouraged Israel to leave
Egypt in the first place. The Lord's response to Moses' misgivings
concerning his own abilities is answered by the promise 'I am with
you' (3:12). As argued in chapter 2, Moses envisions Israel's having
similar misgivings, which prompts the Lord to reveal his name in

---

[6] Greenberg 1971a: 1061 suggests that the charge is driven by the people's fear that
Moses had died, leaving Israel without a leader.

such a way that Israel knows he is present with them (3:14–15). Furthermore, in a time of distress the Lord sought to instil confidence in Israel precisely by promising his presence with Israel (in bringing her into the land, 6:6–8). Israel's confidence, and ultimately her ability to walk out of bondage into freedom, comes in knowing that the Lord is with her.

From the Lord's perspective the mission he intends for Israel likewise comes to an end without his presence with Israel. As we have seen above, after the golden-calf incident the Lord finally and completely restores the covenant in response to Moses' argument that the Lord's intended mission to the nations will come to naught if he is not present with Israel as they go to the land (33:16). Until the golden-calf incident the need for the Lord's presence with Israel, for the sake of his purposes amongst the nations, has not been as starkly apparent. From this point onwards it becomes clear that Israel's faithful obedience depends upon knowing the Lord's presence in her midst. Indeed, as Israel's idolatry stemmed from believing the Lord to be absent, so does unfaithfulness throughout the Scriptures. Examples abound.

> The guilt of the house of Israel and Judah is exceedingly great. The land is full of blood, and the city full of injustice. For they say, 'The LORD has forsaken the land, and the LORD does not see.' (Ezek. 9:9; cf. Pss 10:11; 94:6–7; Isa. 47:10)

In fact, reaching back to the beginning, one could infer that at least one reason why Adam and Eve ate the fruit in Eden was simply because the Lord was not there.

Thus, from both the Lord's and Israel's perspective, the issues raised in 32 – 34 make it abundantly clear that the Lord's dwelling presence with Israel is foundational for Israel's relationship to the Lord as his people and the ongoing purpose to which she is called.

The repentance of Israel

The connection between the Lord's presence with Israel and her faithfulness leads to a second point. A second way that 32 – 34 and the tabernacle material inform one another concerns Israel's repentance. As we have seen in 19 – 24, and most particularly in 19:4–6, the fulfilment of Israel's vocation as a priestly kingdom and holy nation depends upon her obedience. While 32 – 34 suggests that the Lord will not utterly forsake Israel for disobedience, the necessity of obedience has not changed if Israel is to know the Lord's presence and fulfil her calling. If Israel is to know the Lord and fulfil her purpose, she must repent.

As argued in the last chapter, Exodus 33:4–11 indicates that Israel repented of her sin with the calf, the people stripping themselves of their ornaments and mourning at the withdrawal of the Lord's presence. Two observations in the latter tabernacle material confirm that Israel repented. First, Israel brings voluntary freewill offerings for the construction of the tabernacle. The detail and repetition here are important, and worth quoting at length:

> And they came, everyone whose heart stirred him, and everyone whose spirit moved him, and brought the LORD's contribution to be used for the tent of meeting, and for all its service, and for the holy garments. So they came, both men and women. All who were of a willing heart brought brooches and earrings and signet rings and armlets, all sorts of gold objects, every man dedicating an offering of gold to the LORD. And everyone who possessed blue or purple or scarlet yarns or fine linen or goats' hair or tanned rams' skins or goatskins brought them. Everyone who could make a contribution of silver or bronze brought it as the LORD's contribution. And everyone who possessed acacia wood of any use in the work brought it. And every skillful woman spun with her hands, and they all brought what they had spun in blue and purple and scarlet yarns and fine twined linen. All the women whose hearts stirred them to use their skill spun the goats' hair. And the leaders brought onyx stones and stones to be set, for the ephod and for the breastpiece, and spices and oil for the light, and for the anointing oil, and for the fragrant incense. All the men and women, the people of Israel, whose heart moved them to bring anything for the work that the LORD had commanded by Moses to be done brought it as a freewill offering to the LORD. (Exod. 35:21–29)

The description of the offerings is given in great detail, the text carefully noting both the attitude and the scope of the people. The people's attitude is emphasized in the repeated comment that only the willing came to give, emphasizing the gifts were not brought out of compulsion but given gladly. Additionally, the text seems to indicate that all the people were willing, as suggested by the comment that all who were able gave to the construction. This practice continues, according to the text, until the people are actually commanded to stop giving when they have brought enough (36:3–7). The implication is that Israel participated willingly, even gladly, in the construction of the tabernacle. As has often been noted, where the people once gave their gold for the calf, now they freely give it to the Lord. The contrast between Israel's giving to the calf and giving to the tabernacle suggests wholehearted repentance, along the lines of Jesus' later words 'where your treasure is, there your heart will be also' (Matt. 6:21; cf. 2 Cor. 8:1–5).

That Israel repented for her sin with the calf is suggested in another manner. Among the most notable characteristics of the tabernacle material, alluded to above, is the almost verbatim repetition in many places between the tabernacle instructions and the tabernacle construction. Several reasons for this have been suggested. For instance, Goldingay (2003: 415–416) suggests that the repetition suggests the Lord's generosity, that his intention to dwell among Israel had not been withdrawn due to the golden-calf incident, while Blenkinsopp (1997: 113) argues:

> The detailed account of the implementation of the visionary instructions (chs. 35 – 40) was probably the work of a clerical editor anxious to make the point that the instructions retained their validity in spite of the fact that Aaron had compromised himself in the Golden Calf incident.

While there may be elements of truth in both suggestions, more seems to be intended.

The simplest reason, noted by many interpreters, is that the repetition emphasizes Israel's careful obedience. According to Levine (1965: 310), 'The ancient Israelites demonstrated their obedience to God by carrying out his commands with precision and dispatch.' This obedience is stressed, according to Levine, not only by the general repetition throughout the latter tabernacle section, but also through two other literary devices: the repetition of the prescriptive introduction in 35:4–19 and the presence of what he calls the compliance formula ('as/which the LORD commanded Moses' and variants).[7] Again, the contrast with the calf incident is striking.

---

[7] Exod. 35:4, 29; 36:1; 38:22; 39:1, 5, 7, 21, 26, 29, 31, 43; 40:19, 21, 23, 25, 27, 29, 32.

Where there has been flagrant disobedience, now there is whole-hearted devotion.

Conclusion: the glory of God among the nations

The final indication that Israel repented is given in the final words of Exodus: 'Then the cloud covered the tent of meeting, and the glory of the LORD filled the tabernacle' (40:34). Here is the manifestation of the Lord's presence among Israel: the return of the cloud, which, throughout Exodus, has been the manifestation of the Lord's presence (13:21–22; 14:19, 24; 16:10; 19:9, 16; 24:15–16, 18; 33:9; 34:5). The Lord's presence in the tabernacle serves as evidence of Israel's complete restoration. While the Lord had promised that the covenant would be restored (34:10), the Lord's dwelling in the tabernacle becomes the practical realization of that promise. Thus Noth's (1962: 283) comment that the appearance of the cloud 'gave the sign of legitimacy and approval to the newly-built sanctuary', while true, does not go far enough. Further, the practical effect of the Lord's presence, as we are reminded in 33:16, makes Israel distinct, and therefore in a position to fulfil the commission given her to be a priestly kingdom and a holy nation (19:4–6).

The reason that it is crucial to read the latter tabernacle chapters in their canonical order, particularly after Israel's sin with the golden calf, is that they raise questions that get to the very centre of the message of the Bible. What will be the Lord's response to sin? How can the Lord dwell with a people who have walked apart from him? How will the Lord restore his original purposes in creation – to know his people, manifesting his glory while doing them good?

At the close of Exodus Israel has repented, the covenant has been restored, the tabernacle has been built lavishly and willingly, the glory of the Lord has filled the tabernacle and Israel is now poised, the Lord being with her, to carry out her priestly calling to the nations, making the Lord's name known throughout the earth. Yet, even amidst all indications that all has been restored, there remains one hint in Exodus that all is not yet as it should be: Moses is not able to enter the tabernacle (40:35). Thus the problem of sin is reintroduced, Exodus suggesting that the Lord, dwelling in the tabernacle, still cannot dwell directly among his people. This is precisely the reason for Isaiah's cry upon seeing the Lord in his temple: 'Woe is me! For I am lost; for I am a man of unclean lips, and I dwell in the midst of a people of unclean lips; for my eyes have seen the King, the LORD of hosts!' (Isa. 6:5). The restoration in Exodus is real, yet partial. A level of separation still remains.

Once again, that which Exodus speaks of in shadows is brought to fulfilment as the Scriptures continue to make the Lord known. A constant theme throughout the Bible, we see the Lord dwelling with Israel a final time at the end of Revelation:

> I saw the holy city, new Jerusalem, coming down out of heaven from God, prepared as a bride adorned for her husband. And I heard a loud voice from the throne saying, 'Behold, the dwelling place of God is with man. He will dwell with them, and they will be his people, and God himself will be with them as their God.' (Rev. 21:2–4)

While the language of God's dwelling with man is suggested in the tabernacle, the image of a bride adorned for her husband suggests an intimacy impossible in the OT, where a veil shielded the presence of God from the people. In effect, this takes us right back to the garden of Eden, the original sanctuary, where the Lord dwelt and where he met with Adam and Eve, walking with them in the cool of the day. How did we get here?

Again we turn to John 1:14, 'And the Word became flesh and dwelt among us, and we have seen his glory, glory as of the only Son from the Father, full of grace and truth.' In a reference to the tabernacle, Jesus 'tabernacled' (*eskēnōsen*) among his people, fully revealing the glory of God. As we saw in the last chapter, it is in the death of Jesus that the glory of God – the glory of both the Father and the Son – is most clearly revealed. It is also through the death of Jesus that the barrier between God and humanity is removed, as the Word made flesh, full of grace and truth, bears the sin of the world. To use an image from Matthew to illustrate, it is at the death of Jesus that 'the curtain of the temple was torn in two, from top to bottom' (Matt. 27:51; cf. Mark 15:38). The veil guarding the Holy of Holies, with its two cherubim, is in Jesus' death removed, restoring access to God that was characteristic of life in Eden, but impossible since Genesis 3.[8] The point is that, in Jesus, and particularly in his death, fellowship with God is fully restored.

---

[8] For an extended and careful argument that the veil referred to in Matthew is the *pārōket* veil shielding the Holy of Holies, see Gurtner 2007.

This is the point of Jesus' first miracle in John 2, where Jesus 'manifested his glory' by changing water (incidentally, for purification – 2:6) into wine at a wedding feast in Cana. Before extending the wedding celebration by providing more wine (taking the part of the groom – 2:9; cf. 3:29), Jesus is clear with his mother that 'My hour has not yet come' (2:4). It is not until his death that Jesus declares that his hour has come, the hour when he would manifest his glory in full (12:23, 27; 17:1), cleansing his bride and inaugurating the ultimate wedding feast, where he as the bridegroom celebrates a feast, having taken his bride to himself (cf. Eph. 5:25–27). The Lord is present with his people. Thus the presence of the Lord with his people is not simply the means of the mission, but *is itself* the mission. The Lord will be known for who he is, upon whom man can look and not be ashamed. In Paul's words, 'For God, who said, "Let light shine out of darkness," has shone in our hearts to give the light of the knowledge of the glory of God in the face of Jesus Christ' (2 Cor. 4:6). To return to Irenaeus, the glory of God can be seen, face to face – in the face of Jesus. Then, without barrier, God may dwell with all people who are his in Christ Jesus.

Thus, while partial and provisional, at the close of Exodus we have a convergence of Israel's obedience, God's dwelling among his people, and mission, a convergence that will be fulfilled in Christ Jesus. It is in him that the Lord's vision, spoken through Ezekiel in the language of Exodus, will finally be realized:

> They shall not defile themselves any more with their idols and their detestable things, or with any of their transgressions. But I will save them from all the backsliding in which they have sinned, and will cleanse them; and they shall be my people, and I will be their God.
>
> My servant David shall be king over them, and they shall have one shepherd. They shall walk in my rules and be careful to obey my statutes. They shall dwell in the land that I gave to my servant Jacob, where your fathers lived. They and their children and their children's children shall dwell there for ever, and David my servant shall be their prince for ever. I will make a covenant of peace with them. It shall be an everlasting covenant with them. And I will set them in their land and multiply them, and will set my sanctuary in their midst for evermore. My dwelling place shall be with them,

and I will be their God, and they shall be my people. Then the nations will know that I am the LORD who sanctifies Israel, when my sanctuary is in their midst for evermore. (Ezek. 37:23–28)

Conclusion

Exodus is about knowing the Lord. This work has sought to demonstrate this on two levels. First, I have argued that the Lord's commitment to be known as God throughout the earth is the motivation driving everything he does in Exodus, from the manner in which he delivers Israel from Egypt to the reason he gives Israel the law, to the way he responds to Israel's idolatry. Thus the missionary 'heart' of Exodus speaks to both the Lord's governing commitment to be known as God throughout the world and the way that this missionary commitment unites the various materials in the book. The Lord has always had a heart for the world, including a very particular means by which He has sought to reach it.

Secondly, I have argued for the importance of canonical context in interpretation. This also is about knowing God, for if God's people are to know him as he has made himself known, then the manner in which we approach the Scriptures is of great importance. This does not mean that there is no place for critical scholarship, but is rather a recognition that often the impulses at work in critical scholarship may encourage the exegete to settle for a critical solution to explain a theological problem that needs more time, more thought and more prayer. What Proverbs says about wisdom can helpfully be understood as a manner of approaching the Scriptures:

> My son, if you receive my words
>   and treasure up my commandments with you,
> making your ear attentive to wisdom
>   and inclining your heart to understanding;
> yes, if you call out for insight
>   and raise your voice for understanding,
> if you seek it like silver
>   and search for it as for hidden treasures,

then you will understand the fear of the LORD
and find the knowledge of God.

(Prov. 2:1–5)

The implicit hope of this work is for patience and humility as we
approach the Scriptures, realizing that there is much that we don't
understand, and that understanding the Bible takes time.

At the beginning of this work I suggested that our understanding of biblical mission may be distorted if the mission of the church
is considered apart from its expression in the OT. The question of
what it means to follow Jesus' Great Commission is not a NT question alone, or even primarily. In that light the following are several
examples of the way understanding mission from the perspective of
Exodus can help the church bear faithful witness to the Lord.

Exodus demonstrates that mission is tied to community, an
emphasis that can be underappreciated if the Great Commission is
read apart from Israel's call in the OT. The means by which Israel
carried out her missionary calling as a priestly nation was through
keeping the law. What this entailed, in the end, is made plain in
Jesus' summary of the law. Asked 'which is the great commandment
in the Law?' Jesus answers:

You shall love the Lord your God with all your heart and
with all your soul and with all your mind. This is the great and
first commandment. And a second is like it: You shall love
your neighbour as yourself. On these two commandments
depend all the Law and the Prophets. (Matt. 22:37–40)

Loving one another is explicitly foundational for mission for the NT
as well. To obey the call to make disciples, we do well to remember
Jesus' words to his disciples: 'By this all people will know that you
are my disciples, if you have love for one another' (John 13:35). The
practical effect of such love is well illustrated in that, in response to
the Christian community described in Acts 2:42–47, 'the Lord added
to their number day by day those who were being saved' (Acts 2:47).
The mission of the church is not imparting information (admittedly
overstated), but rather living in such a way that the nations take
notice. This is the call of both Israel and the church.

The practical effect of recognizing the importance of community
is (at least) twofold. First, it reminds us that the church *is* before she
does. A church busy about mission that does not love God or one

another builds upon a foundation that cannot last. Yes, the Lord may cause good to come out of such work (see e.g. Phil. 1:15–18), but it is not the way the Lord seeks to bring the nations to himself. In the words of the third commandment, the church bears the Name of the Lord, whether she does it faithfully or unfaithfully, to the blessing or blasphemy of his name (Rom. 2:17). Secondly, it suggests that endeavours that may be considered evangelistic are best rooted in community. Noteworthy is John's given reason for proclaiming the life they know in Jesus: 'that which we have seen and heard we proclaim also to you, so that you too may have fellowship with us; and indeed our fellowship is with the Father and with his Son Jesus Christ' (1 John 1:3). The call is not simply to believe in Jesus, but to take one's place in the fellowship of God's people, fellowship shared with the Father and the Son. To be sure, sometimes community is sparse, particularly when the church moves into areas where there is little or no Christian community. But the witness of a people who love the Lord, love one another, and love their neighbours remains the foundation from which the Lord's mission to be known goes forth.

This leads to a second point, the cost of mission. Exodus reminds us that the cost involved is, in the end, personal, for the Lord will bring his people through trial as he seeks to fit for himself a priestly people who will be holy as the Lord is holy. Not only is this a check to various forms of what has been called 'the prosperity gospel', but it serves as an encouragement not to view difficulty (necessarily) as God's disfavour, but perhaps as a means by which he strengthens a people. God's mission, as he intends it, goes forth as the church is the church, fit for her calling through trial. Piper's (2002: 79) assessment of the modern church is worth considering:

> A typical emotional response to trouble in the church is to think, *If that's the way they feel about me, then I'll just find another church.* We see very few healthy, happy examples today whose lives spell out in flesh and blood the rugged words, 'Count it all joy, my brothers, when you meet trials of various kinds' (James 1:2). When historians list the character traits of America in the last third of the twentieth century, commitment, constancy, tenacity, endurance, patience, resolve, and perseverance will not be on the list. The list will begin with an all-consuming interest in self-esteem. It will be followed by the subheadings of self-assertiveness,

self-enhancement, and self-realization. And if we think that we are not children of our times, let us simply test ourselves to see how we respond when people reject our ideas or spurn our good efforts or misconstrue our best intentions.

Exodus would remind the church that the Lord forges character through trial. Remembering this helps keep the church from discouragement, and serves as a reminder that sometimes the Lord's work in a people takes time.

Thirdly, mission involves making God known for who he is. While perhaps obvious, it bears remembering, for the tendency to understand and present God as we might wish him to be is a tendency that clings closely. In Exodus we see that the Lord makes himself known in a variety of ways, and through judgment as well as through mercy. The Lord judges Pharaoh publicly so that the Egyptians may know that he is God and will not tolerate the oppression of his people. The Lord judges his people in response to the golden calf for the sake of his name among the nations, and yet extends mercy for the very same reason. One tendency in some circles of the church is to underplay God's judgment, and in others to underplay God's mercy. The call, then, is to seek to know God as he has made himself known. Perhaps this sounds obvious, but the line between worshipping the Lord and idolatry is precisely here. To the extent that we create a god in our image, and after our likings, is the extent to which we follow another god.

Finally, to know the Lord for who he is means knowing him as redeemer. Israel never knew the Lord as anyone other than the Lord her God who brought her out of Egypt. In other words whatever else Israel may have known about God, she knew him firstly as her saviour, and did not know him otherwise. To forget this is to undermine the mission of the church. Perhaps the best example of this can be seen in the Pharisees. That the Pharisees had a sense of mission is apparent in Jesus' rebuke 'you travel across sea and land to make a single proselyte, and when he becomes a proselyte, you make him twice as much a child of hell as yourselves' (Matt. 23:15). And yet they appear curiously blind to what it might mean for them to bear witness to the Lord. Why would this be?

All four Gospels consistently portray the Pharisees as people who failed to recognize that they needed a redeemer. The following is representative:

And as Jesus reclined at table in the house, behold, many tax collectors and sinners came and were reclining with Jesus and his disciples. And when the Pharisees saw this, they said to his disciples, 'Why does your teacher eat with tax collectors and sinners?' But when he heard it, he said, 'Those who are well have no need of a physician, but those who are sick. Go and learn what this means, "I desire mercy, and not sacrifice." For I came not to call the righteous, but sinners.' (Matt. 9:10–13)

Self-righteousness and despising others go hand in hand. To the extent that the people of God forget that we are sinners saved by grace is the extent that we will fail to extend grace to others. Faithful mission becomes possible when God's people embrace the Lord as redeemer.

Ultimately, God is known in and through Jesus Christ, his goodness – indeed his glory – manifest most perfectly in the cross. Therefore, faithful mission goes forth with the understanding of Paul, 'I decided to know nothing among you except Jesus Christ and him crucified' (1 Cor. 2:2). It is in Christ that God is present with his people. It is in Christ that God's mission to be known by the nations will be realized. And finally, it is Christ to whom those nations will sing, 'Salvation belongs to our God who sits upon the throne, and to the Lamb!' (Rev. 7:10).

Bibliography

Abba, R. (1961), 'The Divine Name Yahweh', *JBL* 80: 320–328.

Adler, A. (2009), 'What's in a Name? Reflections upon Divine Names and the Attraction of God to Israel', *JBQ* 37.4: 265–269.

Albrektson, B. (1968), 'On the Syntax of אהיה אשר אהיה', in P. R. Ackroyd and B. Lindars (eds.), *Words and Meanings: Essays Presented to David Wynton Thomas*, Cambridge: Cambridge University Press, 15–28.

Albright, W. F. (1924), 'The Name *Yahweh*', *JBL* 43: 370–378.

—— (1957), *From the Stone Age to Christianity: Monotheism and the Historical Process*, 2nd ed., Baltimore: Johns Hopkins Press.

Andersen, F. I. (1974), *The Sentence in Biblical Hebrew*, The Hague: Mouton.

—— (1986), 'Yahweh, the Kind and Sensitive God', in P. T. O'Brien and D. G. Petersen (eds.), *God Who Is Rich in Mercy: Essays Presented to Dr. D. B. Knox*, Australia: Lancer, 41–88.

Arnold, W. R. (1905), 'The Divine Name in Exodus iii. 14', *JBL* 24: 107–165.

Augustine (1853), *Confessions*, tr. E. B. Pusey, Oxford.

Averbeck, R. E. (2003), 'Tabernacle', in T. D. Alexander and D. W. Baker (eds.), *Dictionary of the Old Testament: Pentateuch*, Downers Grove and Leicester: IVP, 807–827.

Baker, D. L. (2010), *Two Testaments, One Bible*, 3rd. ed., Nottingham: Apollos; Downers Grove: InterVarsity Press.

Balentine, S. E. (1999), *The Torah's Vision of Worship*, OBT, Minneapolis: Fortress.

Baltzer, K. (1971), *The Covenant Formulary*, tr. D. E. Green, Philadelphia: Fortress.

Barr, J. (1961), *The Semantics of Biblical Language*, Oxford: Oxford University Press.

—— (1973), 'An Aspect of Salvation in the Old Testament', in E. J. Sharpe and J. R. Hinnells (eds.), *Man and His Salvation*, Manchester: Manchester University Press, 39–52.

Barton, J. (1996), *Reading the Old Testament: Method in Biblical Interpretation*, 2nd ed., London: Darton, Longman & Todd.

Bauckham, R. J. (2003), *Bible and Mission: Christian Witness in a Postmodern World*, Grand Rapids: Baker.

Beale, G. K. (1984), 'An Exegetical and Theological Consideration of the Hardening of Pharaoh's Heart in Exodus 4–14 and Romans 9', *TJ* 5: 129–154.

—— (2004), *The Temple and the Church's Mission*, NSBT 18, Leicester: Apollos; Downers Grove: InterVarsity Press.

Bernhardt, K. H. (1978), 'היה', in *TDOT* 3: 376–381.

Beuken, W. A. M. (1985), 'Exodus 16.5, 23: A Rule Regarding the Keeping of the Sabbath?', *JSOT* 32: 3–14.

Blenkinsopp, J. (1976), 'The Structure of P', *CBQ* 38: 275–292.

—— (1997), 'Structure and Meaning in the Sinai-Horeb Narrative (Exodus 19–34)', in E. E. Carpenter (ed.), *A Biblical Itinerary: Essays in Honor of George W. Coats*, JSOTSup 240, Sheffield: Sheffield Academic Press, 109–125.

Blum, E. (1990), *Studien zur Komposition des Pentateuch*, BZAW 189, Berlin: de Gruyter.

Brichto, H. C. (1983), 'The Worship of the Golden Calf: A Literary Analysis of a Fable on Idolatry', *HUCA* 74: 1–44.

Brueggemann, W. (1979), 'The Crisis and Promise of Presence in Israel', *HBT* 1: 47–86.

—— (1982), *Genesis: Interpretation*, Atlanta: John Knox.

—— (1994), *The Book of Exodus*, NIB 1, Nashville: Abingdon.

—— (1995), 'Pharaoh as Vassal: A Study of a Political Metaphor', *CBQ* 57: 27–51.

—— (1997), *Theology of the Old Testament: Testimony, Dispute, Advocacy*, Minneapolis: Fortress.

Buber, M. (1948), *Israel and the World: Essays in a Time of Crisis*, New York: Schocken.

—— (1958), *Moses: The Revelation and the Covenant*, New York: Harper & Row.

Buber, M., and F. Rosenzweig (1994), *Scripture and Translation*, tr. L. Rosenwald and E. Fox, Indiana Studies in Biblical Literature, Bloomington: Indiana University Press.

Card, M. (2009), *A Better Freedom: Finding Life as Slaves of Christ*, Downers Grove: InterVarsity Press.

Carpenter, E. E. (1997), 'Exodus 18: Its Structure, Style, Motifs', in E. E. Carpenter (ed.), *A Biblical Itinerary: In Search of Method, Form and Content: Essays in Honor of George W.*

Coats, JSOTSup 240, Sheffield: Sheffield Academic Press, 91–108.

Cassuto, U. (1961), *A Commentary on the Book of Genesis*, Jerusalem: Magnes.

—— (1967), *A Commentary on the Book of Exodus*, Jerusalem: Magnes.

Childs, B. S. (1962), *Memory and Tradition in Israel*, SBT 37, London: SCM.

—— (1974), *Exodus*, London: SCM.

—— (1997), 'The Genre of the Biblical Commentary as Problem and Challenge', in M. Cogan, B. L. Eichler and J. H. Tigay (eds.), *Tehillah Le-Moshe: Biblical and Judaic Studies in Honor of Moshe Greenberg*, Winona Lake, Ind.: Eisenbrauns, 185–192.

Clements, R. E. (1965), *God and Temple*, Oxford: Basil Blackwell.

—— (1972), *Exodus*, CBC, Cambridge: Cambridge University Press.

—— (1976), 'Exodus, Book of', in K. Crim (ed.), *Interpreters Dictionary of the Bible*, Supplementary Volume, Nashville: Abingdon, 310–312.

Clines, D. J. A. (1968), 'The Image of God in Man', *TynB* 19: 51–103.

Coats, G. W. (1977), 'The King's Loyal Opposition: Obedience and Authority in Exodus 32–34', in G. W. Coats and B. O. Long (eds.), *Canon and Authority*, Philadelphia: Fortress, 91–109.

Cody, A. (1964), 'When Is the Chosen People Called a Goy?', *VT* 14: 1–6.

—— (1968), 'Exodus 18,12: Jethro Accepts a Covenant with the Israelites', *Bib* 49: 153–166.

Cole, R. A. (1973), *Exodus*, Leicester: Inter-Varsity Press.

Collins, J. J. (1990), 'Is a Critical Biblical Theology Possible?', in W. H. Propp, B. Halpern and D. N. Freedman (eds.), *The Hebrew Bible and Its Interpreters*, Winona Lake, Ind.: Eisenbrauns, 1–17.

Cross, F. M. (1981), 'The Priestly Tabernacle in Light of Recent Research', in A. Biran (ed.), *Temples and High Places in Biblical Times: Proceedings of the Colloquium in Honor of the Centennial of Hebrew Union College-Jewish Institute of Religion, Jerusalem, 14–16 March 1977*, Jerusalem: Nelson Glueck School of Biblical Archaeology, 169–180.

Dale, P. (1985), *Old Testament Law*, Atlanta: John Knox.

Davidson, R. M. (1981), *Typology in Scripture: A Study of Hermeneutical [Typos] Structures*, Andrews University Seminary

Doctoral Dissertation Series 2, Berrien Springs, Mich.: Andrews University Press.

Davies, G. H. (1967), *Exodus*, TBC, London: SCM.

Davies, G. (1999), 'The Theology of Exodus', in E. Ball (ed.), *In Search of True Wisdom: Essays in the Old Testament in Honour of Ronald E. Clements*, JSOTSup 300, Sheffield: Sheffield Academic Press, 137–152.

Davis, D. R. (1982), 'Rebellion, Presence, Covenant', *WTJ* 44: 71–87.

Dawkins, R. (2006), *The God Delusion*, New York: Houghton Mifflin.

Dentan, R. C. (1963), 'The Literary Affinities of Exodus XXXIV 6f', *VT* 13: 34–51.

deVaux, R. (1970), 'The Revelation of the Divine Name YHWH', in J. Durham and J. R. Porter (eds.), *Proclamation and Presence: Old Testament Essays in Honour of Gwynne Henton Davies*, London: SCM, 48–75.

Dohmen, C. (2004), *Exodus 19–40*, HTKAT, Freiburg: Herder.

Dozeman, T. B. (1996), *God at War: Power in the Exodus Tradition*, Oxford: Oxford University Press.

Driver, G. R. (1973), 'Affirmation by Explanatory Negation', *JANESCU* 5: 107–114.

Driver, S. R. (1911), *Exodus*, Cambridge: Cambridge University Press.

—— (1913), *An Introduction to the Literature of the Old Testament*, Edinburgh: T. & T. Clark.

Dumbrell, W. J. (1994), *Covenant and Creation: An Old Testament Covenantal Theology*, Exeter: Paternoster.

Durham, J. (1987), *Exodus*, Waco: Word.

Eichrodt, W. (1961), *Theology of the Old Testament*, tr. J. A. Baker, vol. 1, Philadelphia: Westminster.

Eissfeldt, O. (1955), 'Zwei Verkannte Militär-Technische Termini im Alten Testament', *VT* 5: 232–238.

Elnes, E. E. (1994), 'Creation and Tabernacle: The Priestly Writer's "Environmentalism"', *HBT* 16: 144–155.

Enns, P. (2000), *Exodus*, Grand Rapids: Zondervan.

Eslinger, L. (1991), 'Freedom or Knowledge? Perspective and Purpose in the Exodus Narrative (Exodus 1–15)', *JSOT* 16: 43–60.

Faulkner, W. (1951), *Requiem for a Nun*, New York: Random House.

Firmage, E. (1999), 'Genesis 1 and the Priestly Agenda', *JSOT* 82: 97–114.

Fishbane, M. (1979), *Text and Texture*, New York: Schocken.

Frankel, D. (2002), *The Murmuring Stories of the Priestly School: A Retrieval of Ancient Sacerdotal Lore*, VTSup 89, Leiden: Brill.

Freedman, D. N. (1955), 'God Compassionate and Gracious', *Western Watch* 6: 6–24.

—— (1960), 'The Name of the God of Moses', *JBL* 79: 151–156.

—— (1986), 'חנן', in *TDOT* 5: 443–455.

Fretheim, T. E. (1989), 'Suffering God and Sovereign God in Exodus: A Collision of Images', *HBT* 11: 31–56.

—— (1991a), *Exodus*, Louisville: John Knox.

—— (1991b), 'The Plagues as Ecological Signs of Historical Disaster', *JBL* 110: 385–396.

—— (1991c), 'The Reclamation of Creation: Redemption and Law in Exodus', *Int* 45.4: 354–365.

—— (1996), *The Pentateuch*, Nashville: Abingdon.

Gerstenberger, E. S. (2002), *Theologies in the Old Testament*, tr. J. Bowden, London: T. & T. Clark.

Gianotti, C. R. (1985), 'The Meaning of the Divine Name YHWH', *BSac* 142: 38–48.

Goitein, S. D. (1956), '*YHWH* the Passionate: The Monotheistic Meaning and Origin of the Name *YHWH*', *VT* 6: 1–9.

Goldingay, J. (2003), *Old Testament Theology: Israel's Gospel*, vol. 1, Downers Grove: InterVarsity Press.

Gorman, F. H. (1990), *The Ideology of Ritual: Space, Time, and Status in the Priestly Theology*, JSOTSup 91, Sheffield: Sheffield Academic Press.

Gove, P. B. (ed.) (1968), *Webster's Third New International Dictionary*, Springfield, Mass.: G. and C. Merriam.

Gowan, D. E. (1994), *Theology in Exodus*, Louisville: Westminster John Knox.

Greenberg, M. (1960), 'נסה in Exodus 20:20 and the Purpose of the Sinaitic Theophany', *JBL* 79: 273–276.

—— (1971a), 'Exodus, Book of', in *Encyclopaedia Judaica*, Jerusalem: Keter Publishing House, 6: 1050–1067.

—— (1971b), 'The Redaction of the Plague Narrative in Exodus', in H. Goedicke (ed.), *Near Eastern Studies in Honor of William Foxwell Albright*, Baltimore: Johns Hopkins Press, 243–252.

Gunn, D. M. (1982), 'The Hardening of Pharaoh's Heart: Plot, Character and Theology in Exodus 1–14', in D. J. A. Clines (ed.), *Art and Meaning*, JSOTSup 19, Sheffield: JSOT Press, 72–96.

Gurtner, D. (2007), *The Torn Veil: Matthew's Exposition of the Death of Jesus*, SNTSMS 139, Cambridge: Cambridge University Press.

Hafemann, S. J. (1995), *Paul, Moses, and the History of Israel: The Letter/Spirit Contrast and the Argument from Scripture in 2 Corinthians 3*, WUNT 81, Tübingen: Mohr (Siebeck).

Hamerton-Kelly, R. G. (1970), 'The Temple and the Origins of Jewish Apocalyptic', *VT* 20: 1–15.

Hammer, R. A. (1978), 'New Covenant of Moses', *Judaism* 27: 345–350.

Haran, M. (1978), *Temples and Temple-Service in Ancient Israel: An Inquiry into the Character of Cult Phenomena and the Historical Setting of the Priestly School*, Oxford: Clarendon.

Harris, M. J. (1999), *Slave of Christ: A New Testament Metaphor for Total Devotion to Christ*, NSBT 8, Leicester: Apollos; Downers Grove: InterVarsity Press.

Hasel, G. F. (1991), *Old Testament Theology: Basic Issues in the Current Debate*, 4th ed., Grand Rapids: Eerdmans.

Haugen, G. (1995), *Terrify No More*, Nashville: W Publishing Group.

—— (2005), *Terrify No More*, Nashville: Thomas Nelson.

Hauser, A. J. (1987), 'Two Songs of Victory: A Comparison of Exodus 15 and Judges 5', in E. R. Follis (ed.), *Directions in Biblical Hebrew Poetry*, JSOTSup 40, Sheffield: Sheffield Academic Press, 265–284.

Helfmeyer, F. J. (1998), 'נסה', in *TDOT* 9: 443–455.

Hendel, R. S. (2001), 'The Exodus in Biblical Memory', *JBL* 120: 601–622.

Hilber, J. W. (1996), 'Theology of Worship in Exodus 24', *JETS* 39: 177–189.

House, P. R. (1998), *Old Testament Theology*, Downers Grove: InterVarsity Press.

Houtman, C. (1993), *Exodus 1:1 – 7:13*, tr. S. Woudstra and J. Rebel, HCOT 1, Kampen: Kok.

—— (1996), *Exodus 7:14 – 19:25*, tr. S. Woudstra and J. Rebel, HCOT 2, Kampen: Kok.

—— (2000), *Exodus 20 – 40*, tr. S. Woudstra and J. Rebel, HCOT 3, Kampen: Kok.

Hyatt, J. P. (1971), *Exodus*, London: Oliphants.

Irwin, W. H. (1997), 'The Course of the Dialogue between Moses and Yhwh in Exodus 33:12–17', *CBQ* 59: 629–636.

Isbell, C. D. (2002), *The Function of Exodus Motifs in Biblical*

Narratives: Theological Didactic Drama, Lewiston, N. Y.: Edwin Mellen.

Jacob, B. (1992), *The Second Book of the Bible: Exodus*, tr. W. Jacob, Hoboken, N. J.: KTAV.

Janzen, J. G. (1990), 'The Character of the Calf and its Cult in Exodus 32', *CBQ* 52: 597–607.

—— (1997), *Exodus*, Westminster Bible Companion, Louisville: Westminster John Knox.

Jenson, P. P. (1992), *Graded Holiness: A Key to the Priestly Conception of the World*, JSOTSup 106, Sheffield: JSOT Press.

Josephus, F. (1987), *The Works of Josephus: Complete and Unabridged*, rev. ed., tr. W. Whiston, Peabody: Hendrickson.

Kaiser, W. C., Jr. (1990), *Exodus*, in F. Gaebelein (ed.), *The Expositor's Bible Commentary with the New International Version*, vol. 2, Grand Rapids: Zondervan.

—— (2000), *Mission in the Old Testament: Israel as a Light to the Nations*, Grand Rapids: Baker.

Kapelrud, A. S. (1979), 'Die Theologie der Schopfung im Alten Testament', *ZAW* 91: 159–170.

Kearney, P. J. (1977), 'Creation and Liturgy: The P Redaction of Ex. 25–40', *ZAW* 89: 375–387.

Kitchen, K. A. (2000), 'The Desert Tabernacle: Pure Fiction or Plausible Account?', *BRev* 16: 14–21.

Klein, R. W. (1996), 'Back to the Future: The Tabernacle in the Book of Exodus', *Int* 50.3: 264–276.

Kline, M. G. (1980), *Images of the Spirit*, Eugene, Ore.: Wipf & Stock.

Knierim, R. P. (1965), 'Das Erste Gebot', *ZAW* 77: 20–39.

—— (1995), 'Conceptual Aspects in Exodus 25:1–9', in *Pomegranates and Golden Bells: Studies in Biblical, Jewish, and near Eastern Ritual, Law, and Literature in Honor of Jacob Milgrom*, Winona Lake, Ind.: Eisenbrauns, 113–123.

Knight, G. A. F. (1976), *Theology as Narration*, Edinburgh: Hansel.

Koester, C. R. (2001), *Hebrews*, AB 36, New York: Doubleday.

Köhler, L. (1929), 'Der Decalog', *ThR* NS 1: 161–184.

—— (1957), *Old Testament Theology*, 3rd ed., vol. 49, London: Lutterworth.

Köhler, L., and W. Baumgartner (1996), *The Hebrew and Aramaic Lexicon of the Old Testament*, vol. 3, Leiden: Brill.

—— (1999), *The Hebrew and Aramaic Lexicon of the Old Testament*, vol. 4, Leiden: Brill.

Krašovec, J. (1999), *Reward, Punishment, and Forgiveness: The Thinking and Beliefs of Ancient Israel in the Light of Greek and Modern Views*, VTSup 78, Leiden: Brill.

Kürle, S. (2005), 'The Appeal of Exodus: The Characters of God, Moses, and Israel in the Rhetoric of the Book of Exodus', PhD dissertation, University of Gloucestershire.

Laney, J. C. (2001), 'God's Self-Revelation in Exodus 34:6–8', *BSac* 158: 36–51.

Leder, A. C. (1999), 'Reading Exodus to Learn and Learning to Read Exodus', *CTJ* 34: 11–35.

Leibowitz, N. (1976), *Studies in Shemot*, tr. A. Newman, vol. 1, Jerusalem: Ahva.

Levenson, J. D. (1980), 'The Theologies of Commandment in Biblical Israel', *HTR* 73: 17–33.

—— (1985), *Sinai and Zion*, Minneapolis: Winston.

—— (1988), *Creation and the Persistence of Evil: The Drama of Divine Omnipotence*, San Francisco: Harper & Row.

Levine, B. A. (1965), 'The Descriptive Tabernacle Texts of the Pentateuch', *JAOS* 85: 307–318.

Lindblom, J. (1964), 'Noch Einmal Die Deutung des Jahwe-Names in Ex. 3, 14', in H. Kosmala (ed.), *ASTI*, Leiden: Brill, 4–15.

Lipinski, E. (1999), 'סגלה', in *TDOT* 10: 144–148.

Longacre, R. E. (1995), 'Building for the Worship of God', in W. Bodine (ed.), *Discourse Analysis of Biblical Literature: What It Is and What It Offers*, Atlanta: Scholars Press.

McConville, J. G. (2002), *Deuteronomy*, Apollos Old Testament Commentary 5, Leicester: Apollos.

MacDonald, N. (2003), *Deuteronomy and the Meaning of 'Monotheism'*, vol. 1, FAT, Tübingen: Mohr (Siebeck).

McNeile, A. H. (1908), *The Book of Exodus*, London: Methuen.

Mann, T. W. (1996), 'Passover: The Time of Our Lives', *Int* 50.3: 240–250.

Margaliot, M. (1994), 'The Theology of Exodus 32–34', in *Proceedings of the Eleventh World Congress of Jewish Studies*, Jerusalem: World Union of Jewish Studies.

Martens, E. A. (1994), *God's Design: A Focus on Old Testament Theology*, 2nd ed., Grand Rapids: Baker; Leicester: Apollos.

Milgrom, J. (1970), *Studies in Levitical Terminology*, vol. 14, University of California Publications, Near Eastern Studies, Berkeley: University of California Press.

—— (1975), 'The Compass of Biblical Sancta', *JQR* 65: 205–216.

—— (1990), *Numbers*, JPS Torah Commentary, Philadelphia: Jewish Publication Society.

—— (1991), *Leviticus 1–16*, vol. 3, AB, New York: Doubleday.

Miller, P. (2009), *The Ten Commandments*, Louisville: Westminster John Knox.

Moberly, R. W. L. (1983), *At the Mountain of God: Story and Theology in Exodus 32–34*, JSOTSup 22, Sheffield: JSOT Press.

—— (1992), *The Old Testament of the Old Testament*, Minneapolis: Fortress.

Moran, W. J. (1962), 'A Kingdom of Priests', in J. J. McKenzie (ed.), *The Bible in Current Catholic Thought*, New York: Herder & Herder, 7–20.

Mosis, R. (1978), 'Ex 19:5b, 6a: Syntaktischer Aufbau und lexikalische Semantik', *BZ*: 1–25.

Motyer, J. A. (1959), *The Revelation of the Divine Name*, London: Tyndale.

Mowinckel, S. (1961), 'The Name of the God of Moses', *HUCA* 32: 121–134.

Muilenburg, J. (1968), 'Intercession of the Covenant Mediator', in P. R. Ackroyd and B. Lindars (eds.), *Words and Meanings: Essays Presented to David Wynton Thomas*, Cambridge: Cambridge University Press, 159–181.

Napier, B. D. (1953), 'Community Under Law: On Hebrew Law and Its Theological Presuppositions', *Int* 7.4: 404–417.

Nicholson, E. W. (1977), 'The Decalogue as the Direct Address of God', *VT* 27: 422–433.

—— (1982), 'The Covenant Ritual in Exodus XXIV 3–8', *VT* 32: 74–86.

—— (1986), *God and His People: Covenant and Theology in the Old Testament*, Oxford: Clarendon.

Noth, M. (1962), *Exodus*, London: SCM.

—— (1981), *A History of Pentateuchal Traditions*, tr. B. W. Anderson, Atlanta: Scholars Press.

—— (1983), *The History of Israel*, 2nd ed., New York: Harper & Row.

Olson, D. T. (1985), *The Death of the Old and the Birth of the New: The Framework of the Book of Numbers and the Pentateuch*, BJS 71, Chico, Calif.: Scholars Press.

Paul, S. M. (1970), *Studies in the Book of the Covenant in the Light of Cuneiform and Biblical Law*, VTSup 18, Leiden: Brill.

Peterson, E. H. (2000), *A Long Obedience in the Same Direction*, Downers Grove: InterVarsity Press.

Phillips, A., and L. Phillips (1998), 'The Origin of "I Am" In Exodus 3.14', *JSOT* 78: 81–83.

Philo (1993), *The Works of Philo: Complete and Unabridged*, new updated ed., tr. C. D. Yonge, Peabody: Hendrickson.

Piper, J. (1979), 'Prolegomena to Understanding Romans 9:14–15: An Interpretation of Exodus 33:19', *JETS* 22: 203–216.

—— (1983), *The Justification of God: An Exegetical and Theological Study of Romans 9:1–23*, Grand Rapids: Baker.

—— (2002), *The Roots of Endurance: Invincible Perseverance in the Loves of John Newton, Charles Simeon, and William Wilberforce*. Wheaton, Ill.: Crossway; Leicester: Inter-Varsity Press.

Propp, W. C. (1998), *Exodus 1–18*, vol. 2, AB, New York: Doubleday.

Rad, G. von (1961), *Genesis*, tr. J. H. Marks, Philadelphia: Westminster.

—— (1962), *Old Testament Theology*, vol. 1, New York: HarperCollins.

—— (1966), *The Problem of the Hexateuch and Other Essays*, Edinburgh: Oliver & Boyd.

Räisänen, H. (1976), *The Idea of Divine Hardening*, Helsinki: Finnish Exegetical Society.

Raitt, T. M. (1991), 'Why Does God Forgive?', *HBT* 13: 38–58.

Reno, R. R. (2010), *Genesis*, Grand Rapids: Brazos.

Reuter, E. (2003), 'קנא', in *TDOT* 13: 47–58.

Robinson, B. H. (1985), 'Israel and Amalek: The Context of Exodus 17:8–16', *JSOT* 32: 15–22.

Rodríguez, A. M. (1986), 'Sanctuary Theology in the Book of Exodus', *AUSS* 24: 127–145.

Rowley, H. H. (1948), *From Joseph to Joshua: Biblical Traditions in the Light of Archaeology*, London: Oxford University Press.

—— (1950), *The Biblical Doctrine of Election*, London: Lutterworth.

Ruprecht, E. (1974), 'Stellung und Bedeutung der Erzählung vom Mannawunder (Ex 16) im Aufbau der Priesterschrift', *ZAW* 86: 269–307.

Sæbø, M. (1998), 'God's Name in Exodus 3.13–15: An Expression of Revelation or of Veiling?', in *On the Way to Canon: Creative Tradition History in the Old Testament*, JSOTSup 191, Sheffield: Sheffield Academic Press.

Sailhamer, J. (1991), 'The Mosaic Law and the Theology of the Pentateuch', *WTJ* 53: 241–261.

—— (1992), *The Pentateuch as Narrative: A Biblical-Theological Commentary*, Grand Rapids: Zondervan.

—— (1995), *Introduction to Old Testament Theology: A Canonical Approach*, Grand Rapids: Zondervan.

Sarna, N. M. (1986), *Exploring Exodus: The Heritage of Biblical Israel*, New York: Schocken.

—— (1991), *Exodus*, The JPS Torah Commentary, Philadelphia: Jewish Publication Society.

Scharbert, J. (1957), 'Formgeschichte und Exegese von Ex. 34. 6f und Seiner Parallelen', *Bib* 38: 130–150.

Scharbert, J. (1989), *Exodus*, NEchtB, Würzburg: Echter.

Schenker, A. (1996), 'Drei Mosaiksteinchen: "Königreich von Priestern", "Und Ihre Kinder Gehen Weg", "Wir Tun und Wir Hören" (Exodus 19,6; 21,22; 24,7)', in M. Vervenne (ed.), *Studies in the Book of Exodus: Redaction–Reception–Interpretation*, Louvain: Leuven University Press, 367–380.

Schild, E. (1954), 'On Exodus iii 14 – "I Am That I Am"', *VT* 4: 296–302.

Schultz, R. (2002), 'What Is "Canonical" About a Canonical Biblical Theology?', in S. J. Hafemann (ed.), *Biblical Theology: Retrospect and Prospect*, Downers Grove: InterVarsity Press, 83–99.

Schwartz, B. J. (1995), 'The Bearing of Sin in the Priestly Literature', in D. P. Wright, D. N. Freedman and A. Hurvitz (eds.), *Pomegranates and Golden Bells: Studies in Biblical, Jewish, and Near Eastern Ritual, Law, and Literature in Honor of Jacob Milgrom*, Winona Lake, Ind.: Eisenbrauns, 3–21.

—— (1996), 'The Priestly Account of the Theophany and Lawgiving at Sinai', in M. V. Fox, V. A. Hurowitz, A. Hurvitz, M. L. Klein, B. J. Schwartz and N. Shupak (eds.), *Texts, Temples, and Traditions: A Tribute to Menahem Haran*, Winona Lake, Ind.: Eisenbrauns, 103–134.

Seitz, C. R. (1998), *Word Without End: The Old Testament as Abiding Theological Witness*, Grand Rapids: Eerdmans.

—— (2001), 'The Old Testament, Mission, and Christian Scripture', in *Figured Out*, Louisville: Westminster John Knox, 145–157.

Seybold, K. (1981), 'חלה', in *TDOT* 4: 399–409.

Smith, M. S. (1997), *The Pilgrimage Pattern in Exodus*, JSOTSup 239, Sheffield: Sheffield Academic Press.

Sohn, S.-T. (1999), '"I Will Be Your God and You Will Be My People": The Origin and Background of the Covenant Formula', in R. Chazan, W. W. Hallo and L. H. Schiffman (eds.), *Ki Baruch*

Hu: Ancient Near Eastern, Biblical, and Judaic Studies in Honor of Baruch A. Levine, Winona Lake, Ind.: Eisenbrauns, 355–372.

Sommer, B. D. (2001), 'Conflicting Constructions of the Divine Presence in the Priestly Tabernacle', *BibInt* 9: 41–63.

Speiser, E. A. (1960), '"People" and "Nation" of Israel', *JBL* 79: 157–163.

Spurgeon, C. H. (1991), *Morning and Evening*, Peabody: Hendrickson.

Stamm, J. J., and M. E. Andrew (1967), *The Ten Commandments in Recent Research*, tr. M. E. Andrew, SBT, Second Series 2, Naperville, Ind.: Alec R. Allenson.

Steins, G. (2001), 'Priesterherrschaft, Volk von Priestern oder was sonst? Zur Interpretation von Ex 19,6', *BZ* 45.1: 20–36.

Terrien, S. L. (1978), *The Elusive Presence: Toward a New Biblical Theology*, New York: Harper & Row.

Thiessen, M. (2009), 'Hebrews 12.5–13, the Wilderness Period, and Israel's Discipline', *NTS* 55: 366–379.

Tsutserov, A. (2009), *Glory, Grace, and Truth: Ratification of the Sinaitic Covenant According to the Gospel of John*, Eugene, Ore.: Wipf & Stock.

Van Seters, J. (1994), *The Life of Moses: The Yahwist as Historian in Exodus–Numbers*, CBET 10, Kampen: Kok.

Vervenne, M. (1996), 'Current Tendencies and Developments in the Study of the Book of Exodus', in M. Vervenne (ed.), *Studies in the Book of Exodus: Redaction–Reception–Interpretation*, Leuven: Leuven University Press, 21–55.

Wade, M. L. (2003), *Consistency of Translation Techniques in the Tabernacle Accounts of Exodus in the Old Greek*, Atlanta: Society of Biblical Literature.

Wagner, A. J. (1952), 'An Interpretation of Exodus 20:7', *Int* 6.2: 228–229.

Walzer, M. (1968), 'Exodus 32 and the Theory of Holy War: The History of a Citation', *HTR* 61: 1–14.

Watts, J. W. (1992), *Psalm and Story: Inset Hymns in Hebrew Narrative*, JSOTSup 139, Sheffield: JSOT Press.

—— (1996), 'The Legal Characterization of God in the Pentateuch', *HUCA* 68: 1–14.

Weimar, P. (1988), 'Sinai und Schöpfung: Komposition und Theologie der priesterschriftlichen Sinaigeschichte', *RB* 95: 337–385.

Wellhausen, J. (1885), *Prolegomena to the History of Israel*, tr. J. S. Black and A. Menzies, Edinburgh: Adam & Charles Black.

Wells, J. B. (2000), *God's Holy People*, JSOTSup 305, Sheffield: Sheffield Academic Press.

Wenham, G. J. (1979), *The Book of Leviticus*, NICOT, Grand Rapids: Eerdmans.

—— (1994), 'Sanctuary Symbolism in the Garden of Eden Story', in R. S. Hess and D. T. Tsumura (eds.), *'I Studied Inscriptions from Before the Flood': Ancient Near Eastern, Literary, and Linguistic Approaches to Genesis 1–11*, SBTS 4, Winona Lake, Ind.: Eisenbrauns, 399–404.

Whitney, G. E. (1986), 'Alternative Interpretations of Lô' in Exodus 6:3 and Jeremiah 7:22', *WTJ* 48.1: 151–159.

Whybray, R. N. (1996), 'The Immorality of God: Reflections on Some Passages in Genesis, Job, Exodus and Numbers', *JSOT* 72: 89–120.

Wilson, R. R. (1979), 'The Hardening of Pharaoh's Heart', *CBQ* 41: 18–36.

Wright, C. J. H. (2006), *The Mission of God: Unlocking the Bible's Grand Narrative*, Nottingham: IVP.

Wright, G. E. (1961), 'The Old Testament Basis for the Christian Mission', in G. H. Anderson (ed.), *The Theology of Christian Mission*, New York: McGraw Hill, 17–30.

—— (1971), 'The Divine Name and the Divine Nature', *Perspective* 12: 177–185.

Zevit, Z. (1976), 'The Priestly Redaction and Interpretation of the Plague Narrative in Exodus', *JQR* 66: 193–211.

Zimmerli, W. (1950), 'Das Zweite Gebot', in W. Baumgartner, *Festschrift Alfred Bertholet zum 80 Geburtstag*, Tübingen: J. C. B. Mohr, 550–563.

—— (1978), *Old Testament Theology in Outline*, tr. D. E. Green, Atlanta: John Knox.

—— (1982), *I Am Yahweh*, tr. D. W. Stott, Atlanta: John Knox.

Zyl, D. C. van (1950), 'Exodus 19:3–6 and the Kerygmatic Perspective of the Pentateuch', *OTE* 5: 264–271.

Index of authors

Index of Scripture references

232

Printed and bound by CPI Group (UK) Ltd, Croydon, CR0 4YY

25/03/2025

14647345-0003